MIDDLE LEVEL Six-Way Paragraphs
in the Content Areas

MIDDLE LEVEL

Six-Way Paragraphs
in the Content Areas

100 Passages for Developing
the Six Essential Categories of Comprehension in the
Humanities, Social Studies, Science, and Mathematics

based on
the work of
Walter
Pauk

JAMESTOWN PUBLISHERS

a division of NTC/CONTEMPORARY PUBLISHING GROUP
Lincolnwood, Illinois USA

Readability

Passages 1–25: Level G

Passages 26–50: Level H

Passages 51–75: Level I

Passages 76–100: Level J

ISBN (middle level): 0-8092-0372-3

Published by Jamestown Publishers,
a division of NTC/Contemporary Publishing Group, Inc.
4255 West Touhy Avenue, Lincolnwood (Chicago), Illinois 60712-1975 U.S.A.
© 2001 NTC/Contemporary Publishing Group, Inc.
Manufactured in the United States of America.

6 7 8 9 10 11 12 113 09 08 07 06 05

Contents

To the Student

To succeed in the courses you take, one of the most important skills you can have is good reading ability. Depending on the content, different courses require different types of reading. For example, if material is easy for you or you have studied it before, you may read it quickly. If the material is new or difficult, you may need to read more slowly. In fact, you may need to read it several times. In all the courses you take, you will be able to use the reading skills featured in this book.

The passages in the book are readings in four general categories: the humanities, social studies, science, and mathematics. Each category has several subcategories. For example, social studies may include passages in areas such as history, geography, and anthropology. Mathematics may include consumer and computer topics and puzzles as well as basic mathematical facts. Humanities passages deal with literature, music, art, and architecture.

Certain subject areas may be unfamiliar to you. But this book does not require you to master many new facts. Instead, its purpose is to show you *how to read in the content areas.* You will learn techniques that textbook writers use to organize material. You will see how new information can be applied to things you already know. And you will learn about the six skills that can help you read just about anything.

The Six Types of Questions

In this book, the basic skills necessary for reading factual material are taught through the use of the following six types of questions: main idea, subject matter, supporting details, conclusion, clarifying devices, and vocabulary in context.

Main Idea. While reading anything it is a good idea to ask yourself, What point is the writer trying to make? Once you ask this question, your mind will be looking for an answer, and chances are that you will find one. But if you don't focus in this way, all things seem equal. Nothing stands out.

Try to find the main idea in the following science passage by asking, What point is the writer trying to make?

> The worker ants in an ant colony have many different jobs. Some workers pull the eggs from the royal chamber into a room called the nursery. There, they help larvae climb out of their shells. In the nursery, there are workers who look after the larvae until they become full-grown ants. Some workers look for food and store it in the granary, where seeds are kept. Others dump leftovers in the rubbish room. Ants have their own complete, busy world hidden in tunnels under our feet!

A good answer here is, Worker ants do many different jobs in an ant colony. This passage is fairly easy to figure out because the first sentence is an excellent topic sentence.

The next example, from social studies, does not have a topic sentence. Nevertheless, the question What point is the writer trying to make? can still be answered. This time, think about the passage and come up with your own answer.

> Timbuktu is located in the country of Mali, on the southern edge of the Sahara Desert. It was established in about A.D. 1100 as a camp for nomads traveling across the desert. Within 200 years, it had grown into a fairly large city. Scholarly and religious leaders of Islam, the religion founded by Mohammed, made Timbuktu their home. An important university was built there. There was also a palace for the ruler and many <u>mosques</u> where people could worship. Even when a nonreligious ruler took over, Islamic scholars were used as counselors in religious and legal matters. From Timbuktu, Islam spread across the entire African continent.

This passage may have required a bit more thought, as the correct answer is a summary type answer. Compare your answer with the following main idea statement: Timbuktu developed into an important center of Islam.

Subject Matter. This question looks easy and often is easy. But don't let that fool you into thinking it isn't important. The subject matter question can help you with the most important skill of all in reading and learning: concentration. With it, you comprehend and learn. Without it, you fail.

Here is the secret for gaining concentration: After reading the first few lines of something, ask yourself, What is the subject matter of this passage? Instantly, you will be thinking about the passage. You will be concentrating. If you don't ask this question, your eyes will move across the lines of print, yet your mind may be thinking of other things.

By asking this question as you read each passage in this book, you will master the skill so well that it will carry over to everything you read.

Let's see how this method works. Here is a short passage from science:

> The moon circles Earth on the average of once every 29 days. Its orbit around Earth is not circular; it is more of an oval. So the moon's distance from Earth can vary quite a bit. Sometimes it is about 250,000 miles from Earth. Other times it is only 220,000 miles away.

On finishing the first sentence your thought should have been something like, *Ah, a passage on the moon going around the earth. Maybe I can learn something about this process.* If it was, your head was in the right place. By focusing right away on the subject matter, you will be concentrating, you will be looking for something, your attitude will be superb, and, best of all, you will be understanding, learning, and remembering.

Supporting Details. In common usage, the word *detail* has taken on the meaning of "something relatively unimportant." But details are important. Details are the plaster, board, and brick of a building, while main ideas are the large, strong, steel or wooden beams. A solid, well-written passage must contain both.

The bulk of a factual passage is made up of details that support the main idea. The main idea is often buried among the details. You have to dig to distinguish between them. Here are some characteristics that can help you see the difference between supporting details and main ideas.

First, supporting details come in various forms, such as examples, explanations, descriptions, definitions, comparisons, contrasts, exceptions, analogies, similes, and metaphors.

Second, these various kinds of details are used to support the main idea. The words themselves—supporting details—spell out their job. So when you have trouble finding the main idea, take a passage apart sentence by sentence, asking, "Does this sentence support something, or is this the thing being supported?" In other words, you must not only separate the two but must also see how they help one another. The main idea can often be expressed in a single sentence. But a sentence cannot tell a complete story. The writer must use additional sentences to give a full picture.

The following social studies passage shows how important details are for providing a full picture of what the writer had in mind.

> Objects found with the body told something about the Iceman's life. He wore a well-made fur jacket and pants. He clearly had been hunting, for he carried arrows, and animal bones were nearby. He also had a braided grass mat for sitting or sleeping on. Perhaps he was exhausted when he lay down for the last time.

Here the main idea is in the first sentence. Having stated the main idea, the writer goes on to give example after example showing why it is true. These examples are supporting details.

Conclusion. As a reader moves through a passage, grasping the main idea and supporting details, it is natural for him or her to begin to guess an ending or conclusion. Some passages contain conclusions; others do not. It all depends on the writer's purpose. For example, some passages simply describe a process—how something is done. It is not always necessary to draw a conclusion from such a passage.

In some passages with conclusions, the writer states the conclusion. But in most passages in this book, the conclusion is merely implied. That is, the writer seems to have come to a conclusion but has not stated it. It is up to you to draw that conclusion.

In the following science passage, the writer strongly implies a conclusion but does not state it directly.

> The elephant's great size can sometimes present a heat problem. The larger an object, the harder it is for it to lose heat. Elephants live on the hot plains of Africa, where keeping cool is not an easy task. Elephants' huge ears help them cool their bodies so they can survive in the heat. The large surfaces of the ears have many blood vessels that are very close to the surface of the skin. Blood that is closer to the surface cools more easily.

From this passage, we can draw the conclusion that, without their large ears, elephants probably would not survive in the African heat.

Sometimes a writer will ask you to draw a conclusion by applying what you have learned to a new situation, as in the following passage.

> According to Greek mythology, only one phoenix at a time lived on earth. Legend has it that the single bird lived for exactly 500 years. Just before it was to die, it would build a nest. The mythical bird's last task was to sit patiently on the nest, waiting for the sun to ignite the dry twigs and set the nest ablaze. But as the proud phoenix sacrificed itself in flame, a tiny worm would crawl from beneath the ashes. This worm grew into a new phoenix.

If you were asked what sort of person might be called a phoenix today, you would have to apply your general knowledge to pick the correct answer: someone who rises up again after a defeat.

Looking for a conclusion puts you in the shoes of a detective. While reading, you have to think, *Where is the writer leading me? What conclusion will I be able to draw?* And, like a detective, you must try to guess the conclusion, changing the guess as you get more and more information.

Clarifying Devices. Clarifying devices are words, phrases, and techniques that a writer uses to make main ideas, subideas, and supporting details clear and interesting. By knowing some of these clarifying and controlling devices, you will be better able to recognize them in the passages you read. By recognizing them, you will be able to read with greater comprehension and speed.

Transitional or Signal Words. The largest single group of clarifying devices, and the most widely used, are transitional or signal words. For example, here are some signal words that you see all the time: *first, second, next, last,* and *finally.* A writer uses such words to keep ideas, steps in a process, or lists in order. Other transitional words include *however, in brief, in conclusion, above all, therefore, since, because,* and *consequently.*

When you see transitional words, consider what they mean. A transitional word like *or* tells you that another option, or choice, is coming. Words like *but* and *however* signal that a contrast, or change in point of view, will follow.

Organizational Patterns. Organizational patterns are also clarifying devices. One such pattern is the chronological pattern, in which events unfold in the order of time: one thing happens first, then another, and another, and so on. A time pattern orders events. The event may take place in five minutes or over a period of hundreds of years.

There are other organizational patterns as well. Writers may use spatial descriptions to tell what things look like. They may use lists of examples to make their point. In science writing, they may use scientific data. Seeing the organizational pattern will help you read the material more easily.

Textual Devices. Textbook writers in particular use patterns or particular text styles to make their ideas clear. Bulleted lists, subheads, and boldfaced or italicized words help to highlight important ideas in the text. Charts or diagrams help you to visualize concepts more easily than if they are just explained in words.

Literal Versus Figurative Language. Sometimes a writer's words do not mean exactly what they seem to on first reading. For example, a writer may say, "The great tragedy shattered the hero of the story." You may know *shattered* as meaning "breaking into pieces." The word is often applied to breakable objects, but here it is applied to a person's feelings. Being alert to such special meanings of words can help you better appreciate the writer's meaning.

Two literary devices that writers use to present ideas in interesting ways are similes (SIM-a-lees) and metaphors (MET-a-fors). Both are used to make comparisons that add color and power to ideas. An example of a simile is She has a mind like a computer. In this simile, a person's mind is compared to a computer. A simile always uses the word *like, as,* or *than* to make a comparison. The metaphor, on the other hand, makes a direct comparison: Her mind is a computer.

Vocabulary in Context. How accurate are you in using words you think you already know? Do you know that the word *exotic* means "a thing or person from a foreign country"? So, exotic flowers and exotic costumes are flowers and costumes from foreign countries. *Exotic* has been used incorrectly so often and for so long that it has developed a second meaning. Most people use *exotic* to mean "strikingly unusual, as in color or design."

Many people think that the words *imply* and *infer* mean the same thing. They do not. A writer may imply, or suggest, something. The reader then infers what the writer implied. In other words, to imply is to "suggest an idea." To infer is to "take meaning out."

It is easy to see what would happen to a passage if a reader skipped a word or two that he or she did not know and imposed fuzzy meanings on a few others. The result would inevitably be a gross misunderstanding of the writer's message. You will become a better reader if you learn the exact meanings and different shades of meaning of the words that are already familiar to you.

In this book, you should be able to figure out the meanings of many words from their context—that is, from the words and phrases around them. If this method does not work for you, however, you may consult a dictionary.

Answering the Main Idea Question

The main idea questions in this book are not the usual multiple-choice variety from which you must select the one correct statement. Rather, you are given three statements and are asked to select the statement that expresses the main idea of the passage, the statement that is too narrow, and the statement that is too broad. You have to work hard and actively to identify all three statements correctly. This new type of question teaches you to recognize the differences among statements that, at first, seem almost equal.

To help you handle these questions, let's go behind the scenes to see how the main idea questions in this book were constructed. The true main idea statement was always written first. It had to be neat, succinct, and positive. The main idea tells who or what the subject of the passage is. It also answers the question Does what? or Is what? Next, keeping the main idea statement in mind, the other two statements were written. They are variations of the main idea statement. The "too narrow" statement had to be in line with the main idea but express only part of it. Likewise, the "too broad" statement had to be in line with the main idea but be too general in scope.

Read the science passage below. Then, to learn how to answer the main idea questions, follow the instructions in the box. The answer to each part of the question has been filled in for you. The score for each answer has also been marked.

The Dragonfly's Life Cycle

By far the scariest thing about the dragonfly is its name. This double-winged, fast-flying insect is totally harmless. It has large, deep eyes that can detect the smallest movements. Its body may be bright blue and red or a vivid green. Dragonflies in flight look like dancing spots of color in the light of a midsummer's day.

The dragonfly has a long and respectable history. It was one of the first flying insects on the earth. To see this oldster of the insect world in action, head for a pond. Dragonflies live near water. In fact, they lay their eggs right in water.

A dragonfly goes through several big changes before it becomes a flying insect. From the egg, a tiny creature called a nymph is hatched. It lives in the water, eating other small creatures that live in the pond. As the nymph grows, it becomes too big for its skin. Then it sheds the skin that is too small for it. Soon it grows a new one. This <u>molting</u> happens several times, until the insect is full grown. At this time it crawls up the stem of a water plant, out into the air. It squeezes its way out of its last skin as a full-fledged dragonfly.

After going through all that work to grow up, the dragonfly only lives for about a month. But for this short time it startles the hot summer air with its bright beauty.

Main Idea	1	Answer	Score
Mark the *main idea*		M	15
Mark the statement that is *too broad*		B	5
Mark the statement that is *too narrow*		N	5

a. Dragonflies are harmless, beautiful insects with an interesting life cycle. M 15

[This statement gathers all the important points. It gives a correct picture of the main idea in a brief way: (1) Dragonflies, (2) harmless and beautiful, (3) interesting life cycle.]

b. Dragonflies lay their eggs in water. N 5

[This statement is correct, but it is too narrow. It refers to only a part of the dragonfly's life cycle.]

c. Insects that live near water are harmless and fascinating. B 5

[This statement is too broad. It speaks only of harmless insects, not dragonflies in particular.]

Getting the Most Out of This Book

The following steps could be called "tricks of the trade." Your teachers might call them "rules for learning." It doesn't matter what they are called. What does matter is that they work.

Think about the title. A famous language expert proposes the following "trick" to use when reading. "The first thing to do is to read the title. Then spend a few moments thinking about it."

Writers spend much time thinking up good titles. They try to pack a lot of meaning into them. It makes sense, then, for you to spend a few seconds trying to dig out some meaning. These few moments of thought will give you a head start on a passage.

Thinking about the title can help you in another way too. It helps you concentrate on a passage before you begin reading. Why does this happen? Thinking about the title fills your head with thoughts about the passage. There's no room for anything else to get in to break your concentration.

The Dot Step. Here is a method that will speed up your reading. It also builds comprehension at the same time.

Spend a few moments with the title. Then read quickly through the passage. Next, without looking back, answer the six questions by placing a dot in the box next to each answer of your choice. The dots will be your "unofficial" answers. For the main idea question (question 1) place your dot in the box next to the statement that you think is the main idea.

The dot system helps by making you think hard on your first, fast reading. The practice you gain by trying to grasp and remember ideas makes you a stronger reader.

The Checkmark Step. First, answer the main idea question. Follow the steps that are given above each set of statements for this question. Use a capital letter to mark your final answer to each part of the main idea question.

You have answered the other five questions with a dot. Now read the passage once more carefully. This time, mark your final answer to each question by placing a checkmark (√) in the box next to the answer of your choice. The answers with the checkmarks are the ones that will count toward your score.

The Diagnostic Chart. Now move your final answers to the Diagnostic Chart for the passage. These charts start on page 209.

Use the row of boxes beside Passage 1 for the answers to the first passage. Use the row of boxes beside Passage 2 for the answers to the second passage, and so on. Write the letter of your answer to the left of the dotted line in each block.

Correct your answers using the Answer Keys on pages 204–207. When scoring your answers, do not use an *x* for incorrect or a *c* for correct. Instead, use this method: If your choice is incorrect, write the letter of the correct answer to the right of the dotted line in the block.

Thus, the row of answers for each passage will show your incorrect answers. And it will also show the correct answers.

Your Total Comprehension Score. Go back to the passage you have just read. If you answered a question incorrectly, draw a line under the correct choice on the question page. Then write your score for each question on the line provided. Add the scores to get your total comprehension score. Enter that number in the box marked Total Score.

Graphing Your Progress. After you have found your total comprehension score, turn to the Progress Graphs that begin on page 214. Write your score in the box under the number of the passage. Then put an *x* along the line above the box to show your total comprehension score. Join the *x*'s as you go. This will plot a line showing your progress.

Taking Corrective Action. Your incorrect answers give you a way to teach yourself how to read better. Take the time to study these answers.

Go back to the questions. For each question you got wrong, read the correct answer (the one you have underlined) several times. With the correct answer in mind, go back to the passage itself. Read to see why the given answer is better. Try to see where you made your mistake. Try to figure out why you chose an incorrect answer.

The Steps in a Nutshell

Here's a quick review of the steps to follow. Following these steps is the way to get the most out of this book. Be sure you have read and understood everything in this To the Student section before you begin.

1. **Think about the title of the passage.** Try to get all the meaning the writer put into it.
2. **Read the passage quickly.**
3. **Answer the questions, using the dot system.** Use dots to mark your unofficial answers. Don't look back at the passage.
4. **Read the passage again—carefully.**
5. **Mark your final answers.** Put a checkmark (√) in the box to note your final answer. Use capital letters for each part of the main idea question.

6. **Mark your answers on the diagnostic chart.** Record your final answers on the diagnostic chart for the passage. Write your answers to the left of the dotted line in the answer blocks for the passage.

7. **Correct your answers.** Use the answer keys on pages 204–207. If an answer is not correct, write the correct answer in the right side of the block, beside your incorrect answer. Then go back to the question page. Place a line under the correct answer.

8. **Find your total comprehension score.** Find this by adding up the points you earned for each question. Enter the total in the box marked Total Score.

9. **Graph your progress.** Enter and plot your score on the progress graph for that passage.

10. **Take corrective action.** Read your wrong answers. Read the passage once more. Try to figure out why you were wrong.

To the Teacher

The Reading Passages

Each of the 100 passages included in the book is related to one of four general content areas: the humanities, social studies, science, or mathematics. Each of these areas has several subcategories; humanities, for example, includes passages that deal with literature, music, art, and architecture. The graphic accompanying the title of each piece identifies the general content area to which it belongs.

In addition, each piece had to meet the following two criteria: high interest level and appropriate readability level.

The high interest level was assured by choosing passages of mature content that would appeal to a wide range of readers. In essence, students read passages that will convey interesting information in a content area, whether that area is the student's chosen field of study or not.

The readability level of each passage was computed by applying Dr. Edward B. Fry's *Formula for Estimating Readability*, thus enabling the arrangement of passages according to grade levels within the book. *Six-Way Paragraphs in the Content Areas, Introductory Level* contains passages that range from reading level 4 to reading level 7, with 25 passages on each level. *Six-Way Paragraphs in the Content Areas, Middle Level* contains passages that range from reading level 7 to reading level 10, with 25 passages on each reading level. The passages in *Six-Way Paragraphs in the Content Areas, Advanced Level,* range from reading level 10 to reading level 12$^+$, with 25 passages on each reading level.

The Six Questions

This book is organized around six essential questions. The most important of these is the main idea question, which is actually a set of three statements. Students must first choose and label the statement that expresses the main idea of the passage; then they must label each of the other statements as being either too narrow or too broad to be the main idea.

In addition to the main idea question, there are five other questions. These questions are within the framework of the following five categories: subject matter, supporting details, conclusion, clarifying devices, and vocabulary in context.

By repeated practice with answering the questions within these six categories, students will develop an active, searching attitude about what they read. These six types of questions will help them become aware of what they are reading at the time they are actually seeing the words and phrases on a page. This type of thinking-while-reading sets the stage for higher comprehension and better retention.

The Diagnostic Chart

The Diagnostic Chart provides the most dignified form of guidance yet devised. With this chart, no one has to point out a student's weaknesses. The chart does that automatically, yielding the information directly and personally to the student, making self-teaching possible. The organization of the questions and the format for marking answers on the chart are what make it work so well.

The six questions for each passage are always in the same order. For example, the question designed to teach the skill of drawing conclusions is always the fourth question, and the main idea question is always first. Keeping the questions in order sets the stage for the smooth working of the chart.

The chart works automatically when students write the letter of their answer choices for each passage in the spaces provided. Even after completing only one passage, the chart will reveal the type or types of questions answered correctly, as well as the types answered incorrectly. As the answers for more passages are recorded, the chart will show the types of questions that are missed consistently. A pattern can be seen after three or more passages have been completed. For example, if a student answers question 4 (drawing conclusions) incorrectly for three out of four passages, the student's weakness in this area shows up automatically.

Once a weakness is revealed, have your students take the following steps: First, turn to the instructional pages in the beginning of the book and study the section in which the topic is discussed. Second, go back and reread the questions that were missed in that particular category. Then, with the correct answer to a question in mind, read the entire passage again, trying to see how the writer developed the answer to the question. Do this for each question that was missed. Third, when reading future passages, make an extra effort to correctly answer the questions in that particular category. Fourth, if the difficulty continues, arrange to see your teacher.

MIDDLE LEVEL Six-Way Paragraphs
in the Content Areas

Each of the 100 passages included in this book is related to one of four general content areas: humanities, social studies, science, or mathematics. The graphic accompanying the title of each piece identifies the general content area to which it belongs.

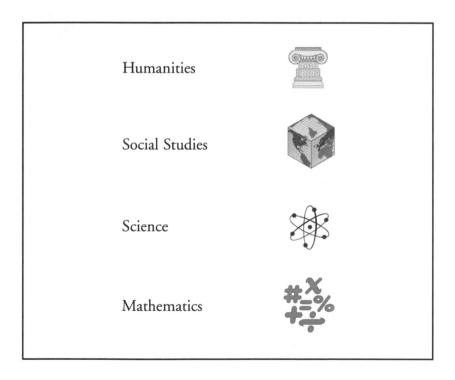

Humanities

Social Studies

Science

Mathematics

1 Life Science and Physical Science

There are many branches of science that you may study. Basically, though, all of these fall into two major areas—life science and physical science.

Life science is the study of life and living things. This is the organic world. This is where each living thing carries out life processes. (Life processes are things like growing and reproducing.) Physical science is the study of the <u>inorganic</u> world. It studies nonliving things. Nonliving things do not carry out life processes.

Life science is also called biology. Two areas of biology are zoology and botany. Zoology is the study of animals. Botany is the study of plants. Some biologists study how organisms carry out life processes. This is physiology. Other scientists study how parents and offspring are alike and different. This is genetics. Some biologists specialize in a combination of subjects. An example is paleontology. It is the study of ancient life. It combines the studies of earth science, zoology, and botany.

The area of physical science includes four big subjects. One is physics. It is the study of energy. It includes the structure and behavior of atoms. Another is chemistry. It is the study of matter. It studies matter's properties and structure and the ways it changes. A third is astronomy. This is the science of the entire universe beyond Earth. It also studies Earth when Earth interacts with other bodies in the solar system. A fourth is earth science. This is the study of Earth and the space surrounding it. Different branches of earth science study land, water, and air. These are the sciences of geology, oceanography, and meteorology.

Main Idea   1

	Answer	Score
Mark the *main idea*	M	15
Mark the statement that is *too broad*	B	5
Mark the statement that is *too narrow*	N	5

a. Our universe is studied scientifically. ☐ _____

b. Life science is the study of life and living things. ☐ _____

c. Science involves two major areas, life science and physical science. ☐ _____

Subject Matter　2　The purpose of this passage is mainly to
- ☐ a. give a history of science study.
- ☐ b. define life science and physical science.
- ☐ c. explore careers in science.
- ☐ d. predict future trends in science.

_____

Supporting Details　3　Chemistry
- ☐ a. is one of the life sciences.
- ☐ b. is the study of matter and its properties.
- ☐ c. looks at life processes.
- ☐ d. studies the organic world.

_____

Conclusion　4　An area that would be studied in life science would be
- ☐ a. human diseases.
- ☐ b. sunspots.
- ☐ c. snow.
- ☐ d. volcanoes.

_____

Clarifying Devices　5　The writer helps to make clear the four categories of physical science by
- ☐ a. using signal and transitional words.
- ☐ b. using similes and metaphors.
- ☐ c. presenting them in order of importance.
- ☐ d. presenting them in chronological order.

_____

Vocabulary in Context　6　The word <u>inorganic</u> means
- ☐ a. physical.
- ☐ b. scientific.
- ☐ c. nonliving.
- ☐ d. living.

_____

Add your scores for questions 1–6. Enter the total here and on the graph on page 214.　　**Total Score**

_____

2 A Great American Playwright

You may not have heard of playwright Eugene O'Neill. He died in 1953. Most of his plays were serious or even tragic. Yet when critics look at the large number of works he produced and their general excellence, most agree that he is America's greatest playwright.

O'Neill had the theater around him for most of his life. His father was a Shakespearean actor, and the family—his wife, his older son, and young Eugene—often accompanied him on tour. Before he began writing plays, O'Neill worked at various jobs. He was a sailor and a gold prospector as well as an actor.

O'Neill brought new techniques to the American theater. For example, in one play the characters turn aside and speak their thoughts out loud. In another, the characters wear various masks. These show their inner and outer personalities.

Many of O'Neill's life experiences found their way into his plays. Several of his early short plays, for example, were set at sea. *The Iceman Cometh,* a later work, presents a group of alcoholic do-nothings sitting in a bar. Their lives seem modeled on O'Neill's early years. Other famous works deal directly with his immediate family. One, *Long Day's Journey into Night,* is almost a family portrait. It explores the complicated and bitter relations between a vain, loudmouthed father, his morphine-addicted wife, his alcoholic older son, and his sickly younger one. Another, *A Moon for the Misbegotten,* deals with the older brother's sad life. O'Neill tries to suggest a way that things might have turned out better.

O'Neill is a major force in American theater. His best works are often put on in influential playhouses. Famous actors <u>vie</u> for the chance to play his best roles.

Main Idea   1

	Answer	Score
Mark the *main idea*	M	15
Mark the statement that is *too broad*	B	5
Mark the statement that is *too narrow*	N	5

a. Eugene O'Neill became famous for his new techniques as well as his family-based plays.   ☐   _____

b. In one of O'Neill's plays the characters wear masks.   ☐   _____

c. O'Neill was an important writer.   ☐   _____

Score 15 points for each correct answer.   Score

Subject Matter   2   This passage deals mainly with O'Neill's
☐ a. early life.
☐ b. major plays.
☐ c. family.
☐ d. popularity.   _____

Supporting   3   *A Moon for the Misbegotten* is about O'Neill's
Details
☐ a. whole family.
☐ b. mother.
☐ c. father.
☐ d. brother.   _____

Conclusion   4   You can conclude from this passage that
☐ a. O'Neill's family had a lot of problems.
☐ b. O'Neill hated his family.
☐ c. O'Neill wrote only about his family.
☐ d. O'Neill wrote only a few plays.   _____

Clarifying   5   The topic of the third paragraph is developed
Devices   through
☐ a. comparison and contrast.
☐ b. examples.
☐ c. steps in a process.
☐ d. a spatial description.   _____

Vocabulary   6   The word <u>vie</u> means to
in Context
☐ a. gain weight.
☐ b. cheat.
☐ c. compete.
☐ d. spend money.   _____

Add your scores for questions 1–6. Enter the total here   Total
and on the graph on page 214.   Score   _____

3 How Much Do You Save?

Stores often use percents to attract customers to sales. A store might display a large sign such as Clearance Sale! Everything 30 Percent Off! To determine the savings on an article that is 30 percent off, you need to know how to do computations with percents.

Most people recognize that 50 percent equals one-half and that 25 percent equals one-fourth, but other percents such as 30 percent or 45 percent may be real mysteries. A percent can be expressed as a fraction with a bottom number of 100. Here are two examples using 50 percent and 25 percent. The reduced forms of the fractions show why 50 percent equals one-half and 25 percent equals one-fourth.

$$50 \text{ percent} = \frac{50}{100} = \frac{1}{2} \qquad 25 \text{ percent} = \frac{25}{100} = \frac{1}{4}$$

An essential concept that will assist you in computing percents is that any fraction is a different way of writing division. The following examples show two percents written as both fractions and division statements.

$$30 \text{ percent} = \frac{30}{100} = 30 \div 100 \qquad 45 \text{ percent} = \frac{45}{100} = 45 \div 100$$

To compute 30 percent of a price, perform these two steps: multiply by 30, then divide by 100. This two-step strategy can help you solve any percent. To prove to yourself that it works, experiment with a problem such as 50 percent of $18. (You know before you start that the answer should be $9.) Using a calculator, multiply 50 times 18 to get 900; then divide 900 by 100 to get 9.

You probably won't <u>employ</u> this strategy with percents that you can easily calculate on your own. But when you encounter more challenging percents, the multiply-divide strategy will always work.

Main Idea   1

	Answer	Score
Mark the *main idea*	M	15
Mark the statement that is *too broad*	B	5
Mark the statement that is *too narrow*	N	5

a. Computing percents can be done by multiplying and then dividing by 100. ☐ _____

b. Computing percents is difficult for many people. ☐ _____

c. A savings of 25 percent means that you save one-fourth of the regular price. ☐ _____

Subject Matter   **2**   Another good title for this passage would be
- ☐ a. Avoiding Trouble with Fractions.
- ☐ b. Comparing Prices on Sale Merchandise.
- ☐ c. Multiplying and Dividing.
- ☐ d. Finding a Percent of a Price.

_____

Supporting Details   **3**   A percent can be expressed as
- ☐ a. a fraction with a top number of 100.
- ☐ b. a fraction with a bottom number of 100.
- ☐ c. always a very large number.
- ☐ d. a way of not getting cheated at a sale.

_____

Conclusion   **4**   To figure out 45 percent of $30,
- ☐ a. multiply 45 times 30 and divide the answer by 100.
- ☐ b. multiply 100 times 30 and divide the answer by 45.
- ☐ c. make $30 into a fraction.
- ☐ d. realize that 45 percent equals one-fourth.

_____

Clarifying Devices   **5**   The writer introduces this passage by
- ☐ a. discussing what 25 percent and 50 percent are equal to.
- ☐ b. telling what the word _percent_ means.
- ☐ c. describing how percents are used in advertising sales.
- ☐ d. telling how percents are done on a calculator.

_____

Vocabulary in Context   **6**   In this passage the word <u>employ</u> means to
- ☐ a. forget.
- ☐ b. hire.
- ☐ c. use.
- ☐ d. understand.

_____

Add your scores for questions 1–6. Enter the total here and on the graph on page 214.   **Total Score**   _____

4 Gold and Silver Worth $30 Million

The Spanish explorer Francisco Pizarro was exploring South America in the 1530s when he saw a large raft. It carried silver, gold, emeralds, and rich cloth. This was his first look at the riches of the Inca Empire. At one time this empire covered much of western South America.

Atahualpa was ruler of the Inca Empire. One of his messengers visited Pizarro's camp and invited Pizarro to visit the city of Cajamarca. Pizarro and his men were looking for glory and gold. They wanted to expand the Spanish Empire. So Pizarro and about 160 horsemen and soldiers accepted the invitation. They set off into the Andes Mountains. When Pizarro and his men came out of the mountains, they looked down on Cajamarca Valley. The tents of the Inca army were below them.

To greet Pizarro, Atahualpa had put on embroidered clothes and an emerald collar. He was carried on a special throne to Cajamarca's central square. He arrived with about 5,000 men. Without warning, the Spaniards attacked. The unarmed Inca soldiers tried to escape, but the Spaniards killed thousands of them. They captured Atahualpa.

Atahualpa's people tried to get him back. They gathered gold and silver worth 30 million dollars to give to Pizarro. It was one of the largest <u>ransoms</u> in history. Pizarro agreed to the ransom. But then he did not keep his promise. Instead he accused Atahualpa of sending for an army. The Spaniards sentenced him to death. He was executed in Cajamarca Square.

Pizarro's stolen treasure was 11 tons of gold objects. He melted down almost all of it. Few gold objects survived the Spanish conquest.

Main Idea	1	Answer	Score
	Mark the *main idea*	M	15
	Mark the statement that is *too broad*	B	5
	Mark the statement that is *too narrow*	N	5

a. The Spanish explorers stole from and conquered the Incas. ☐ _____

b. Pizarro met the Inca ruler in a public square. ☐ _____

c. The Spanish explored South America. ☐ _____

Score 15 points for each correct answer.　　　　　　**Score**

Subject Matter　　2　Another good title for this passage is
　　　　　　☐ a. A Meeting in the Andes.
　　　　　　☐ b. The Wealth of the Incas.
　　　　　　☐ c. The Downfall of an Inca Leader.
　　　　　　☐ d. Atahualpa and His 5,000 Men.　　　____

Supporting　　3　The value of the ransom was
Details
　　　　　　☐ a. paid mostly in emeralds.
　　　　　　☐ b. 11 million dollars.
　　　　　　☐ c. 30 million dollars.
　　　　　　☐ d. 5,000 dollars.　　　____

Conclusion　　4　This passage clearly demonstrates Pizarro's
　　　　　　☐ a. bad temper.
　　　　　　☐ b. honesty.
　　　　　　☐ c. greed.
　　　　　　☐ d. fairness.　　　____

Clarifying　　5　The basic pattern used to develop this passage is
Devices
　　　　　　☐ a. question and answer.
　　　　　　☐ b. a spatial description.
　　　　　　☐ c. comparison and contrast.
　　　　　　☐ d. chronological order.　　　____

Vocabulary　　6　The word ransoms means
in Context
　　　　　　☐ a. prices paid for someone's release.
　　　　　　☐ b. searches.
　　　　　　☐ c. agreements between two people.
　　　　　　☐ d. gatherings of military troops.　　　____

Add your scores for questions 1–6. Enter the total here　　**Total**
and on the graph on page 214.　　**Score**　　____

5 Plate Tectonics: A Very Slow Ride

The surface of the earth may seem very <u>stable</u> to you. But you might be amazed if you knew some of the things that were going on under that surface.

The earth has an outer shell of rigid pieces called *tectonic plates*. The plates include both ocean floor and dry land. Some have whole continents on top of them. These plates are estimated to be about six to ten miles thick under the oceans, and as much as 120 miles thick under some continents. The continents on top of the plates are just going along for a slow ride, moving only about four inches per year. But even this small movement causes three types of big interactions.

One type is ocean ridges. These ridges develop in places where two plates are moving away from each other. As the plates separate, hot magma flows up to fill the space. New crust builds up on the plate boundaries and causes ocean ridges. These ridges form long mountain ranges, which only rise above the ocean surface in a few places.

Another type of reaction—trenches—occurs between two plates that are moving toward each other. As the plates meet, one bends downward and plunges underneath the other. This forms deep ocean trenches. The Marianas Trench off Guam in the western Pacific Ocean has a depth of more than 36,000 feet. This is the lowest point on the ocean floor. If the leading edges of the two colliding plates carry continents, then the layers of rock in the overriding plate crumple and fold. A plate that carried what is now India collided with the southern edge of the plate that carried Europe and most of Asia. This caused the Himalayas, the world's highest mountains.

The third reaction is transform faults. These faults occur where two plates that are traveling in opposite directions slide past each other. Severe earthquakes can occur. The San Andreas Fault in California is a good example of this type of movement.

Main Idea	1			
			Answer	**Score**
	Mark the *main idea*		M	15
	Mark the statement that is *too broad*		B	5
	Mark the statement that is *too narrow*		N	5

a.	Tectonic plates cause three types of movements of the earth's surface.	☐	___
b.	The movement of tectonic plates may cause earthquakes.	☐	___
c.	The earth has a shell of tectonic plates.	☐	

Score 15 points for each correct answer.　　　　Score

Subject Matter　2　This passage is mostly about
- ☐ a. effects of movements of the earth's plates.
- ☐ b. types of continents.
- ☐ c. the Marianas Trench.
- ☐ d. transform faults.　　　＿＿＿

Supporting Details　3　The San Andreas Fault is an example of
- ☐ a. a California rock formation.
- ☐ b. a severe earthquake.
- ☐ c. a trench.
- ☐ d. two plates traveling in opposite directions.　＿＿＿

Conclusion　4　According to information in this passage, the earth
- ☐ a. is always changing.
- ☐ b. never changes.
- ☐ c. is shrinking.
- ☐ d. is melting.　　　＿＿＿

Clarifying Devices　5　To explain an effect of trenches, the writer gives the example of
- ☐ a. the sea floor near Guam.
- ☐ b. India.
- ☐ c. the San Andreas Fault.
- ☐ d. the Himalayan Mountains.　　＿＿＿

Vocabulary in Context　6　In this passage the word <u>stable</u> means
- ☐ a. a place for horses.
- ☐ b. calm and easygoing.
- ☐ c. steady or firm.
- ☐ d. a collection of animals.　　＿＿＿

Add your scores for questions 1–6. Enter the total here and on the graph on page 214.　　Total Score　＿＿＿

11

6 Cubism

Painters often want to show things in a new way. They want to experiment with techniques that fit their own artistic vision. Sometimes this means they want to paint entirely differently from others around them. This was certainly true of Georges Braque and Pablo Picasso and the painting movement called *Cubism*.

Picasso and Braque began developing their new artistic ideas in the early 1900s. Much of the painting they saw around them was beautiful and <u>sensual</u>. These two artists, however, were more interested in appealing to the viewer's mind. And so they put less emphasis on painting things exactly the way they looked. Instead, they took three-dimensional objects and tried to make them look flat. A painting of a woman, for example, might show her front, back, and sides all at the same time. You might see a face in such a painting, and a vague body shape. But you would probably also see a lot of geometric shapes that represented the other parts of the body. These shapes were often cones and cubes. The finished paintings were more abstract than realistic.

So who founded cubism, Picasso or Braque? It is really impossible to say. The two began exchanging ideas and paintings almost as soon as they met, in 1907. Picasso did a painting of young women that is sometimes considered the first work of Cubism. But Braque was the one who contributed much of the emphasis on geometric forms. For a time the artists' works were so similar that it was hard to tell who painted what.

Cubism as an art movement lasted fewer than 20 years. Both Braque and Picasso went on to other painting styles. But Cubism was a strong break with realistic painting. The way it dealt with the world would have an enormous influence on painters for the rest of the 20th century.

Main Idea   1

	Answer	Score
Mark the *main idea*	M	15
Mark the statement that is *too broad*	B	5
Mark the statement that is *too narrow*	N	5

a. Braque was particularly influenced by geometric shapes.   ☐   _____

b. Cubism was an art movement that presented three-dimensional objects in a new way.   ☐   _____

c. Trends in art often change.   ☐   _____

Subject Matter   **2**   Another good title for this passage would be
☐ a. Why Picasso Is Famous.
☐ b. What Is a Cube?
☐ c. Painting in the Twentieth Century.
☐ d. A Startling New Way of Painting.   _____

Supporting   **3**   Picasso and Braque were interested in
Details
☐ a. doing beautiful paintings.
☐ b. appealing to the viewer's mind.
☐ c. having an art movement named after them.
☐ d. confusing the viewer as much as possible.   _____

Conclusion   **4**   The name *Cubism* comes from the
☐ a. painters' desire to paint objects rather
   than people.
☐ b. heavy square chalks the painters used.
☐ c. painters' interest in young animals.
☐ d. geometric shapes the painters used.   _____

Clarifying   **5**   In the final paragraph, the term *strong break* means a
Devices
☐ a. sudden stop.
☐ b. big change.
☐ c. serious fall.
☐ d. shattering of an object.   _____

Vocabulary   **6**   In this passage the word <u>sensual</u> means
in Context
☐ a. emotional.
☐ b. lazy.
☐ c. appealing to the mind.
☐ d. appealing to the senses.   _____

Add your scores for questions 1–6. Enter the total here   **Total**
and on the graph on page 214.   **Score**   _____

7 Not Just a White Man's War

President Abraham Lincoln's first call for volunteers to fight in the Civil War was for whites only. The Civil War was a white man's war, northern whites insisted. Its purpose was to preserve the Union. It was not being fought to end slavery. But by September of 1862, the <u>sentiment</u> toward black volunteers had changed. Lincoln had hoped that the war would be short, but it had already lasted nearly a year and a half. Union manpower had fallen dangerously low.

Lincoln had a plan. He issued the *Emancipation Proclamation.* It stated that as of January 1, 1863, all slaves residing in the rebellious Southern states would be forever free. And starting immediately, Union armies would accept black volunteers.

The Southern Rebels' response to Lincoln's call for black troops was a deadly one. Captives of any Union regiment with black troops were to be given "no quarter." They were to be put to death immediately.

African-American troops throughout the war distinguished themselves in battle at places like Milliken's Bend, Fort Wagner, and the Crater at St. Petersburg. As to their conduct on the battlefield, Colonel Thomas Wentworth Higginson wrote: "Nobody knows anything about these men who has not seen them in battle. No officer in this regiment now doubts that the successful prosecution of the war lies in the unlimited employment of black troops." By the war's end 186,000 black troops had participated. They made up nearly 10 percent of Union forces. These black soldiers saw action in more than 250 battles. Black soldiers also gave their lives. By the war's end about 38,000 black troops had died. They died from disease, in battle, and after capture by Rebel troops.

Main Idea 1

	Answer	Score
Mark the *main idea*	M	15
Mark the statement that is *too broad*	B	5
Mark the statement that is *too narrow*	N	5

a. Abraham Lincoln's first call for Union troops was for whites only. ☐ _____

b. African-American troops played an important part in the Civil War. ☐ _____

c. Many men served in the Civil War. ☐ _____

Subject Matter 2 This passage is mainly about
- [ ] a. causes of the Civil War.
- [ ] b. the Emancipation Proclamation.
- [ ] c. black soldiers in the Civil War.
- [ ] d. why Lincoln was a good President.   _____

Supporting Details 3 Feelings about having black volunteers in the Union army changed because
- [ ] a. Colonel Higginson changed everyone's mind.
- [ ] b. Union captives were being put to death.
- [ ] c. there were not enough Union troops.
- [ ] d. slavery had ended.   _____

Conclusion 4 The writer of this passage wants the reader to reach the conclusion that
- [ ] a. Lincoln acted too late to free the slaves.
- [ ] b. blacks fought well for the Union cause.
- [ ] c. the Civil War changed American history.
- [ ] d. the South nearly won the Civil War.   _____

Clarifying Devices 5 Which sentence from the passage helps clarify the phrase *no quarter?*
- [ ] a. They were to be put to death immediately.
- [ ] b. Black troops throughout the war distinguished themselves.
- [ ] c. Nobody knows anything about these men.
- [ ] d. Union armies would accept black volunteers.   _____

Vocabulary in Context 6 The word <u>sentiment</u> means
- [ ] a. newspaper editorials.
- [ ] b. people who keep watch.
- [ ] c. poetry.
- [ ] d. thought and feeling.   _____

Add your scores for questions 1–6. Enter the total here and on the graph on page 214.   **Total Score**   _____

8 Beyond the Domino

Dominoes is a familiar game played with rectangular tiles. Each domino consists of a rectangle formed by joining two squares. Domino-like shapes can also be formed by joining more than two squares. Such geometric shapes are called *polyominoes*. The most popular polyominoes are the *pentominoes,* those made with five squares. (*Pento-* means "five.") Below are the 12 possible pentominoes:

The pentominoes, which can be made by cutting the shapes from graph paper, are used for a wide variety of puzzles. Each puzzle has the same basic rule: you are to use all 12 pentominoes to build a shape. Only the outline of the shape is given, and the puzzle is to arrange the pieces to fill the given outline. For example, a number of different rectangles are possible, such as the one shown. The shapes don't allow you to fill in a square, but you can make squares with "holes" in them.

If you become fascinated with pentomino puzzles, you have many hours of enjoyment ahead of you. You will probably start creating your own puzzles to solve. The pieces have many interesting qualities to discover. For example, each pentomino can be built using nine of the others. Pentominoes are a great way to improve your <u>visual</u> thinking skills. And they are lots of fun!

Main Idea	1		
		Answer	**Score**
	Mark the *main idea*	**M**	15
	Mark the statement that is *too broad*	**B**	5
	Mark the statement that is *too narrow*	**N**	5
	a. A pentomino is made up of five squares.	☐	____
	b. Pentominoes are geometric shapes that can be used in visual puzzles.	☐	____
	c. Many people enjoy geometric puzzles.	☐	____

Score 15 points for each correct answer.   Score

Subject Matter   2   This passage is mainly about
- ☐ a. how to solve geometric puzzles.
- ☐ b. why geometric puzzles are popular.
- ☐ c. dominos.
- ☐ d. pentominoes and pentomino puzzles.   _____

Supporting Details   3   A pentomino piece is made of
- ☐ a. 5 squares.
- ☐ b. 12 squares.
- ☐ c. 5 rectangles.
- ☐ d. 12 rectangles.   _____

Conclusion   4   You can conclude from this passage that
- ☐ a. you can make a complete square from pentomino pieces.
- ☐ b. rectangles can be of different lengths and widths.
- ☐ c. pentominoes can be bought in toy stores.
- ☐ d. pentominoes are a fairly new game.   _____

Clarifying Devices   5   The writer pictures the 12 pentominos to
- ☐ a. help you see how many kinds there are.
- ☐ b. prove that they are easy to make.
- ☐ c. show that they are fun to play with.
- ☐ d. show that each one has four sides.   _____

Vocabulary in Context   6   In this passage <u>visual</u> means having
- ☐ a. to do with hearing.
- ☐ b. to do with vision.
- ☐ c. many shapes.
- ☐ d. many sizes.   _____

Add your scores for questions 1–6. Enter the total here and on the graph on page 214.   Total Score   _____

9 An Essential Scientific Process

All life on the earth depends upon green plants. Using sunlight, the plants produce their own food. Then animals feed upon the plants. They take in the nutrients the plants have made and stored. But that's not all. Sunlight also helps a plant produce oxygen. Some of the oxygen is used by the plant, but a plant usually produces more oxygen than it uses. The <u>excess</u> oxygen is necessary for animals and other organisms to live.

The process of changing light into food and oxygen is called *photosynthesis*. Besides light energy from the sun, plants also use water and carbon dioxide. The water gets to the plant through its roots. The carbon dioxide enters the leaves through tiny openings called *stomata*. The carbon dioxide travels to chloroplasts, special cells in the bodies of green plants. This is where photosynthesis takes place. Chloroplasts contain the chlorophylls that give plants their green color. The chlorophylls are the molecules that trap light energy. The trapped light energy changes water and carbon dioxide to produce oxygen and a simple sugar called *glucose*.

Carbon dioxide and oxygen move into and out of the stomata. Water vapor also moves out of the stomata. More than 90 percent of the water a plant takes in through its roots escapes through the stomata. During the daytime, the stomata of most plants are open. This allows carbon dioxide to enter the leaves for photosynthesis. As night falls, carbon dioxide is not needed. The stomata of most plants close. Water loss stops.

If photosynthesis ceased, there would be little food or other organic matter on the earth. Most organisms would disappear. The earth's atmosphere would no longer contain oxygen. Photosynthesis is essential for life on our planet.

Main Idea   1 ───────────────────────────────

	Answer	Score
Mark the *main idea*	M	15
Mark the statement that is *too broad*	B	5
Mark the statement that is *too narrow*	N	5

a. Stomata allow carbon dioxide to enter leaves for photosynthesis. ☐ _____

b. Life on the earth depends upon green plants. ☐ _____

c. The process of changing light into food and oxygen is called photosynthesis. ☐ _____

Subject Matter   **2**   Another good title for this passage would be

☐ a. Oxygen and Carbon Dioxide.

☐ b. Plants and Their Roots.

☐ c. How Photosynthesis Works.

☐ d. Why Our Earth Needs Water.   _____

Supporting Details   **3**   Which of the following does *not* move through a plant's stomata?

☐ a. carbon dioxide

☐ b. water vapor

☐ c. oxygen

☐ d. food   _____

Conclusion   **4**   In the title, the term *Essential Scientific Process* refers to

☐ a. photosynthesis.

☐ b. the formation of glucose.

☐ c. global warming.

☐ d. water getting to the roots of plants.   _____

Clarifying Devices   **5**   This passage is primarily developed by

☐ a. explaining a process.

☐ b. telling a story.

☐ c. comparing and contrasting.

☐ d. convincing the reader of plants' importance.   _____

Vocabulary in Context   **6**   In this passage excess means

☐ a. heavy.

☐ b. extra.

☐ c. green.

☐ d. liquid.   _____

Add your scores for questions 1–6. Enter the total here and on the graph on page 214.   **Total Score**   _____

10 Scraping the Sky

These buildings are huge. One of them—the Petronas Towers in Malaysia—is 1,483 feet tall. This makes it the tallest building in the world, but others are close behind. The Sears Tower in Chicago is 1,450 feet, and the World Trade Center in New York City is 1,368 feet. No wonder they are called skyscrapers!

You might wonder why people wanted to build tall buildings in the first place. Actually, American architects and business people had been thinking about it through most of the 19th century. But toward the end of the century, the <u>climate</u> was right. People were streaming into large American cities. There was no place to put them. There was also a boom in business and much optimism about the future. And in Chicago, where many early skyscrapers were built, there was both opportunity and need. The whole downtown of the city had been destroyed by fire in 1871.

Certain things had to happen before it was possible to build tall buildings. The higher you wanted to build a building of stone, the thicker the walls and foundation you had to construct in order to support its weight. Then in the 1880s an architect named William Le Baron Jenney used a new method of support, a lightweight steel frame, that allowed him to build a taller building with wider windows. This early skyscraper—the Home Insurance Building in Chicago—was all of nine stories tall!

From there, however, techniques developed rapidly. Architects learned how to support each floor of a building on beams that bore their entire weight. Since the walls were only like a skin, they could be light and filled with windows, as in the modern skyscrapers we see today. And high-speed elevators, the descendants of an invention from the 1850s, make it possible to reach the highest floors in seconds.

Main Idea	1		Answer	Score
	Mark the *main idea*		M	15
	Mark the statement that is *too broad*		B	5
	Mark the statement that is *too narrow*		N	5

		Answer	Score
a.	Skyscrapers developed because of new architectural methods and cities' needs.	☐	____
b.	One of the earliest skyscrapers was nine stories tall.	☐	____
c.	Skyscrapers are huge buildings.	☐	____

Score 15 points for each correct answer.   **Score**

Subject Matter 2 This passage is mainly about
☐ a. the development of the skyscraper.
☐ b. modern skyscrapers.
☐ c. American cities in the 19th century.
☐ d. William Le Baron Jenney.   _____

Supporting Details 3 The World Trade Center is in
☐ a. Malaysia.
☐ b. Chicago.
☐ c. Los Angeles.
☐ d. New York City.   _____

Conclusion 4 Skyscrapers could not be built until
☐ a. their walls did not have to bear all the weight of the building.
☐ b. people began to appreciate large windows.
☐ c. cities had successful downtown areas.
☐ d. businesses were willing to pay for them.   _____

Clarifying Devices 5 In the first paragraph the writer's purpose is to
☐ a. interest you with some surprising facts.
☐ b. compare modern skyscrapers with older ones.
☐ c. define the word *skyscraper*.
☐ d. show that American skyscrapers are no longer the tallest.   _____

Vocabulary in Context 6 In this passage <u>climate</u> means
☐ a. weather.
☐ b. conditions or feelings.
☐ c. heat.
☐ d. height.   _____

Add your scores for questions 1–6. Enter the total here and on the graph on page 214.   **Total Score**   _____

11 Prime and Composite Numbers

One important way of classifying a whole number is by whether it is prime or composite. A prime number is a whole number greater than 1. It can have only two factors, or numbers that can be multiplied to produce it. These are the number itself and the number 1. The number 6 is not prime because it has the factors 2 and 3. If a number is not prime, like the example number 6, then it is composite—it is "composed" of its different factors.

To identify all prime numbers less than 100, start with a grid. Shade in all the multiples of two: 4, 6, and so on (as shown below). Shade in the multiples of 3, 5, and 7. The unshaded numbers are prime numbers.

You'll see from your diagram that a prime number greater than 2 has to end in the digit 1, 3, 7, or 9. But other than that, there apparently isn't any obvious pattern to the frequency of the primes. In fact, many renowned mathematicians have been fascinated with prime numbers, wondering if there *is* a complex pattern to their occurrence.

	2	3	4	5	6	7	8	9	10
11	12	13	14	15	16	17	18	19	20
21	22	23	24	25	26	27	28	29	30
31	32	33	34	35	36	37	38	39	40
41	412	43	44	45	46	47	48	49	50
51	52	53	54	55	56	57	58	59	60
61	62	63	64	65	66	67	68	69	70
71	72	73	74	75	76	77	78	79	80
81	82	83	84	85	86	87	88	89	90
91	92	93	94	95	96	97	98	99	100

Prime numbers have recently been put to an important use. Let's say a very large number, one with 120 digits, has only four factors: 1, itself, and two roughly equal prime numbers. (Those prime numbers might have 40 or 50 digits themselves.) Mathematicians believe that figuring out what those factors are can take years, even on the fastest computers. So these sorts of numbers are used in creating a procedure called *oblivious transfer,* a method of providing <u>secure</u> Internet transactions.

Main Idea 1

	Answer	Score
Mark the *main idea*	M	15
Mark the statement that is *too broad*	B	5
Mark the statement that is *too narrow*	N	5

a. The only even prime number is 2. ☐ _____

b. Prime numbers are part of mathematics. ☐ _____

c. Mathematicians consider prime numbers both interesting and useful. ☐ _____

Subject Matter 　**2**　This passage is mainly concerned with
- ☐ a. prime numbers and their use.
- ☐ b. prime numbers between 1 and 200.
- ☐ c. whether there is a pattern in how often prime numbers occur.
- ☐ d. composite numbers and their use.

_____

Supporting Details 　**3**　The number 6 is not a prime number because it
- ☐ a. is less than 100.
- ☐ b. is an even number.
- ☐ c. has other factors besides itself and 1.
- ☐ d. is not a whole number.

_____

Conclusion 　**4**　This passage leads the reader to conclude that
- ☐ a. there are no prime numbers over 100.
- ☐ b. prime numbers can be very large.
- ☐ c. prime numbers cannot end in 3.
- ☐ d. mathematicians have identified every prime number that exists.

_____

Clarifying Devices 　**5**　The diagram helps show that prime numbers
- ☐ a. are only even numbers.
- ☐ b. are greater than 2.
- ☐ c. require multiplication skills.
- ☐ d. have no obvious repeating pattern.

_____

Vocabulary in Context 　**6**　In this passage the word <u>secure</u> means
- ☐ a. unlikely.
- ☐ b. simple.
- ☐ c. safe.
- ☐ d. inexpensive.

_____

Add your scores for questions 1–6. Enter the total here and on the graph on page 214.　　**Total Score**

_____

12 Pavlov's Bewitched Dogs

Is behavior learned? Psychologists have discussed this question for years. They began thinking about it because of the work of Ivan Pavlov. He was a Russian professor of physiology. Here is his story.

In carefully controlled experiments, Pavlov showed that dogs could be taught to salivate. Critics said the dogs were bewitched. And Pavlov was probably as surprised as his critics. But the evidence was there.

The discovery was accidental. Pavlov was doing research on digestion and on the central nervous system. For his research, he collected saliva from the animals in his laboratory. To get the saliva, he had an experimenter put meat powder in the laboratory dogs' mouths. The meat powder was a stimulus to get the dogs' mouths to water. Soon he noticed that the dogs' mouths watered even before they got the meat powder. In fact, their mouths began to water at the sight of the experimenter. The experimenter had become the stimulus!

Pavlov wondered if other stimuli could get the dogs to salivate. He paired the meat powder with the sound of a tuning fork, the turning on of a light, and the ringing of a bell. He got the same results. An automatic physical response, called a *reflex,* is one of the most basic actions animals perform. Sneezing in a dusty place and shivering in the cold are reflex actions. But Pavlov's experiments showed that reflexes could be taught. This led the way to further thinking on whether behavior is natural or learned.

It may not sound so <u>incredible</u> today, but at the turn of the 20th century Pavlov's research seemed remarkable. It brought about new research methods and ideas. Pavlov continued his work on the nervous system of the dog. He experimented with different stimuli. His work became the basis for much of modern psychology.

Main Idea 1	Answer	Score
Mark the *main idea*	M	15
Mark the statement that is *too broad*	B	5
Mark the statement that is *too narrow*	N	5
a. Ivan Pavlov was a Russian scientist.	☐	_____
b. Pavlov's dogs salivated to such stimuli as bells and lights.	☐	_____
c. Pavlov's experiments led to important psychological findings.	☐	_____

24

Score 15 points for each correct answer. **Score**

Subject Matter   2   This passage is mostly about
- ☐ a. experiments with different kinds of dogs.
- ☐ b. the meaning of *salivate*.
- ☐ c. how Ivan Pavlov's work with stimuli changed ideas about behavior.
- ☐ d. the life of Ivan Pavlov.

_____

Supporting Details   3   Pavlov's dogs responded to
- ☐ a. newspapers.
- ☐ b. the sound of a bell.
- ☐ c. forks, knives, and spoons.
- ☐ d. saliva.

_____

Conclusion   4   From this passage it is reasonable to conclude that
- ☐ a. bells should be rung at meal times.
- ☐ b. Pavlov enjoyed being a famous person.
- ☐ c. dogs can be taught to do anything.
- ☐ d. Pavlov became more interested in dogs' brains than in their digestion.

_____

Clarifying Devices   5   People said the dogs were bewitched because
- ☐ a. Pavlov seemed like an evil wizard.
- ☐ b. the dogs were salivating without a direct stimulus.
- ☐ c. the dogs performed in a circus sideshow.
- ☐ d. the dogs never slept after Pavlov's experiment.

_____

Vocabulary in Context   6   The word <u>incredible</u> means
- ☐ a. unpleasant.
- ☐ b. new.
- ☐ c. confusing.
- ☐ d. unbelievable.

_____

Add your scores for questions 1–6. Enter the total here and on the graph on page 214.

Total Score

_____

13 Black Holes

Most scientists agree that black holes exist but are nearly impossible to locate. A black hole in the universe is not a solid object, like a planet, but it is shaped like a sphere. Astronomers think that at the center of a black hole there is a single point in space with infinite density (in other words, there are no limits to its denseness). This single point is called a *singularity*. If the singularity theory is correct, it means that when a <u>massive</u> star collapses, all the material in it disappears into the singularity. The center of a black hole would not really be a hole at all, but an infinitely dense point.

A black hole also has no surface. It begins at a gravitational place whose outer limits are called the event horizon. The event horizon is the point of no return. Anything that crosses the event horizon is pulled in by the black hole's great gravity.

Although black holes do exist, they are difficult to observe. These are the reasons.

- No light or anything else comes out of black holes. As a result, they are invisible to a telescope.
- In astronomical terms, black holes are truly tiny. For example, a black hole formed by the collapse of a giant star would have an event horizon only 18 miles across.
- The nearest black holes would be dozens of light years away from Earth. One light year is the distance light travels in a year. It is about 6 trillion miles. Even the most powerful telescopes could not pick out an object so small at such a great distance.

In 1994 the Hubble Space Telescope provided evidence that black holes exist. There are still answers to be found, however, so black holes remain one of the mysteries of the universe.

Main Idea	1		Answer	Score
	Mark the *main idea*		M	15
	Mark the statement that is *too broad*		B	5
	Mark the statement that is *too narrow*		N	5
	a. Black holes are part of space.		☐	_____
	b. Black holes exist but are difficult to observe.		☐	_____
	c. Black holes are infinitely dense.		☐	_____

Subject Matter   2   Another good title for this passage would be
- ☐ a. Black Holes Allow Nothing to Escape!
- ☐ b. Black Holes: A Mystery to Be Solved.
- ☐ c. The Universe Holds Many Secrets.
- ☐ d. Traveling to a Black Hole.

_____

Supporting Details   3   The center of a black hole is
- ☐ a. infinite in size.
- ☐ b. not really a hole at all.
- ☐ c. empty.
- ☐ d. a huge, massive star.

_____

Conclusion   4   A black hole is like a planet in that both
- ☐ a. support life.
- ☐ b. are spherical in shape.
- ☐ c. are solid.
- ☐ d. are invisible to telescopes.

_____

Clarifying Devices   5   The three bulleted points support the statement that
- ☐ a. black holes are difficult to find.
- ☐ b. no light can escape from black holes.
- ☐ c. black holes do exist.
- ☐ d. black holes do not exist.

_____

Vocabulary in Context   6   The word <u>massive</u> means very
- ☐ a. bright.
- ☐ b. fast.
- ☐ c. far away.
- ☐ d. large.

_____

Add your scores for questions 1–6. Enter the total here and on the graph on page 214.   **Total Score**

_____

14 The Nuyorican Poets Cafe

Do you know the word *Nuyorican?* Some say it refers to Puerto Ricans living in New York City. Others say it means Puerto Ricans who have returned from New York to Puerto Rico. There is another meaning as well. The word is part of the name of the Nuyorican Poets Cafe. This is a group—and place—that has existed in New York since 1974.

The Nuyorican Poets Cafe was, in fact, begun by New York Puerto Ricans. Its mission from the very beginning has been to showcase new art. At first this was just material from the Caribbean islands and Hispanic America. But now it has expanded to include any group that is not part of the mainstream American community.

What does "art" mean to the Nuyoricans? Actually, it includes a variety of things. Most of these involve performance. Much of the earliest work they presented was poetry through poetry slams. They have also had dance and jazz performances. Featured as well have been singers and theater presentations. The group did a collection of poetry, *Aloud! Voices from the Nuyorican Poets Cafe.* It won an American Book Award.

Large portions of the program at the Nuyorican Poets Cafe are <u>spontaneous</u> rather than planned. One segment, for example, might feature an open microphone. Here poets and singers can perform while a jazz band provides appropriate background music. The tone of much of the work is designed to get the audience to think and respond. Performers express political and gender views—in fact, whatever is on their minds.

A schedule for a recent week at the Cafe shows its variety. Included were talks by authors, a one-man show, a comedy presentation, a short play, and a "Latin jazz jam." The Cafe more than does its part to bring new and exciting voices to audiences.

Main Idea	1	Answer	Score
	Mark the *main idea*	**M**	15
	Mark the statement that is *too broad*	**B**	5
	Mark the statement that is *too narrow*	**N**	5

a. The Nuyorican Poets Cafe presents many varieties of performances. ☐ ____

b. A book of poetry published by the Nuyorican Poets Cafe won an award. ☐ ____

c. Performers need a place to perform. ☐

Score 15 points for each correct answer.   **Score**

Subject Matter   2   Another good title for this passage is
      ☐ a. A Showcase for Many Kinds of Talent.
      ☐ b. A Place for Performers.
      ☐ c. A Place for Minorities Only.
      ☐ d. Performing in New York City.   _____

Supporting   3   Performers at the Nuyorican Poets Cafe may be from
Details
      ☐ a. Puerto Rico only.
      ☐ b. a few countries in South America.
      ☐ c. any group that wants to present its art.
      ☐ d. mostly Mexico and Guatemala.   _____

Conclusion   4   You can conclude from the passage that the
      Nuyorican Poets Cafe would be a good place to
      ☐ a. present original music.
      ☐ b. present a photography exhibit.
      ☐ c. get recipes for multiethnic food.
      ☐ d. meet travelers from all over the world.   _____

Clarifying   5   Questions are used in this passage to
Devices
      ☐ a. surprise the reader.
      ☐ b. show two sides of the story.
      ☐ c. help introduce important points.
      ☐ d. compare the present and the future.   _____

Vocabulary   6   The word <u>spontaneous</u> means
in Context
      ☐ a. confusing.
      ☐ b. long.
      ☐ c. lively.
      ☐ d. unplanned.   _____

Add your scores for questions 1–6. Enter the total here   **Total**
and on the graph on page 214.   **Score**   _____

15 Random Numbers

What does the word *random* mean to you? You might think of events that are unpredictable. Or you might think of a series of numbers with no obvious pattern. Most people agree that tossing a coin results in a random outcome. Many have a false belief, though, that after a long sequence of heads the toss is more than 50 percent likely to be tails. Such a belief is known, for reasons you can imagine, as the "gambler's <u>fallacy</u>."

The need for random numbers or procedures occurs more often than you might think. In statistics, a sequence of outcomes or number choices is defined as random if each outcome is not influenced by the previous ones. So anyone who buys a ticket for a lottery wants to be sure that the results are truly random. And when doing such things as polling, statisticians need to pick random samples. This way, they ensure that their poll results will have validity. Computers are used to generate lists of random numbers for statistical and scientific work.

When might you need to use random numbers? People today use numbers in secret passwords for computer or banking access. Many people do not choose these numbers wisely. It is *not* a good idea, for example, to use part of your telephone number, social security number, or address. You could instead pick a number from a table of random numbers. But you might not have such a table handy. Consider this simpler, more practical way of getting a random number. Write the digits 0 through 9 on ten slips of paper. Then put them in a bag, and draw the needed number of digits. The key idea behind secret passwords is to use numbers that would be almost impossible for someone to guess.

Main Idea	1		Answer	Score
	Mark the *main idea*		M	15
	Mark the statement that is *too broad*		B	5
	Mark the statement that is *too narrow*		N	5

a. Random numbers are needed in many everyday transactions.	☐	_____
b. Tossing a coin is a random procedure.	☐	_____
c. Number patterns can be described in different ways.	☐	_____

Score 15 points for each correct answer.   Score

Subject Matter   **2**   This passage is mainly about
- ☐ a. ways of winning at games of chance.
- ☐ b. setting up statistical experiments.
- ☐ c. remembering computer passwords.
- ☐ d. choosing and using random numbers. _____

Supporting Details   **3**   If two events are random, then
- ☐ a. they are closely related.
- ☐ b. they occur at the same time.
- ☐ c. the second event does not depend on the first event.
- ☐ d. the events must involve large numbers. _____

Conclusion   **4**   Random numbers must be selected
- ☐ a. from a hat.
- ☐ b. with a number pattern in mind.
- ☐ c. with no way to control or influence the choice.
- ☐ d. from a random number table. _____

Clarifying Devices   **5**   In the final paragraph the writer shows how random numbers
- ☐ a. can be used to pick passwords.
- ☐ b. are important in statistical work.
- ☐ c. are organized into tables.
- ☐ d. are composed of one-digit numerals. _____

Vocabulary in Context   **6**   In this passage the word <u>fallacy</u> means
- ☐ a. a lie.
- ☐ b. a mistaken belief.
- ☐ c. an argument.
- ☐ d. a choice. _____

Add your scores for questions 1–6. Enter the total here and on the graph on page 214.

Total Score _____

16 Where in the World?

You probably know your postal address and your zip code, right? But did you know that you can pinpoint your global address too? For example, the global address for downtown Chicago, Illinois, looks like this: 41°50'N 87°45'W. These numbers and symbols tell the latitude and longitude of the city.

Lines of latitude and longitude are the imaginary grid geographers use to locate places on the earth. Latitude is the position of a point on the earth's surface in relation to the equator. The distance is measured in degrees beginning at the equator and going toward one of the earth's poles. Any point on the equator has a latitude of zero degrees. This is written 0°. The North Pole has a latitude of 90° north, and the South Pole has a latitude of 90° south. So a point halfway between the North Pole and the equator would be located at 45 degrees north (45°N). The distance between degrees is divided into 60 minutes. The symbol for minutes is '. So a latitude of 48°40'N would be somewhere between 48° and 49° north.

Lines of longitude are imaginary lines running north and south. They divide the globe into 360 equal slices. The main lines of longitude are called meridians. All meridians pass through the North and the South poles. The prime meridian, or first meridian, is the imaginary great circle that passes through the North and South poles and Greenwich, England, just outside London. This line is 0° longitude. The prime meridian divides the earth into an eastern hemisphere and a western hemisphere. Each hemisphere has 180 degrees. Similar to latitude, each degree of longitude is divided into 60 minutes. The distance between meridians is greatest at the equator and gradually decreases as the meridians near the poles.

So now, can you find your global address? Where in the world are YOU?

Main Idea 1

	Answer	Score
Mark the *main idea*	M	15
Mark the statement that is *too broad*	B	5
Mark the statement that is *too narrow*	N	5

a. Locations on the earth can be pinpointed by latitude and longitude. ☐ _____

b. Every place has an address. ☐ _____

c. Global distances are measured in degrees. ☐ _____

Score 15 points for each correct answer.   Score

Subject Matter   **2**   The information in this passage would most
likely be found in a
☐ a. psychology book.
☐ b. sociology book.
☐ c. world history book.
☐ d. geography book.   _____

Supporting   **3**   The equator is at
Details   ☐ a. 0° latitude.
☐ b. 45°N latitude.
☐ c. 45°S latitude.
☐ d. 180° latitude.   _____

Conclusion   **4**   A latitude of 75°20'S would be closest to
☐ a. the South Pole.
☐ b. the North Pole.
☐ c. the Equator.
☐ d. Canada.   _____

Clarifying   **5**   The example 41°50'N 87°45'W is an address
Devices   ☐ a. for the suburban areas of Chicago.
☐ b. showing latitude only.
☐ c. showing longitude only.
☐ d. showing both latitude and longitude.   _____

Vocabulary   **6**   In this passage the word <u>prime</u> means
in Context   ☐ a. flat.
☐ b. most important.
☐ c. first.
☐ d. long.   _____

Add your scores for questions 1–6. Enter the total here   Total
and on the graph on page 214.   Score   _____

17 Unlocking the Human Genome

A project to unlock secrets—what scientist could resist that challenge? This is what many scientists are doing as they work on the Human Genome Project. The aim of the project is to decode all of the some 100,000 genes in the human body. Scientists are using DNA fingerprinting techniques to do the decoding.

DNA is the substance found in the chromosomes of a cell. A chromosome is a chain of genes. Each gene carries a piece of information. At any one moment in a cell, thousands of genes are turned on and off to produce proteins. The challenge for scientists is to find out what role each gene plays in protein production. At some point this decoding will be complete. Then scientists will have a map of an ideal genome, or a picture of the total genetic nature of a human being. The ideal genome is called a consensus genome. Everything works well in a consensus genome.

But no one in the world has a consensus genome. Everyone's genome is different from the ideal. These differences are referred to as genetic <u>mutations</u>. Genetic mutations in a person's genome mean that the person has a greater than average chance of suffering from health problems. Some problems are not life-threatening. These would include things like baldness, stuttering, or mild headaches. Other problems are serious, such as schizophrenia, heart disease, or diabetes.

It will take years to identify the role of each of the 100,000 genes. The short-term goal of the project is to find the physical and mental health problems a person is likely to encounter during his or her lifetime. The long-term goal is to have each person live a longer, healthier life.

Main Idea	1		
		Answer	**Score**
	Mark the *main idea*	M	15
	Mark the statement that is *too broad*	B	5
	Mark the statement that is *too narrow*	N	5
	a. The human body has about 100,000 genes.	☐	_____
	b. The Human Genome Project is trying to decode the genes in the human body.	☐	_____
	c. Scientists unlock secrets.	☐	_____

Score 15 points for each correct answer.   Score

Subject Matter   **2**   This passage is mostly about
☐ a. how DNA works.
☐ b. decoding all the genes in the human body.
☐ c. illnesses like diabetes.
☐ d. the future of science.   _____

Supporting Details   **3**   A chromosome is a
☐ a. fingerprint.
☐ b. substance called DNA.
☐ c. colorful cell.
☐ d. chain of genes.   _____

Conclusion   **4**   The Human Genome Project is mainly a scientific
☐ a. challenge.
☐ b. agreement.
☐ c. debate.
☐ d. law.   _____

Clarifying Devices   **5**   The first sentence in this passage is intended to
☐ a. make you angry.
☐ b. arouse your interest.
☐ c. confuse you.
☐ d. present the main idea.   _____

Vocabulary in Context   **6**   Mutations are
☐ a. experiments.
☐ b. disagreements
☐ c. differences or changes.
☐ d. people who do not live on Earth.   _____

Add your scores for questions 1–6. Enter the total here and on the graph on page 214.   Total Score   _____

18 Novels of War

War has been the topic of many great novels. The situation of constantly dealing with death is a dramatic one. It is one in which writers can explore a wide range of emotions.

The Red Badge of Courage, a novel of the Civil War, was written by an author who had never been in battle. Yet this author, Stephen Crane, was able to recreate the feelings of a common soldier very realistically. The reader follows the soldier through romantic notions of war to overwhelming fear to final acceptance of his duty. Though written long ago, this novel deals with feelings in a way that seems almost modern.

All Quiet on the Western Front is a novel about World War I. It too explores the emotions of a young soldier in battle. Much of the story takes place in the trenches. Here the young man and his companions must deal with the brutality all around them. In the end, war has become everything to them—their past, present, and future. They feel they have nothing to rely on but each other. They are fighting for nothing.

Many novels have been written about World War II. *The Naked and the Dead* is generally thought to be the best of these. It was written by Norman Mailer, and is set on an island in the Pacific. Mailer explores the lives of a platoon of soldiers, both through the day-to-day details of war and through flashbacks into their past. This novel presents another realistic picture of war and how soldiers cope with it.

The Things They Carried is about Vietnam. Author Tim O'Brien tells 22 related stories about a narrator and his fellow soldiers. Some of the stories occur outside Vietnam, such as a story in which the narrator considers escaping to Canada instead of being drafted.

Three of these four novels are based on personal experience. Seeing the horror of war firsthand no doubt helped the writers take the romance out of it.

Main Idea	1		
		Answer	**Score**
	Mark the *main idea*	M	15
	Mark the statement that is *too broad*	B	5
	Mark the statement that is *too narrow*	N	5

a. Many great novels have been written about war. ☐ _____

b. Authors write about things they know. ☐ _____

c. In war novels, many soldiers come to hate war. ☐ _____

Score 15 points for each correct answer.   **Score**

Subject Matter   2   Another good title for this passage would be
- [ ] a. From Stephen Crane to Norman Mailer.
- [ ] b. Four Great Wartime Novels.
- [ ] c. How the War Novel Began.
- [ ] d. Soldiers in Battle.   _____

Supporting Details   3   *All Quiet on the Western Front* is about
- [ ] a. Vietnam.
- [ ] b. World War II.
- [ ] c. the Civil War.
- [ ] d. World War I.   _____

Conclusion   4   To write a good war novel, one should deal with
- [ ] a. the everyday situations that soldiers face.
- [ ] b. how generals make battle decisions.
- [ ] c. why one side is right and the other is wrong.
- [ ] d. faraway settings.   _____

Clarifying Devices   5   The statement that "war has become . . . their past, present, and future" means that
- [ ] a. the soldiers think constantly about the past.
- [ ] b. the war goes on for at least 10 years.
- [ ] c. the soldiers forget about their real past and don't look forward to the future.
- [ ] d. the soldiers' families don't understand them.   _____

Vocabulary in Context   6   In this passage the word <u>platoon</u> means
- [ ] a. flat boat.
- [ ] b. squad or company.
- [ ] c. group that always argues.
- [ ] d. battle.   _____

Add your scores for questions 1–6. Enter the total here and on the graph on page 214.   **Total Score**   _____

19 "Monday's Child Is Fair of Face"

When the Kaminsky sisters were children, their grandmother taught them a nursery rhyme. According to this rhyme, the day of the week you were born on determined your <u>dominant</u> character trait: "Monday's child is fair of face. Tuesday's child is full of grace," and so on. Victoria's older sister Alexandra used to brag about how "fair of face" she was because she had been born on a Monday. She asserted that Victoria's birth day was a Wednesday and thus her sister was "full of woe." (Vicky vehemently denied this, although she wasn't absolutely certain what *woe* meant.) Their mom said she couldn't recall the days they were born on and she wished they would stop arguing.

When she was old enough to figure out the problem mathematically, Victoria set out to discover whether or not her birth date, November 26, 1954, had truly fallen on a Wednesday. She started with Pearl Harbor Day, December 7, 1941, because she knew it had been a Sunday. Victoria calculated that she had been born almost 13 years later (1954 − 1941 = 13). She multiplied 13 × 365 days for a product of 4,745 days. Then she added 3 leap days (because 1944, 1948, and 1952 were leap years). Her total, 4,748, was the number of days between December 7, 1941 and December 7, 1954.

Victoria then subtracted 11 days (the number of days between November 26 and December 7) for a difference of 4,737. Next, she needed to calculate how many extra days beyond a week that was. Dividing 4,737 by 7, she got an answer of about 676 and $\frac{7}{10}$ weeks. That $\frac{7}{10}$ translated into 5 days. This meant that November 26, 1954, fell on a *Friday* (Sunday + 5 days)! Friday's child was "loving and giving."

She was even more pleased to discover that Alexandra's birthday, October 16, 1952, was actually a Thursday. Thursday's child, says the old rhyme, "has far to go."

Main Idea	1			
			Answer	Score
	Mark the *main idea*		M	15
	Mark the statement that is *too broad*		B	5
	Mark the statement that is *too narrow*		N	5
	a. Vicky used math to prove her sister wrong.		☐	_____
	b. Sisters often tease each other.		☐	_____
	c. Victoria was born on a Friday, and Alexandra was born on a Thursday.		☐	_____

Subject Matter   **2**   Another good title for this passage might be
- ☐ a. Proving a Point with Math.
- ☐ b. Children's Nursery Rhymes.
- ☐ c. The Kaminsky Sisters.
- ☐ d. Pearl Harbor Day.

_____

Supporting Details   **3**   Victoria started her calculations with Pearl Harbor Day because
- ☐ a. it was her birthday.
- ☐ b. it was her sister's birthday.
- ☐ c. she knew it was on a Sunday.
- ☐ d. it occurred in 1941.

_____

Conclusion   **4**   We can conclude from reading the passage that
- ☐ a. Victoria did not get good grades in math.
- ☐ b. Victoria was 13 years old on Pearl Harbor Day.
- ☐ c. the sisters seldom argued.
- ☐ d. the sisters were competitive with each other.

_____

Clarifying Devices   **5**   This passage is developed mainly through
- ☐ a. giving examples to support a main idea.
- ☐ b. listing events in reverse time order.
- ☐ c. explaining the steps in a process.
- ☐ d. comparing and contrasting.

_____

Vocabulary in Context   **6**   In this passage <u>dominant</u> means
- ☐ a. largest.
- ☐ b. least noticeable.
- ☐ c. most important or influential.
- ☐ d. loudest.

_____

Add your scores for questions 1–6. Enter the total here and on the graph on page 214.   **Total Score**

_____

20 Shirley Chisholm, Political Trailblazer

"I stand before you today as a candidate for the Democratic <u>nomination</u> for the presidency of the United States. I am not the candidate of black America, although I am black and proud. I am not the candidate for the women's movement of this country, although I am a woman, and I am equally proud of that. . . . I am the candidate of the people."

With this announcement on January 25, 1972, Shirley Chisholm made political history. She was the first black woman to run for the presidential nomination of a major party. Who was Shirley Chisholm?

Shirley St. Hill was born in Brooklyn, New York, in 1924. From the age of three to nearly 10, she lived with her grandmother in Barbados. When she returned to her family in Brooklyn, she attended New York public schools. She received a degree in sociology from Brooklyn College. She met and married Conrad Chisholm.

In the early 1960s, Chisholm and others formed the Unity Democratic Club. Although unsupported by the males in the club, she ran for the New York State Assembly in 1964. She won and two years later was reelected. In 1968, she ran for Congress. She won the primary election, then beat her Republican opponent. She became the first black woman in the House of Representatives. She served seven terms.

In the 1970s, both the civil rights and the women's movements were asking, "Why not a woman president?" In 1972, Chisholm was urged to run. Although her primary election percentages were small, she stayed in the race to give America's neglected groups a choice. In the end, she was not the Democratic Party's nominee, but she had proven that a black woman could be a serious candidate.

Main Idea	1		
		Answer	**Score**
	Mark the *main idea*	M	15
	Mark the statement that is *too broad*	B	5
	Mark the statement that is *too narrow*	N	5
	a. Shirley Chisholm was active in politics.	☐	_____
	b. Shirley Chisholm was the first black woman to run for President.	☐	_____
	c. Shirley Chisholm lived for a time in Barbados.	☐	_____

Subject Matter 2 This passage deals mainly with
- [ ] a. the personal life of Shirley Chisholm.
- [ ] b. the political career of Shirley Chisholm.
- [ ] c. U.S. history in the 1970s.
- [ ] d. the history of presidential campaigns.   _____

Supporting Details 3 Shirley Chisholm was one of the founders of the
- [ ] a. Unity Democratic Club.
- [ ] b. New York State Assembly.
- [ ] c. women's movement.
- [ ] d. Republican Party.   _____

Conclusion 4 This passage leads the reader to believe that
- [ ] a. women politicians in the 1960s and 1970s were not unusual.
- [ ] b. Chisholm became President of the United States.
- [ ] c. Chisholm's presidential campaign was an important milestone in U.S. history.
- [ ] d. a women will never be president.   _____

Clarifying Devices 5 The basic pattern used to develop this passage is
- [ ] a. personal narrative.
- [ ] b. question and answer.
- [ ] c. comparison and contrast.
- [ ] d. chronological order.   _____

Vocabulary in Context 6 The word <u>nomination</u> means
- [ ] a. naming as a candidate for office.
- [ ] b. winner of a political race.
- [ ] c. fund-raiser.
- [ ] d. religious group.   _____

Add your scores for questions 1–6. Enter the total here   **Total**
and on the graph on page 214.   **Score**   _____

21 Sunspots

It's not surprising that sunspots were observed by ancient astronomers. The largest sunspots on the sun can be seen without a telescope. It was not until the invention of the telescope in the early 17th century, however, that systematic studies of sunspots could be undertaken. The great astronomer Galileo was among the first to make telescopic observations of sunspots.

Sunspots are regions of extremely strong magnetic fields found on the sun's surface. A sunspot has a dark central core known as the *umbra*. The umbra is surrounded by a dark ring called the *penumbra,* where the magnetic field spreads outward. Sunspots appear dark because they are giving off less radiation. They are cooler than the rest of the sun's surface.

Sunspots are frequently observed in pairs or in paired groups. The members of a spot pair are identified as the leading spot and the following spot. They are identified by their position in the pair in terms of the direction in which the sun rotates.

The number of sunspots at any one time varies. Sometimes there may be as many as 10 groups and 300 spots across the sun. A large spot group may consist of as many as 200 spots. The number of spots changes in a fairly regular pattern called the *sunspot cycle*. The largest number occurs about every 11 years. At sunspot minimum, there are at most just a few small spots.

The average lifetime of an individual spot group is roughly one solar rotation, which is about 25 days. The most <u>persistent</u> large spots, however, can survive for two to three months.

Main Idea	1			
			Answer	**Score**
	Mark the *main idea*		M	15
	Mark the statement that is *too broad*		B	5
	Mark the statement that is *too narrow*		N	5
	a.	Sunspots appear on the sun.	☐	_____
	b.	Sunspots, regions of magnetic fields on the sun's surface, occur at fairly regular intervals.	☐	_____
	c.	Large sunspots can be seen without a telescope.	☐	_____

Subject Matter   2   This passage is mainly
☐ a. a description of sunspots.
☐ b. a discussion of why sunspots occur.
☐ c. an explanation of the sun's movements.
☐ d. a biography of Galileo.
_____

Supporting Details   3   Leading spot and following spot are
☐ a. the names of spots in a spot pair.
☐ b. the direction of the sun's rotation.
☐ c. names of the two largest sunspots.
☐ d. names of a sunspot's central core and the ring around the core.
_____

Conclusion   4   If there had been heavy sunspot activity in 1857, the next heavy outbreak would have been in
☐ a. 1858.
☐ b. 1862.
☐ c. 1865.
☐ d. 1868.
_____

Clarifying Devices   5   The first paragraph presents sunspots through
☐ a. an explanation of how they work.
☐ b. a descriptive perspective.
☐ c. a historical perspective.
☐ d. a cause and effect perspective.
_____

Vocabulary in Context   6   In this passage persistent means
☐ a. quickly disappearing.
☐ b. large.
☐ c. lasting.
☐ d. having a dark, reddish brown color.
_____

Add your scores for questions 1–6. Enter the total here and on the graph on page 214.   **Total Score**   _____

22 Classical Music

If you don't understand its structure, classical music may be something of a mystery to you. Things become a lot clearer if you know what you are listening to.

Many of the pieces you hear being played by full orchestras are *symphonies*. The symphony is a type of composition that developed its basic form in the 1700s. It usually consists of four sections, or movements, of music. The first movement is generally quick and often lively. It introduces a musical theme and then plays with it by doing variations of it. The second movement usually has a slow tempo, while the third is quick again. The fourth movement is often even quicker. It builds up in intensity to a very lively finale. Throughout the symphony the theme introduced in the first movement recurs and is developed.

Joseph Haydn and Wolfgang Mozart were two of the early popular writers of symphonies. Their music was delicate and melodic. It uses mostly string instruments and a few trumpets, horns, flutes, and clarinets. Ludwig van Beethoven, writing slightly later, expanded the symphonic form. He introduced several more instruments. He raised the loudness and intensity of the music. The quick pace of the third movement was also his <u>innovation</u>. Beethoven wrote only nine symphonies (compared to more than 100 by Haydn). But his ideas influenced many later composers.

Similar in some ways to the symphony is the *concerto*. The concerto, though, is written to showcase one instrument. This is often the violin or piano. Also unlike the symphony, the concerto has only three movements. It moves from fast to slow to fast. Sometimes the featured player plays along with the orchestra. At other times he or she is given solo sections to show off playing skills.

Main Idea	1		Answer	Score
	Mark the *main idea*		M	15
	Mark the statement that is *too broad*		B	5
	Mark the statement that is *too narrow*		N	5

a. Beethoven was a great composer of symphonies. ☐ _____

b. Symphonies and concertos are two forms of classical music. ☐ _____

c. Classical music uses certain formats. ☐ _____

Subject Matter　2　Another good title for this passage would be

☐ a. Three Great Composers.

☐ b. Symphonies and Concertos.

☐ c. Old Music, New Formats.

☐ d. The Music of the World.　　_____

Supporting Details　3　A symphony usually has

☐ a. two movements.

☐ b. three movements.

☐ c. four movements.

☐ d. five movements.　　_____

Conclusion　4　You can conclude that after Beethoven

☐ a. the symphony did not change at all.

☐ b. writers used some of his new ideas.

☐ c. writers ignored what he had done.

☐ d. no more symphonies were written.　　_____

Clarifying Devices　5　The writer explains concertos mainly by

☐ a. comparing and contrasting them with symphonies.

☐ b. mentioning several famous ones.

☐ c. talking about the instruments they are written for.

☐ d. describing their first and third movements.　　_____

Vocabulary in Context　6　The word <u>innovation</u> means

☐ a. new building.

☐ b. orchestra.

☐ c. piece of music.

☐ d. new idea.　　_____

Add your scores for questions 1–6. Enter the total here and on the graph on page 214.　　**Total Score**　_____

23 Making a Budget

Making a budget can help many people save for an important purchase or just get their finances under control. Budgeting requires very little math, but it does mean keeping track of expenditures.

Start by selecting several large categories such as rent, <u>utilities</u>, telephone, food, and transportation. Then add a final category called "other" for the rest of your expenses. The categories you select will depend on how you spend your money. Next, pull out your checkbook and credit card statements. Use at least three months worth of numbers—six months is even better. When you add up what you've been spending for each category, the results may surprise you! You may not realize how much you spend on items such as clothing, eating out, and entertainment.

If you want a visual picture of your expenditures, you can use a circle graph. To create such a graph, you'll need a tool called a *protractor,* a plastic device used to draw angles that can be found in any stationery store. As an example, let's say a person spent $4,325 in the last month. Of that amount, $725 went for rent. To draw the section on the graph for rent, divide the category amount ($725) by the total ($4,325). Then multiply by 360 degrees. You would get 60.3 degrees, the angle for the "rent" section on the graph.

60.3 degrees

Once you fully understand how you are spending your money, you can make better-informed decisions about financial matters. If you want to save for a big purchase, you can decide which categories you can trim down.

Main Idea   1

	Answer	Score
Mark the *main idea*	M	15
Mark the statement that is *too broad*	B	5
Mark the statement that is *too narrow*	N	5

a. When making a budget, it is best to break down spending into categories like food and rent. ☐ _____

b. Circle graphs are useful items. ☐ _____

c. Making a budget requires an understanding of past expenditures. ☐ _____

Subject Matter   2   This passage mostly focuses on
☐ a. the importance of using graphs.
☐ b. saving money for important purchases.
☐ c. an introduction to making a personal budget.
☐ d. using a protractor to draw angles.   _____

Supporting Details   3   A protractor is a
☐ a. circle graph.
☐ b. budget.
☐ c. category of expenditures.
☐ d. tool for drawing angles.   _____

Conclusion   4   A completed circle graph for a budget should show
☐ a. all the money that is spent over a month or other period.
☐ b. mainly amounts for food and transportation.
☐ c. the amount a person plans to make in the future.
☐ d. all rent increases for the past three years.   _____

Clarifying Devices   5   The diagram of the circle graph in the passage is intended to show
☐ a. a completed sample budget.
☐ b. the categories to use in making a budget.
☐ c. a sample first step in figuring out spending.
☐ d. how to use a protractor.   _____

Vocabulary in Context   6   In this passage the word <u>utilities</u> means
☐ a. useful devices or machines.
☐ b. services such as electricity, gas, and water.
☐ c. computer programs for specific tasks.
☐ d. all large expenses.   _____

Add your scores for questions 1–6. Enter the total here and on the graph on page 214.   **Total Score**   _____

24 The Homeless

People without homes have always been present in America. In the past they were called *hoboes, bums,* or *drifters*. But it was not until the early 1980s that these people received a new name, when activists named them *the homeless*.

The types of people who were homeless also changed in the 1980s. No longer were they primarily older men. They were younger, with an average age of 35. Their numbers consisted of women, children, adolescents, and entire families. They were of many races and cultures. No longer were they only in the inner city. They lived in rural areas and in large and small cities. No longer were they invisible to the people with homes and jobs. The homeless of the 1980s lived in packing crates and doorways. They slept on sidewalks and in public parks. They begged money from passersby and pushed their possessions in shopping carts.

Counting the numbers of homeless people is difficult. However, in 1984 the Department of Housing and Urban Development estimated the homeless population at between 250,000 and 350,000. In 1990 the Census Bureau counted about 459,000 people in shelters, in cheap hotels, and on the streets. In 1995 the National Alliance to End Homelessness estimated that there were 750,000 homeless Americans.

The homeless of the 1980s also began to speak out for themselves. Some spoke to Congress and to government committees controlling funding for social programs. Street newspapers, such as Chicago's *Streetwise* and Boston's *Spare Change,* had stories, poems, and essays that expressed the homeless viewpoint. The visible and vocal presence of the homeless prompted help from volunteers and government agencies. But what is still needed is a solution to the <u>plight</u> of America's homeless.

Main Idea	1		Answer	Score
	Mark the *main idea*		M	15
	Mark the statement that is *too broad*		B	5
	Mark the statement that is *too narrow*		N	5
	a. Homelessness is a real problem.		☐	_____
	b. Homelessness in America changed in the 1980s.		☐	_____
	c. Some homeless people live in packing crates.		☐	_____

Subject Matter   2   This passage is mainly about
- [ ] a. the history of the homeless.
- [ ] b. the homeless in the 1980s and 1990s.
- [ ] c. one homeless person's story.
- [ ] d. a way to provide homes for the homeless.   _____

Supporting Details   3   One way the homeless spoke out about their problem was by
- [ ] a. writing books.
- [ ] b. expressing their viewpoints in street newspapers.
- [ ] c. moving to rural areas.
- [ ] d. being elected to government office.   _____

Conclusion   4   Homelessness in the 1980s was
- [ ] a. less of a problem than in earlier years.
- [ ] b. a problem mostly of older men.
- [ ] c. more widespread than earlier.
- [ ] d. easier to count with each passing year.   _____

Clarifying Devices   5   The size of the homeless population is indicated through
- [ ] a. agency statistics.
- [ ] b. adjectives such as "many" and "few."
- [ ] c. a graph.
- [ ] d. a quoted expert.   _____

Vocabulary in Context   6   The word <u>plight</u> means
- [ ] a. hopelessness.
- [ ] b. fight.
- [ ] c. distressing situation.
- [ ] d. lack of money.   _____

Add your scores for questions 1–6. Enter the total here and on the graph on page 214.   **Total Score**   _____

25 Recognizing Volcanoes

Volcanoes may assume a variety of shapes. These are determined by the composition of the magma, or hot melted rock, that lies within them. The shapes are also determined by their past eruptions. The four main volcano forms are identified by the shape of their cones. These include cinder cones, shield volcanoes, composite cones, and domes.

Cinder cones are the simplest type of volcano. They form when an eruption throws out mostly rocks and ash but little flowing lava. Cinder cones usually consist of small volcanic fragments that are as fine as ash or as large as a pebble. The cinder cone of Paricutín in Mexico began in a flat cornfield in 1943. It reached a height of 1,300 feet before becoming <u>dormant</u>.

Nonexplosive eruptions with easy flowing lava produce *shield volcanoes.* The flow pours out in all directions, building a broad, gently sloping cone. The lava flows from shield volcanoes are usually only 3 to 33 feet thick, but they may spread out for long distances. The name *shield* comes from their resemblance to the shields of early Germanic warriors. The volcanoes of Hawaii and Iceland are shield volcanoes.

Alternating eruptions of ash and rocks followed by quiet lava flows form strong, steep-sided volcanic cones called *composite cones.* Most of the tallest volcanoes on the continents are composite volcanoes. Mount St. Helens in Washington is an example of such a volcano.

Domes are built by a lava so thick that it barely flows. When a dome plugs the vent of a volcano, pressure builds up under the dome. This may result in a future eruption. Domes often form in the craters of composite volcanoes, such as the one that has recently developed in the crater of Mount St. Helens.

Main Idea 1

	Answer	Score
Mark the *main idea*	**M**	15
Mark the statement that is *too broad*	**B**	5
Mark the statement that is *too narrow*	**N**	5

a. The tallest volcanoes on the continents are composite volcanoes. ☐ _____

b. Volcanic forms are identified by the shape of their cones. ☐ _____

c. Volcanoes have a variety of shapes. ☐ _____

Subject Matter   **2**   Which fictional Internet Website would most likely produce the information found in this passage?

☐ a. volcano_dwellers@botany.gov

☐ b. reachingskyward@astronomy.net

☐ c. rocks-lava-ashes@geology.com

☐ d. old.old.stuff@paleontology.edu   _____

Supporting Details   **3**   Paricutín is an example of a

☐ a. shield volcano.

☐ b. dome.

☐ c. cinder cone.

☐ d. composite cone.   _____

Conclusion   **4**   This passage leads the reader to conclude that

☐ a. all volcanoes have cinder cones.

☐ b. volcanoes can be grouped by their similarities.

☐ c. like snowflakes, no two volcanoes are alike.

☐ d. all volcanoes explode regularly.   _____

Clarifying Devices   **5**   The words in _italic_ type are

☐ a. supporting details.

☐ b. names of important places.

☐ c. key words.

☐ d. definitions.   _____

Vocabulary in Context   **6**   In this passage <u>dormant</u> means

☐ a. inactive.

☐ b. tired.

☐ c. lively.

☐ d. noticeable.   _____

Add your scores for questions 1–6. Enter the total here and on the graph on page 214.   **Total Score**   _____

26 The Art of Frida Kahlo

For years her reputation was overshadowed by that of her husband, muralist Diego Rivera. In the last several years, however, the work of painter Frida Kahlo has come to be regarded as just as important, if not more so, than that of her spouse.

Kahlo was born near Mexico City and at one point considered becoming a doctor. But physical difficulties <u>plagued</u> her. She contracted polio as a child and developed a limp. When she was 18, she was involved in a serious bus accident that crippled her and caused intense pain for the rest of her life. She began to paint while recuperating from that accident. She showed some of her early work to Rivera, whom she had met earlier when she was a student. This was the beginning of their stormy relationship.

Many of Kahlo's paintings are self-portraits. They often relate to her accident or other important events in her life. For example, one shows her painting while seated in a wheelchair. Another shows her confined to bed with a skeletal form above her. Portraits with thorn necklaces represent her physical suffering. A portrait of her with Rivera suggests their difficult marriage: he is shown cutting up her body. Others show her head on the body of a wounded deer or her dressed in men's clothing, which she often wore. In most of her paintings she uses bright, intense colors and a simple, almost childlike style.

Both Kahlo and Rivera were very involved in promoting all things Mexican. Though she was born in 1907, Kahlo usually gave her birth date as 1910, the first year of the Mexican Revolution. Kahlo promoted Mexican art and handicrafts and often dressed in the same sort of shawls and jewelry as the native women wore.

Main Idea	1	Answer	Score
	Mark the *main idea*	M	15
	Mark the statement that is *too broad*	B	5
	Mark the statement that is *too narrow*	N	5

a. Frida Kahlo's paintings express her suffering as well as important events in her life. ☐ _____

b. Frida Kahlo was a Mexican painter. ☐ _____

c. Frida Kahlo was married to Diego Rivera. ☐ _____

Score 15 points for each correct answer.   **Score**

Subject Matter   **2**   This passage is mainly about
     ☐ a. Frida Kahlo's marriage.
     ☐ b. Frida Kahlo's works.
     ☐ c. the Mexican Revolution.
     ☐ d. Frida Kahlo's polio.
          _____

Supporting Details   **3**   Many of Kahlo's paintings are
     ☐ a. of animals.
     ☐ b. of her husband.
     ☐ c. self-portraits.
     ☐ d. painted in a sophisticated style.
          _____

Conclusion   **4**   It is fair to conclude from this passage that Kahlo
     ☐ a. was bright and well-educated.
     ☐ b. relied on her husband to help her with painting.
     ☐ c. had several children.
     ☐ d. wanted to live in the United States.
          _____

Clarifying Devices   **5**   The term *stormy* in the second paragraph refers to a relationship
     ☐ a. spent much of the time outdoors.
     ☐ b. involving many disagreements and fights.
     ☐ c. where both people were interested in weather.
     ☐ d. with many embraces and other public signs of affection.
          _____

Vocabulary in Context   **6**   In this passage <u>plagued</u> means
     ☐ a. made happy.
     ☐ b. painted.
     ☐ c. caused disease.
     ☐ d. bothered.
          _____

Add your scores for questions 1–6. Enter the total here and on the graph on page 215.   **Total Score**   _____

27 The Quadragenarian in the Quadrangle

If you know French or Spanish, you should have an easy time understanding words based on Latin or Greek number forms. The chart below <u>illustrates</u> this.

	1	2	3	4	5	6	7	8	9	10
French	un	deux	trois	quatre	cinq	six	sept	huit	neuf	dix
Spanish	uno	dos	tres	cuatro	cinco	seis	siete	ocho	nueve	diez
Latin	uni-	duo-	tri-	quadr-	quin-	sex-	sept-	oct-	novem-	decem-
Greek	mono-	di-	tri-	tetra-	penta-	hex-	hepta-	oct-	ennea-	deca-

Use the chart to help you read this paragraph. See that quadragenarian leading a quadruped through the quadrangle? In November he will have triple bypass surgery. He has completed his insurance forms in quintuplicate, but he still has a myriad of things to do before entering the hospital. Next year he hopes to enter a pentathlon; he has a monomania about sports that I find unique. His friends unite in the hope that a decade from now, when he is a quinquagenarian, he will slow down a little—they tell him that a century ago he wouldn't have lived this long.

Now read the numerical "translation." See that man between 40 and 49 leading a four-footed creature through the courtyard surrounded on four sides by buildings? In the ninth month of the year (according to an early Roman calendar) he will have heart surgery bypassing three of his arteries. He has completed five copies of his insurance forms, but he still has a great many things to do before entering the hospital (*myria* means "10,000" or "a great many" in Greek). Next year he hopes to enter an athletic competition involving five different events. He has a craziness that makes him focus on one topic—in this instance, sports. I think he is the only one who is this way. His friends are one in the hope that 10 years from now, when he is between 50 and 59, he will slow down a little. Had he lived 100 years ago, he wouldn't have lived this long.

Main Idea   1

	Answer	Score
Mark the *main idea*	**M**	15
Mark the statement that is *too broad*	**B**	5
Mark the statement that is *too narrow*	**N**	5

a. *Penta-* means "five" in Greek. ☐ _____

b. Greek and Latin number words can help you understand unfamiliar words. ☐ _____

c. Many words have foreign roots. ☐ _____

Score 15 points for each correct answer. Score

Subject Matter 2 Another good title for this passage might be
- ☐ a. Triple Bypass Surgery.
- ☐ b. Studying Greek and Latin.
- ☐ c. The History of Our Language.
- ☐ d. Greek and Latin Number Words.

_____

Supporting Details 3 A quinquagenarian is someone
- ☐ a. between 40 and 59.
- ☐ b. between 50 and 59.
- ☐ c. who is crazy about sports.
- ☐ d. who does a task five times.

_____

Conclusion 4 After reading this passage you can conclude that
- ☐ a. very few words are based on Latin or Greek.
- ☐ b. many words are based on Latin and Greek.
- ☐ c. to understand numbers, it's important to know French or Spanish.
- ☐ d. words with Latin or Greek roots are rarely useful in math.

_____

Clarifying Devices 5 In the final paragraph, the author puts quotation marks around _translation_ to show that
- ☐ a. "translation" isn't exactly the right word for what follows.
- ☐ b. someone's exact words are being quoted.
- ☐ c. "translation" has a Greek root.
- ☐ d. you need to know Latin to understand what follows.

_____

Vocabulary in Context 6 In this passage <u>illustrates</u> means
- ☐ a. draws a picture.
- ☐ b. helps write a book.
- ☐ c. makes clear.
- ☐ d. draws lines and boxes.

_____

Add your scores for questions 1–6. Enter the total here and on the graph on page 215.
Total Score

_____

28 The Sahara

The name *Sahara* derives from the Arabic word for "desert" or "steppe." At 3.5 million square miles, an area roughly the size of the United States, the Sahara Desert in northern Africa is the largest desert in the world. It spans the continent from the Atlantic Ocean to the Red Sea. Daytime temperatures can reach as high as 130°F. The humidity sometimes gets into the teens. But it can also be as low as 2.5 percent, the lowest in the world. Most of the Sahara receives less than five inches of rain per year, while large areas sometimes have no rainfall at all for years.

At the heart of the Sahara is the landlocked north African country of Niger. Here the sand dunes can be 100 feet tall and several miles long. Here sand plains stretch over an area larger than Germany where there is neither water nor towns. Yet sitting in the midst of the surrounding desert is the town of Bilma. Suddenly there are pools of clear water. Surprisingly, there are groves of date palms. Underground water resources, or oases, sufficient to support irrigated agriculture are found in dry stream beds and depressions. Irrigation ditches run off a creek to water fields. Corn, cassava, tea, peanuts, hot peppers, and orange, lime, and grapefruit trees grow in these fields. Donkeys and goats graze on green grass.

The Sahara of Niger is still a region where you can see a camel <u>caravan</u> of 500 camels tied together in loose lines as long as a mile, traveling toward such oasis towns. There a caravan will collect life-sustaining salt, which is mined from watery basins, and transport it up to 400 miles back to settlements on the edges of the desert. The round trip across the vast sands takes one month.

Main Idea 1		Answer	Score
	Mark the *main idea*	M	15
	Mark the statement that is *too broad*	B	5
	Mark the statement that is *too narrow*	N	5
	a. Africa has desert lands.	☐	_____
	b. The Sahara is a large, forbidding African desert.	☐	_____
	c. Lines of camels still cross the Sahara through Niger.	☐	_____

Subject Matter   2   This passage is mostly about
- ☐ a. life in the Sahara.
- ☐ b. the deserts of Africa.
- ☐ c. Bilma.
- ☐ d. how camels travel in the desert.   _____

Supporting Details   3   Rainfall in most of the Sahara is
- ☐ a. less than five inches per year.
- ☐ b. less than ten inches per year.
- ☐ c. less than twenty inches per year.
- ☐ d. zero.   _____

Conclusion   4   The Sahara can be described as
- ☐ a. a place of contrasts.
- ☐ b. a place where no one lives.
- ☐ c. an area where the winters are cold.
- ☐ d. an area that appeals to many tourists.   _____

Clarifying Devices   5   The phrase "an area roughly the size of the United States" gives an indication of the size of
- ☐ a. northern Africa.
- ☐ b. Niger.
- ☐ c. the Sahara.
- ☐ d. all of Africa.   _____

Vocabulary in Context   6   In this passage <u>caravan</u> means
- ☐ a. traveling circus.
- ☐ b. group traveling together through difficult country.
- ☐ c. railroad train.
- ☐ d. a small, fast sailing ship.   _____

Add your scores for questions 1–6. Enter the total here and on the graph on page 215.   **Total Score**   _____

29 Making Silicon Chips

It was originally called the *monolithic integrated circuit.* Since its development in 1958, it has gotten smaller and more complex, but its name has become less complicated. Today it is called the *silicon chip,* and it is contained in many things that you use every day. You'll find it in your pocket calculator, computer, microwave oven, and cellular phone.

This powerful, <u>miniaturized</u> electrical circuit begins with quartz crystal, or silica. Quartz is the main ingredient in a silicon chip. Found in many stones and sand, it is the earth's second most abundant element. The quartz crystal is mined and sent to the chip factory. There it is converted into a 264-pound rod of pure silicon. The rod is sliced into very thin wafers. Each wafer is washed, polished, cleaned, and carefully inspected. Then the wafers are coated with a layer of electrical insulation.

Meanwhile, designers have used a computer to map out the electrical circuit they need. They make a mask, or pattern, of the circuit. Then they reduce the mask and duplicate it hundreds of times. The masks are used to stencil many circuit patterns at one time onto the wafer. This process is performed several times, overlaying layers of the circuit. A complicated chip might have as many as 20 overlaid masks.

The finished, individual chips are cut from the wafer, and connecting wires are bonded onto each chip. Because the chip is usually less than the size of a fingernail, each one is placed into a frame. The frame is sealed in a plastic case, and legs are bent down ready to be inserted into a circuit board. The process—from wafer to chip—includes several hundred steps and takes about 45 days.

Main Idea 1

	Answer	Score
Mark the *main idea*	M	15
Mark the statement that is *too broad*	B	5
Mark the statement that is *too narrow*	N	5

a. Silicon chips are very useful. ☐ _____

b. Quartz is the main ingredient in a silicon chip. ☐ _____

c. Silicon chips are produced in a lengthy, complicated process. ☐ _____

Score 15 points for each correct answer.   **Score**

Subject Matter   **2**   This passage is primarily about
- [ ] a. mining.
- [ ] b. computers.
- [ ] c. the making of miniature electrical circuits.
- [ ] d. products that are used every day.

_____

Supporting Details   **3**   Wafers are washed and polished
- [ ] a. after the wafers are cut from the rod.
- [ ] b. before the wafers are cut from the rod.
- [ ] c. after the mask is laid on the wafers.
- [ ] d. when the quartz crystal is mined.

_____

Conclusion   **4**   The final sentence is a reference to the
- [ ] a. simplicity of making a silicon chip.
- [ ] b. size of a silicon chip.
- [ ] c. complexity of making a silicon chip.
- [ ] d. quality of a silicon chip.

_____

Clarifying Devices   **5**   The structure of this passage is
- [ ] a. steps in a process.
- [ ] b. cause and effect.
- [ ] c. question and answer.
- [ ] d. compare and contrast.

_____

Vocabulary in Context   **6**   The word <u>miniaturized</u> in this passage means
- [ ] a. involving tiny toys.
- [ ] b. involving a difficult process.
- [ ] c. made larger.
- [ ] d. made smaller.

_____

Add your scores for questions 1–6. Enter the total here and on the graph on page 215.   **Total Score**   _____

30 The Harlem Renaissance

You've seen the word *Renaissance* before. You probably remember that it means "rebirth." And that is basically what the period called the Harlem Renaissance was. It was a time during the 1920s in which African-American writers, artists, and performers took a new look at the ideas and feelings they expressed. This movement took place largely in New York City, in Harlem. It reflected the talents of blacks from all over the country, as well as from the West Indies, who were moving into the area.

Until the beginning of the Harlem Renaissance, many black writers had felt that to be successful they needed to mimic the ideas of white writers. But now they began branching out in new directions. Their writing expressed pride in their race. It also made clear their contributions to American culture. One important writer of the movement was Langston Hughes. Hughes wrote poetry, fiction, plays, essays, and autobiographies. In his works he portrayed the hard lives, but also the triumphs, of his people. Another important author was Zora Neale Hurston. She wrote many stories in dialect. Some of her associates disapproved of this. But she showed African Americans, especially African-American women, as being strong-willed and able to stand up for themselves.

Music was another important <u>facet</u> of the Harlem Renaissance. The nightclub called the Cotton Club brought in both black and white audiences. Here such musicians as Duke Ellington and Louis Armstrong could be heard. Singers, including Billie Holiday and Lena Horne, also appeared here. There were also sensational dancers.

The Harlem Renaissance flourished through the 1920s. It came to an end in 1929, when the Great Depression hit America and the rest of the world.

Main Idea	1		Answer	Score
		Mark the *main idea*	M	15
		Mark the statement that is *too broad*	B	5
		Mark the statement that is *too narrow*	N	5
	a.	Harlem is part of New York City.	☐	_____
	b.	The Harlem Renaissance was a rebirth in black writing and arts.	☐	_____
	c.	The Harlem Renaissance included people like Duke Ellington.	☐	_____

Score 15 points for each correct answer.   Score

Subject Matter   **2**   This passage is mainly about
☐ a. blacks in New York.
☐ b. Langston Hughes.
☐ c. accomplishments of the Harlem Renaissance.
☐ d. the end of the Harlem Renaissance.   _____

Supporting   **3**   Zora Neale Hurston
Details
☐ a. wrote many stories in dialect.
☐ b. wrote a lot of poetry.
☐ c. performed at the Cotton Club.
☐ d. was married to Duke Ellington.   _____

Conclusion   **4**   Participants in the Harlem Renaissance exhibited
a lot of
☐ a. fear.
☐ b. scandalous behavior.
☐ c. self-confidence.
☐ d. posters.   _____

Clarifying   **5**   The word *Renaissance* is explained through
Devices
☐ a. a definition.
☐ b. comparison and contrast.
☐ c. a chronological list of events.
☐ d. an explanation of music played in the 1920s.   _____

Vocabulary   **6**   In this passage <u>facet</u> means
in Context
☐ a. a cut in a diamond.
☐ b. side or view.
☐ c. description or picture.
☐ d. something moving very quickly.   _____

Add your scores for questions 1–6. Enter the total here   **Total**
and on the graph on page 215.   **Score**   _____

31 The Highest Court

There is a <u>motto</u> carved over the entrance to the United States Supreme Court Building in Washington, D.C. The words are "Equal Justice Under Law." Supreme Court justices are dedicated to this motto.

The writers of the 1787 Constitution of the United States provided for a Supreme Court in Article III. Surprisingly, the Constitution does not specify the number of justices. Nor does it tell what their duties are. It also does not say when or where they are to meet.

In its early history, the Supreme Court had a relatively weak role in government. Its job was to interpret the Constitution. At that time there weren't many interpretations to be made. As the United States grew, the Constitution was more often challenged. The Supreme Court responded to those challenges. Its strong responses helped to keep the Constitution up to date. They also strengthened the power of the court. It became a highly respected and equal third branch of government.

Today's court is made up of a Chief Justice and eight associate justices. All justices are appointed by the President. The appointments must be confirmed by the Senate. These are lifetime appointments. Lifetime appointments ensure that a justice's decisions do not affect his or her position in office. A justice can make decisions without fear of being fired, voted out of office, or replaced on political whim. On the other hand, lifetime appointments can be a problem. An aging justice's questionable health may hinder his or her ability to do the job. It is interesting to note that few justices have ever stepped down. Usually it is death rather than retirement that removes a justice from the Supreme Court bench.

Main Idea	1		Answer	Score
	Mark the *main idea*		M	15
	Mark the statement that is *too broad*		B	5
	Mark the statement that is *too narrow*		N	5

a. Supreme Court justices have lifetime appointments. ☐ _____

b. The Supreme Court has become an important part of the U.S. government. ☐ _____

c. The Constitution calls for a Supreme Court. ☐ _____

Subject Matter   **2**   The content of this passage deals mainly with
- ☐ a. how to get appointed to the Supreme Court.
- ☐ b. the cases of the Supreme Court.
- ☐ c. a brief explanation of the Supreme Court.
- ☐ d. the phrase "Equal Justice Under Law."

     _____

Supporting Details   **3**   Supreme Court justices are
- ☐ a. appointed by the President and confirmed by the Senate.
- ☐ b. voted into office by popular election.
- ☐ c. appointed by the President.
- ☐ d. chosen by the writers of the Constitution.

     _____

Conclusion   **4**   The Supreme Court concerns itself with
- ☐ a. writing the Constitution.
- ☐ b. deciding whether laws are allowed by the Constitution.
- ☐ c. making laws.
- ☐ d. advising the President.

     _____

Clarifying Devices   **5**   The information in the final paragraph
- ☐ a. gives information in narrative form.
- ☐ b. presents two sides of an issue.
- ☐ c. uses chronological order.
- ☐ d. tries to persuade the reader.

     _____

Vocabulary in Context   **6**   The word <u>motto</u> means
- ☐ a. a phrase adopted as a rule.
- ☐ b. an address.
- ☐ c. a title.
- ☐ d. a decorative picture.

     _____

Add your scores for questions 1–6. Enter the total here and on the graph on page 215.   **Total Score**   _____

32 Converting Measurements

Every once in a while, you may need to change a measurement from one unit to another. You might measure a window in inches and then need to find the number of yards of fabric for a curtain.

Unit conversion of this sort is based on a simple mathematics principle: Multiplying a number times 1 does not change its value. To use the principle in converting measurements, start by finding the conversion factor; for example, 1 yard = 36 inches. Conversion factors can be found in dictionaries or encyclopedias. Write the conversion factor as a fraction, with 1 yard on the top and 36 inches on the bottom. This fraction equals the number 1 because, even though they are in different measures, the top and bottom quantities have the same value. If a window is 60 inches long, multiply 60 inches times the fraction to change the measurement to yards.

$$\frac{1 \text{ yard}}{36 \text{ inches}} \times 60 \text{ inches} = \frac{60}{36} \text{ (or } 60 \div 36\text{)} = 1\frac{2}{3} \text{ yards}$$

Here is a more complicated example that shows how to change 50 miles per hour into meters per second. Two fractions are used, one to convert the miles to meters and another to convert the hours to seconds.

$$\frac{50 \text{ miles}}{1 \text{ hour}} \times \frac{1609 \text{ m}}{1 \text{ mile}} \times \frac{1 \text{ hour}}{3600 \text{ sec}} = \frac{50 \times 1609}{3600} \text{ (or } 50 \times 1609 \div 3600\text{)} = 22.3 \text{ m/sec}$$

Notice that miles is on the *top* of the first fraction and on the *bottom* of the second fraction. Positioned in this way, the units cancel each other out. This second example may look complicated but remember, all you have done is multiply 50 miles per hour times the number 1 twice. You haven't <u>altered</u> the actual quantity, only the units in which it is named.

Main Idea	1		Answer	Score
		Mark the *main idea*	M	15
		Mark the statement that is *too broad*	B	5
		Mark the statement that is *too narrow*	N	5
	a.	Unit conversions use math.	☐	_____
	b.	To convert a unit of measurement, multiply by an appropriate fraction.	☐	_____
	c.	To change inches to yards, divide the number of inches by 36.	☐	_____

Score 15 points for each correct answer.　　　　　　**Score**

Subject Matter　**2**　This passage is mainly about
　　　　　　　□ a. multiplying and dividing.
　　　　　　　□ b. inches and yards.
　　　　　　　□ c. converting units of measurement.
　　　　　　　□ d. estimating with measurements.　　　_____

Supporting　**3**　A conversion fraction equals 1 because
Details　　　□ a. all fractions equal 1.
　　　　　　　□ b. the top and bottom quantities have the
　　　　　　　　　same value.
　　　　　　　□ c. the top and bottom numbers are the same.
　　　　　　　□ d. the two numbers are found in a dictionary.　_____

Conclusion　**4**　Understanding conversion factors can be useful
　　　　　　　□ a. in a job where you must change feet to meters.
　　　　　　　□ b. when buying running shoes.
　　　　　　　□ c. when weighing apples in a fruit market.
　　　　　　　□ d. in a job where you use computers.　　_____

Clarifying　**5**　The writer explains converting units of
Devices　　　measurement by
　　　　　　　□ a. describing something that actually happened.
　　　　　　　□ b. defining *conversion*.
　　　　　　　□ c. giving two mathematical examples.
　　　　　　　□ d. giving a history of this type of conversion.　_____

Vocabulary　**6**　In this passage the word <u>altered</u> means
in Context　　□ a. changed.
　　　　　　　□ b. prayed for.
　　　　　　　□ c. destroyed.
　　　　　　　□ d. measured.　　　　　　　　_____

Add your scores for questions 1–6. Enter the total here　**Total**
and on the graph on page 215.　　　　　　　**Score**　_____

33 A Little Lamp to Read By

Thomas A. Edison said he would invent an inexpensive incandescent bulb that would burn for hundreds of hours. He was sure that people really wanted a soft, mellow little lamp to read by. The problem was the filament. This was the thin wire inside the vacuum-sealed globe that would provide the light. He couldn't find a material with such a high resistance and melting point that only a small amount of electric current would make it glow for thousands of hours.

Then, on October 21, 1879, a horseshoe-shaped filament of sewing thread in a vacuum-sealed glass globe burned for $14\frac{1}{2}$ hours. Edison knew he was on the right track. The thread had been coated with powdered carbon and cooked in a furnace. It had been carbonized. In the months to come, Edison and his assistants would have everything in sight carbonized—wood shavings, fishing line, cork, even a hair from an assistant's beard—in his search for the right material.

After months of methodical testing, the answer came quite by accident. As Edison idly ran his fingers along a palm-leaf fan, the texture of the hard bamboo rim caught his attention. Well, why not? They'd tried everything else. The bamboo fibers, carbonized and carefully assembled into a paper-thin filament, proved sturdier and longer-lasting than anything else.

Immediately the Great Bamboo Hunt began. Edison sent out <u>scouts</u> to bring back samples of every variety on earth. They brought back more than 6,000 bamboo samples. All were carbonized and tested, but the best came from a plantation in Japan. In the years to come this plantation would supply the filament material for millions of lamps around the world.

Main Idea	1		
		Answer	**Score**
Mark the *main idea*		M	15
Mark the statement that is *too broad*		B	5
Mark the statement that is *too narrow*		N	5
a. Thomas A. Edison was a famous inventor.		☐	_____
b. The best filament material came from Japan.		☐	_____
c. Incandescent bulbs were not useful until the right filament was found.		☐	_____

Subject Matter 2 Another good title for this passage would be
- [ ] a. The Search for the Right Filament.
- [ ] b. Edison, The Great Inventor.
- [ ] c. Hunting for Bamboo.
- [ ] d. Working with a Vacuum Tube.

_____

Supporting Details 3 Edison looked for
- [ ] a. a filament material with high resistance and a high melting point.
- [ ] b. a vacuum-sealed glass globe.
- [ ] c. an electric current.
- [ ] d. a palm-leaf fan with a hard bamboo rim.

_____

Conclusion 4 Edison's discovery was the result of his personal
- [ ] a. appearance.
- [ ] b. friends.
- [ ] c. persistence.
- [ ] d. property.

_____

Clarifying Devices 5 Wood shavings, fishing line, cork, and hair are examples of
- [ ] a. the right filament materials.
- [ ] b. materials that Edison tested.
- [ ] c. things that will burn in a furnace.
- [ ] d. things that can be made into thread.

_____

Vocabulary in Context 6 In this passage scouts means
- [ ] a. people sent to get information.
- [ ] b. young members of a pack or troop.
- [ ] c. Native American guides.
- [ ] d. rude, unpleasant people.

_____

Add your scores for questions 1–6. Enter the total here and on the graph on page 215.   **Total Score**

_____

34 Native American Pottery

There are several American Indian groups in the Southwest that still make beautiful pottery. Some of this pottery may be sold at fairly high prices. But the makers consider their work as more than a <u>commercial</u> enterprise. By using methods handed down for generations, the potters express their pride in their cultural inheritance.

Some of the most interesting pottery is made by the Pueblo Indians. There are 21 individual pueblos in Arizona and New Mexico. Several are famous for their craftsmanship. To make a pot, these potters use a clay base and add long, thin coils of clay to it in a spiral pattern. When they have reached the size they want, they use an implement such as a rock or shell to smooth the surfaces of the pot.

How a pot is decorated and fired depends on the traditions of the group making it. Traditional pottery produced by the Acoma, who have lived for centuries on a high mesa in New Mexico, is first painted with a clay slip. The resulting pots, which are prized for their delicacy and strength, may be left white. They may also be painted with black and white patterns or with a combination of black, orange, and brown.

Very distinctive black pottery comes from the San Ildefonso and Santa Clara pueblos. The black color is the result of carbon being released from the animal manure in which the pot is fired. Some artisans hand-rub this ware to a shiny gloss. Others cut patterns into it, resulting in a part shiny, part flat surface. Potters at San Ildefonso make many types of wares. Potters at Santa Clara are especially known for wedding jars—jars with two necks connected by a handle.

Other groups such as the Hopi and the Cochiti also make pottery. Each group uses distinctive methods and produces distinctive forms and designs.

Main Idea	1		Answer	Score
		Mark the *main idea*	**M**	15
		Mark the statement that is *too broad*	**B**	5
		Mark the statement that is *too narrow*	**N**	5
	a.	Making pottery is an ancient art.	☐	_____
	b.	Some potters add long, thin coils of clay to a clay base.	☐	_____
	c.	Several Southwest Indian groups are known for beautiful pottery.	☐	_____

Score 15 points for each correct answer.   **Score**

Subject Matter 2 Another good title for this passage would be
☐ a. How to Make a Pot.
☐ b. Living on a High Mesa.
☐ c. The Indians of Arizona and New Mexico.
☐ d. An Old Art Still Practiced.   _____

Supporting Details 3 The San Ildefonso pueblo is known for
☐ a. black pottery.
☐ b. wedding jars.
☐ c. thin and delicate shapes.
☐ d. black, brown, and orange pots.   _____

Conclusion 4 Traditional methods of making pottery
☐ a. are rarely used anymore.
☐ b. take a lot of time.
☐ c. are not of interest to pottery collectors.
☐ d. will soon be completely replaced.   _____

Clarifying Devices 5 The second paragraph in this passage is developed mainly through
☐ a. steps in a process.
☐ b. descriptions of objects.
☐ c. the telling of a story.
☐ d. examples.   _____

Vocabulary in Context 6 In this passage the word <u>commercial</u> means
☐ a. having to do with advertising products on TV.
☐ b. having to do with selling and business.
☐ c. large-scale.
☐ d. artistic.   _____

Add your scores for questions 1–6. Enter the total here and on the graph on page 215.   **Total Score**   _____

35 The British in India

Around A.D. 1500 European traders began arriving in India. They wanted to take India's spices, rice, silk, and sugar cane back to Europe. The most successful trading company was the British East India Company, which was founded in 1600. With the help of the British government, this company gained great control over India.

British rule had some benefits for India. Important crops—including tea, coffee, and indigo—were introduced into India and a national railroad system was built to help export goods. English was used across the many regions of India, providing one common language for the people.

But the British caused hardships too. For example, farmers in the Bengal region were forced to grow the export crop of indigo, used to make blue dye, instead of food. As a result, in 1770 about 10 million people died of famine. Britain also caused hardship in the Indian cloth industry by putting a 30 percent import tax on Indian cloth. This made Indian cloth too expensive to sell in Britain. When the Indians lost their British customers, their cloth industry was ruined. Then British cloth factories profited by selling British cloth to the Indians.

The Indian people were discontent under British rule. In 1930 Mohandas Gandhi took up the cause of Indian independence. He encouraged Indians to protest in nonviolent ways. He encouraged them not to pay taxes to the British and advocated a <u>boycott</u> of British-made products. After great struggle, both nonviolent and violent, the British withdrew, and in 1947 India became a self-governing, independent country.

Main Idea   1

	Answer	Score
Mark the *main idea*	M	15
Mark the statement that is *too broad*	B	5
Mark the statement that is *too narrow*	N	5

a. The British ruled India.	☐	_____
b. Mohandas Gandhi took up the cause of Indian independence in 1930.	☐	_____
c. British rule of India had benefits and hardships.	☐	_____

Score 15 points for each correct answer.   **Score**

Subject Matter **2** This passage is mainly about
☐ a. the history of India.
☐ b. Britain's role in the history of India.
☐ c. the export crop of indigo.
☐ d. India's struggle for independence.   _____

Supporting Details **3** A benefit of British rule was
☐ a. famine.
☐ b. decline of India's cloth industry.
☐ c. an independent Indian government.
☐ d. a national railroad system.   _____

Conclusion **4** The Indian people were discontent because they did not
☐ a. like British cloth.
☐ b. like British taxes or British rule.
☐ c. want to speak English.
☐ d. want to be farmers.   _____

Clarifying Devices **5** Benefits and hardships of British rule are contrasted in paragraphs
☐ a. 2 and 3.
☐ b. 1 and 2.
☐ c. 1 and 4.
☐ d. 3 and 4.   _____

Vocabulary in Context **6** The word <u>boycott</u> means to
☐ a. buy a great deal of.
☐ b. allow only men and boys to use.
☐ c. refuse to buy, sell, or use.
☐ d. advertise.   _____

Add your scores for questions 1–6. Enter the total here and on the graph on page 215.   **Total Score**   _____

36 Storing a Million Dollars at Home

The only trouble with being rich these days is that you can't really interact with your riches. Novelist George Eliot wrote of a miser named Silas Marner who kept his loot concealed under his floor. Every night he had the pleasure of counting his fortune, basking in the glow of golden coins in candlelight. Today if you were a millionaire, you would probably bank your money or perhaps invest it in mutual funds or real estate. But if you *were* to store a million dollars at home, how much space would be involved?

Picture a shoebox about 5 inches wide, 12 inches long, and 5.5 inches tall. Now imagine your million is stored in quarter rolls (each contains $10 and is a cylinder about 2.75 inches long and an inch in diameter). You can easily fit four rows of four rolls into the bottom of your box, and you can stack the rolls four layers high (that's 64 rolls, or $640). Now visualize a small empty room in your home—a closed-in porch, perhaps—about nine feet square. Envision yourself laying down a layer of wall-to-wall shoeboxes (each box is weighty since it's chock-full of quarter rolls); the layer is 21 boxes wide and eight boxes long, for a total of 168 boxes.

After stacking up 9 layers of quarter-filled boxes, you've constructed a rectangular solid about 49.5 inches tall (about chest high). Absolutely exhausted, you sit down to compute the amount you've stacked so far. Nine layers of 168 = 1,512 boxes. Since each box contains $640, you've already stacked up $967,680! The amount you have yet to stack, $32,320, means that you have 50.5 boxes of $640 to go. Crawling on hands and knees atop your <u>edifice</u>, you lay down 50 more boxes, thereby accounting for $32,000. There is still $320 remaining from your million to stack, or 32 quarter rolls in your last shoebox—two layers of 16 rolls. Your porch is out of commission, but you've got your million at home where you can gloat over it!

Main Idea	1			
			Answer	**Score**
		Mark the *main idea*	M	15
		Mark the statement that is *too broad*	B	5
		Mark the statement that is *too narrow*	N	5
		a. In quarter rolls, $640 fills one shoebox.	☐	_____
		b. Some people store money at home.	☐	_____
		c. You can visualize $1,000,000 by figuring out how much space it fills.	☐	_____

Subject Matter   2   Another good title for this passage would be

☐ a. Counting by Candlelight.

☐ b. Visualizing a Fortune.

☐ c. Putting Quarters in Shoeboxes.

☐ d. Multiplying and Dividing.   _____

Supporting Details   3   The money storage described in this passage is done by putting

☐ a. 9 layers of quarter rolls in each shoebox.

☐ b. 640 quarter rolls in each shoebox.

☐ c. $64 in each shoebox.

☐ d. 64 quarter rolls in each shoebox.   _____

Conclusion   4   The author wants readers to conclude that

☐ a. it is unsafe to invest in real estate.

☐ b. Silas Marner was a dishonest person.

☐ c. it is fun to imagine keeping $1,000,000 at home, but it is not a practical idea.

☐ d. you can keep a lot of money at home if you are willing to work hard at storing it.   _____

Clarifying Devices   5   The idea of quarter rolls in shoeboxes helps readers to

☐ a. picture a large amount of money.

☐ b. recall the main character in *Silas Marner*.

☐ c. review multiplication and division skills.

☐ d. figure out why banks do not store coins.   _____

Vocabulary in Context   6   The word <u>edifice</u> means

☐ a. structure.

☐ b. room.

☐ c. sculpture.

☐ d. lesson.   _____

Add your scores for questions 1–6. Enter the total here and on the graph on page 215.   **Total Score**   _____

37 The Good Mother Dinosaur

Jack Horner was on a fossil-hunting trip in Montana in 1978 when a stony bump in a pasture caught his attention. Pebbles and gray-black stone were scattered over it. Horner and fellow fossil-hunter Bob Makela had found the bones of two baby duckbilled dinosaurs. These were the bones of Hadrosaurus, some of the most commonly found dinosaur fossils in the American West. So Horner and Makela had not found anything unusual yet. When they dug further, however, they realized that they had found the first dinosaur nest ever discovered in North America.

Over the next six summers, Horner and his crew returned to the Montana pasture. They uncovered seven more nests. All were found in the same layer of sedimentary rock. All were about 23 feet apart. Adult dinosaurs were known to be up to 23 feet long, so that meant that there was just enough room for these big creatures to walk between the nests. Horner realized that the dinosaurs had nested together. He had discovered the first dinosaur nesting colony.

The nests contained mostly crushed and broken shells. The baby dinosaurs in the nests were different sizes. The smallest ones, with no wear on their teeth, were new hatchlings, and the bigger ones showed signs that they had been eating for a while. Horner concluded that the adult dinosaurs were feeding the babies in the nest until they grew big enough to leave. Until Jack Horner's discovery, no one had ever thought that these colony-nesting dinosaurs were also <u>nurturing</u> parents. Horner and Makela called these dinosaurs *Maiasaura peeblesorum.* The *peeblesorum* part was for the Peebles family who owned the pasture where the nests were found. *Maiasura* means "good mother lizard."

Main Idea	1		Answer	Score
	Mark the *main idea*		M	15
	Mark the statement that is *too broad*		B	5
	Mark the statement that is *too narrow*		N	5

a. Dinosaur fossils are found in the American West. ☐ _____

b. The dinosaur nests were about 23 feet apart. ☐ _____

c. Horner's and Makela's fossil discovery led to new facts about dinosaur life. ☐ _____

Score 15 points for each correct answer.   **Score**

Subject Matter   **2**   This passage is mainly about the
- [ ] a. discovery of dinosaur nesting colonies.
- [ ] b. size and shape of Hadrosaurus.
- [ ] c. Peebles family's land.
- [ ] d. lives of Jack Horner and Bob Makela.   _____

Supporting Details   **3**   The dinosaur nests were
- [ ] a. 23 feet long.
- [ ] b. 23 feet apart.
- [ ] c. on top of the ground.
- [ ] d. stomped on by adult dinosaurs.   _____

Conclusion   **4**   This passage leads the reader to conclude that
- [ ] a. we now know all there is to know about dinosaurs.
- [ ] b. we still don't know everything about dinosaurs.
- [ ] c. Horner made a lot of money on his discovery.
- [ ] d. nearly all dinosaurs are found in Montana.   _____

Clarifying Devices   **5**   The author explains *Maiasaura peeblesorum* by
- [ ] a. telling a story about digging in the rock.
- [ ] b. relating the history of the Peebles family.
- [ ] c. telling what each word means.
- [ ] d. giving reasons why Latin words are used in naming species.   _____

Vocabulary in Context   **6**   The word <u>nurturing</u> means
- [ ] a. nervous.
- [ ] b. caring.
- [ ] c. curious.
- [ ] d. nesting.   _____

Add your scores for questions 1–6. Enter the total here and on the graph on page 215.   **Total Score**   _____

38 The Romantic Poets

Most readers realize that in poetry, especially lyric poetry, writers are usually trying to express their feelings or emotions. For a long time, though, expressing feelings was not seen as a function of poetry. This idea was overturned, however, through the work of the English poets who are now known as the Romantics.

The Romantic poets were writing in the years just before and after 1800. Two occurrences that affected them greatly were the French and the American revolutions. These were seen as symbols of the mental and personal freedom that all people deserved.

What did the Romantic poets write about? One common topic was nature. Some of the most beautiful natural descriptions ever written come from these poets. But, in holding with their views of poetry, nature was only a starting point. It was a <u>vehicle</u> that caused them to think about and express their own feelings. Another common topic was the supernatural or unusual human experience. Poet William Blake commonly wrote about visions and dreams. So did Samuel Taylor Coleridge. Percy Bysshe Shelley was interested in the occult. Lord Byron explored the appeal of a Satanic hero. John Keats often told supernatural tales.

These poets' belief in individual freedom was reflected in their personal lives. Shelley married very young but quickly tired of his even younger wife. When he met Mary Wollstonecraft Godwin, he ran away with her to France. There he invited his wife to come and live with them, as a sister. Coleridge began taking drugs prescribed for physical ailments., and he soon became addicted. He wrote the famous poem "Kubla Khan" after taking opium. Byron had many sexual affairs, including one relationship which caused such a scandal that he had to leave England forever.

Main Idea   1

	Answer	Score
Mark the *main idea*	M	15
Mark the statement that is *too broad*	B	5
Mark the statement that is *too narrow*	N	5

a. The Romantic poets believed in personal freedom and expression of emotion. ☐ _____

b. Poets all have their own ideas of what to write about. ☐ _____

c. Many Romantic poems deal with dreams or visions. ☐ _____

Subject Matter   2   This passage is mostly about
- [ ] a. Byron and Blake.
- [ ] b. the Romantic poets' ideas and lives.
- [ ] c. the influence of the French Revolution.
- [ ] d. nature poetry.

_____

Supporting Details   3   Samuel Taylor Coleridge
- [ ] a. is known mainly for his nature poetry.
- [ ] b. ran away to France with a woman who was not his wife.
- [ ] c. often wrote of dreams and visions.
- [ ] d. fought in the French Revolution.

_____

Conclusion   4   A Romantic poet would be most likely to write about
- [ ] a. a beautiful room in a mansion.
- [ ] b. a museum.
- [ ] c. a walk along a river.
- [ ] d. two gossipy old men.

_____

Clarifying Devices   5   The third and fourth paragraphs of this passage are developed mainly
- [ ] a. through examples.
- [ ] b. in chronological order.
- [ ] c. through spatial description.
- [ ] d. by giving steps in a process.

_____

Vocabulary in Context   6   In this passage the word <u>vehicle</u> means
- [ ] a. a car or bus.
- [ ] b. a means for communicating something.
- [ ] c. a sign pointing in a certain direction.
- [ ] d. an emotion.

_____

Add your scores for questions 1–6. Enter the total here and on the graph on page 215.   **Total Score**   _____

39 Cargo Cults

The term *cargo cult* is used by anthropologists to describe South Pacific island religious movements that began in the 1860s. Island natives saw the economic <u>disparity</u> between themselves and white colonialists. Surely, they reasoned, the white men's ships being unloaded each day were the source of the white man's power. If the islanders could copy the arrival of cargo ships exactly, they would please their ancestral gods. Then they too would receive the same wealth.

World War II brought U.S. military troops to the islands of the South Pacific. The islanders had scarcely seen a piece of steel, let alone huge ships, airplanes, thousands of white men, Jeeps, radios, refrigerators, and mobile hospitals. They were impressed and confused. The goods simply appeared. It could only be explained by magic. Again, as islanders did in the 19th century, the 20th century islanders reasoned that if the white man's magic were copied accurately, the islanders' cargo would come as well.

Cult rituals developed that often included preparations to receive the cargo. Airstrips were hacked out of the jungle; lookouts were posted to watch for airplanes; wooden radios were built with vines running out the back as antennae. Cult members dressed in makeshift U.S. Army uniforms and held military drills using bamboo "rifles." Military radio commands such as "Roger, out" and "You have landing clearance" were preserved as an oral tradition and passed down through the generations.

Not surprisingly, the results were disappointing. The planes and ships did not return. The cargo of the white man's world did not come to the islanders. Today, cargo cultism is rare, and most islanders have gone on to other things.

Main Idea	1		
		Answer	**Score**
Mark the *main idea*		M	15
Mark the statement that is *too broad*		B	5
Mark the statement that is *too narrow*		N	5

a. Cargo cults try to duplicate military uniforms and drills. ☐ _____

b. Cargo cults are a result of South Pacific islanders' exposure to material goods. ☐ _____

c. An unusual religion was practiced in the South Pacific Islands. ☐ _____

Score 15 points for each correct answer.   **Score**

Subject Matter 2 This passage deals mainly with
☐ a. the work of South Pacific islanders.
☐ b. islanders' reaction to modern society's wealth.
☐ c. colonialism in the South Pacific.
☐ d. World War II in the South Pacific.
_____

Supporting Details 3 In this passage, uniforms, drills, bamboo rifles, and radio commands are examples of
☐ a. 19th century colonialism.
☐ b. military training in the South Pacific.
☐ c. U.S. military troop activity.
☐ d. islanders' attempts to copy the white man's magic.
_____

Conclusion 4 Cargo cults may be described as
☐ a. a result of the white man's greed.
☐ b. an unusual effect when two cultures meet.
☐ c. a good way for islanders to make money.
☐ d. against the law, but practiced illegally.
_____

Clarifying Devices 5 The quotation marks around the word *rifles* in the third paragraph shows that
☐ a. this is an important word in this passage.
☐ b. the items being discussed aren't really rifles.
☐ c. the word is quoted from someone's speech.
☐ d. this is a title of a short story.
_____

Vocabulary in Context 6 The word <u>disparity</u> means
☐ a. lack of organization.
☐ b. difference.
☐ c. two or double of something.
☐ d. unhappiness.
_____

Add your scores for questions 1–6. Enter the total here and on the graph on page 215.   **Total Score**   _____

40 Patching Things Up with Your Bank

Reconciliation can refer to the act of patching up a lovers' quarrel; similarly, when you reconcile your checkbook, you and your bank hash out "misunderstandings." Suppose Akira Horikoshi's checking account register for the new year begins like this:

NUMBER	DATE	DESCRIPTION OF TRANSACTION	PAYMENT/DEBIT (-)	✓	FEE IF ANY (-)	DEPOSIT/CREDIT (-)	BALANCE $ 6,000 00
90	1/2	John Scandellari (landlord)	$700.00		$	$	5,300 00
91	1/5	Health Conscious Insurance	130.00				5170 00

On January 7 Akira deposits $1,000 and writes a check for $60; on 1/8 he writes a check for $80; on 1/9 he writes a check for $50. A little adding and subtracting shows that his balance is now $5,980. Aki keeps <u>meticulous</u> track of his account, dutifully subtracting the amount of each check right after he writes it, but then he suddenly gets a baffling bank statement saying he has $5,150, almost $1,000 less than he thought.

If such a discrepancy has ever occurred with your bank statement, you might follow Akira's procedure to reconcile it. First, he noted that the statement says "covers transactions through January 6"—so one reason he and his bank "disagree" is that this statement doesn't account for anything that happened after that date. All it covers is the initial $6,000 deposit, the first two checks he wrote (for $700 and $130), and a pair of items he'd forgotten: a $10 monthly checking fee and a $10 check printing charge.

Subtracting these two items from his $5,980 balance gave Aki $5,960. He then totaled out any transactions occurring after January 6. The three checks he wrote add up to $190; subtracted from his 1/7 deposit of $1,000, this leaves $810—the exact difference between the $5,960 he believes he has and the $5,150 the bank said he has.

Main Idea	1			
			Answer	**Score**
	Mark the *main idea*		M	15
	Mark the statement that is *too broad*		B	5
	Mark the statement that is *too narrow*		N	5

a. It is fairly simple to balance a checking account. ☐ _____

b. Many people write checks. ☐ _____

c. Subtract the amount of each check after you write it. ☐ _____

Subject Matter 2 This passage is mainly about
☐ a. writing checks to pay bills.
☐ b. patching up lovers' quarrels.
☐ c. balancing a checking account.
☐ d. thinking like a bank manager. _____

Supporting Details 3 Akira began the new year with an opening balance of
☐ a. $1,000.
☐ b. $5,150.
☐ c. $5,940.
☐ d. $6,000. _____

Conclusion 4 An important thing to figure out in balancing a checkbook is
☐ a. which checks have and have not cleared.
☐ b. how many checks you write every month.
☐ c. how many deposits you make in a year.
☐ d. how many deposits are more than $1,000. _____

Clarifying Devices 5 The two meanings for *reconciliation* suggest a connection between balancing a checking account and
☐ a. opening a savings account.
☐ b. patching up a lovers' quarrel.
☐ c. adding several outstanding checks.
☐ d. juggling a career and a love life. _____

Vocabulary in Context 6 Meticulous means extremely
☐ a. sloppy.
☐ b. difficult.
☐ c. careful.
☐ d. metallic. _____

Add your scores for questions 1–6. Enter the total here and on the graph on page 215. **Total Score** _____

41 How Snow Begins

You can roll it, pack it, throw it, and shovel it. You can snowboard and ski on it. But do you know how snow begins?

Snow begins when water vapor or a supercooled droplet of water forms a hexagonal-shaped ice crystal. This crystal forms around a <u>nucleus</u> of a tiny particle that is suspended in the lower atmosphere. These particles might be clay silicate, bits of volcanic ash, or even extraterrestrial material. The ice crystals may fall to the ground in this icy form, as they do in the very cold regions of the Arctic and Antarctic, or they may grow into snow crystals. Snow crystals form by means of sublimation. Sublimation occurs when water vapor turns directly into ice without passing through a liquid stage.

The shape of a snow crystal is determined mostly by temperature and the amount of water vapor present in the air. Two things can happen to falling snow crystals. They can meet with other snow crystals to form aggregations. These are our familiar snowflakes. Or they can meet supercooled water droplets. When this happens, the droplets freeze immediately. The crystals become snow pellets that are called *graupel.*

Have you ever heard that no two snowflakes look exactly alike? This idea probably came from the work of Wilson Alwyn Bentley of Jericho, Vermont. In 1885, Bentley took photographs of snowflakes through a microscope. Thousands of his photomicrographs were collected in a 1931 book titled *Snow Crystals.* Not one of the snowflakes that Bentley photographed was identical to another. No two snowflakes being exactly alike is an interesting idea, but it is difficult to prove.

Main Idea   1 ——————————————————————

	Answer	Score
Mark the *main idea*	M	15
Mark the statement that is *too broad*	B	5
Mark the statement that is *too narrow*	N	5

a. Snow crystals form aggregations. ☐ _____

b. Snow is all around us. ☐ _____

c. Snow forms in several different ways. ☐ _____

Score 15 points for each correct answer.   **Score**

Subject Matter   **2**   This passage is mainly about
  ☐ a. what people do with snow.
  ☐ b. how to photograph snow.
  ☐ c. snowfall in the Arctic and Antarctic.
  ☐ d. the formation of snow.   _____

Supporting   **3**   Aggregations of snow crystals are
Details
  ☐ a. ice crystals.
  ☐ b. graupel.
  ☐ c. snowflakes.
  ☐ d. supercooled water droplets.   _____

Conclusion   **4**   According to the last paragraph, Bentley's photos
  ☐ a. proved that a book about snowflakes could
       be a commercial success.
  ☐ b. proved that snowflakes could not be
       photographed.
  ☐ c. did not prove that no two snowflakes are
       alike.
  ☐ d. proved that no two snowflakes are alike.   _____

Clarifying   **5**   The final paragraph of the passage
Devices
  ☐ a. continues talking about how snow is formed.
  ☐ b. introduces a new but related topic.
  ☐ c. introduces a new, totally unrelated topic.
  ☐ d. is meant to make the reader laugh.   _____

Vocabulary   **6**   In this passage <u>nucleus</u> means
in Context
  ☐ a. core.
  ☐ b. starting point.
  ☐ c. stopping point.
  ☐ d. ice cube.   _____

Add your scores for questions 1–6. Enter the total here   **Total**
and on the graph on page 215.   **Score**   _____

42 Cajun and Zydeco

Only a few sections of the United States have developed their own local music. One of these is southern Louisiana. Here not only Cajun music but its "cousin"—zydeco—originated.

The Cajuns are descendants of the Acadians, who were French Catholics forced to leave Canada in the 1700s. The music they brought to Louisiana was French folk music, but it grew and changed to reflect the new life and environment. There were songs, for example, about the loneliness people suffered. And there were musical influences from others in the area, including the Creoles of French-African <u>descent</u>.

The earliest Cajun tunes were played mostly on violins. Then accordions were added and became a dominant part of the music. Other instruments such as the steel guitar and the bass fiddle were included. The singing was in Cajun French. Typically, Cajun music would be played at a *fais-do-do,* a community dance. There the music accompanied waltzes and two-steps.

As Cajun Louisiana became less isolated, some feared that the music would die out. But a successful performance at the Newport Jazz Festival in 1964 introduced Cajun music to a new, national audience.

Zydeco, developed by the Creoles, is a mixture of traditional music and more modern rhythm and blues. It only started up after World War II. As time has passed, it has picked up elements from many other kinds of music including soul and reggae. Zydeco was originally sung in French, but is now often performed in English. It influenced Cajun music, and vice versa. Both are ways for people to express their culture and heritage.

Main Idea	1		Answer	Score
	Mark the *main idea*		M	15
	Mark the statement that is *too broad*		B	5
	Mark the statement that is *too narrow*		N	5

a. Some sections of the United States have their own forms of music. ☐ _____

b. Cajun and zydeco are types of music developed by peoples of Louisiana. ☐ _____

c. Cajun music was often played at community dances. ☐ _____

Score 15 points for each correct answer.

Score

Subject Matter   **2**   Another good title for this passage would be
     ☐ a. Music from Louisiana.
     ☐ b. An Acadian Treat.
     ☐ c. Music Rarely Heard Today.
     ☐ d. Dancing and Playing the Fiddle.

_____

Supporting Details   **3**   An essential part of Cajun music is
     ☐ a. singing in English.
     ☐ b. the piano.
     ☐ c. the accordion.
     ☐ d. rhythm and blues.

_____

Conclusion   **4**   It is fair to conclude from this passage that
     ☐ a. Cajun music is more modern and zydeco is more traditional.
     ☐ b. zydeco is more modern and Cajun is more traditional.
     ☐ c. people who can play one type of music usually can't play the other.
     ☐ d. no one plays Cajun music anymore.

_____

Clarifying Devices   **5**   The beginning of the second paragraph provides a
     ☐ a. description of French Canada.
     ☐ b. brief history of the Cajuns.
     ☐ c. definition of the word _Creole._
     ☐ d. list of instruments used in Cajun music.

_____

Vocabulary in Context   **6**   The word <u>descent</u> in this passage means
     ☐ a. wholesome and proper.
     ☐ b. the act of removing the smell from.
     ☐ c. the act of going down.
     ☐ d. heritage.

_____

Add your scores for questions 1–6. Enter the total here and on the graph on page 215.

Total Score

_____

43 Xi'an Warriors

In the city of Xi'an in central China lies one of archaeology's most astonishing discoveries. Two thousand years ago, the strong and powerful emperor Qin Shihuangdi died and was buried. What a burial it must have been! The gravesite is guarded by more than 8,000 life-size soldiers and horses made of clay. The figures are arranged in great military formations. They wear brightly painted military uniforms. They are also lifelike in their postures and facial expressions. The figures are known as the Terra Cotta Warriors.

The site, discovered in 1974, is just 23 miles east of the ancient city of Xi'an. Three areas were <u>unearthed</u>. They are named Pit Number 1, Pit Number 2, and Pit Number 3. Pit Number 1 holds a huge rectangular military formation. There are about 6,000 terra cotta figures, horses, and chariots. The formation includes infantrymen and chariot soldiers. They stand in rows as vanguard, rearguard, and right and left flanks of a strong army. Pit Number 2 contains a battle formation of more than 1,400 terra cotta figures and horses. There are crossbowmen, charioteers, and cavalrymen. Pit Number 3 is divided into three sections, including an area with chariots and horses. There are only 64 armored warriors in this pit. It is thought to represent the command headquarters of the emperor's army.

The discovery of the huge burial pits was an important find. It has provided an opportunity for archaeologists and historians to study the culture of Qin Shihuangdi. Qin Shihuangdi was clearly a powerful ruler. But could he have imagined his power reaching so far beyond his time?

Main Idea	1	Answer	Score
	Mark the *main idea*	M	15
	Mark the statement that is *too broad*	B	5
	Mark the statement that is *too narrow*	N	5

a. Qin Shihuangdi's burial site is an amazing archaeological find. ☐ _____

b. The three pits contain terra cotta figures. ☐ _____

c. Chinese archaeological sites are valuable. ☐ _____

Subject Matter   2   The passage mainly describes
☐ a. the life and times of Qin Shihuangdi.
☐ b. the chariots.
☐ c. the contents of the burial pits.
☐ d. the facial expressions of the warriors.   _____

Supporting Details   3   All three pits contained
☐ a. crossbowmen.
☐ b. cavalrymen.
☐ c. Qin Shihuangdi.
☐ d. horses.   _____

Conclusion   4   Qin Shihuangdi's power reaches beyond his time because
☐ a. he is still emperor.
☐ b. his burial pit provides information about his life and the era.
☐ c. he ruled a large portion of China.
☐ d. he was emperor for a very long time.   _____

Clarifying Devices   5   The question at the end suggests that the reader should
☐ a. visit this site.
☐ b. consider the historical and archaeological importance of the site today.
☐ c. imagine the extent of Qin Shihuangdi's influence on modern warfare.
☐ d. investigate careers in archaeology.   _____

Vocabulary in Context   6   The word <u>unearthed</u> means
☐ a. dug up.
☐ b. reburied.
☐ c. covered with mud.
☐ d. sent into space.   _____

Add your scores for questions 1–6. Enter the total here and on the graph on page 215.   **Total Score**   _____

44 Tracking Down HIV

In the summer of 1980, a patient had a strange purplish spot removed from below his ear. It was Kaposi's sarcoma, a rare form of skin cancer. This patient also had lymph node swelling and exhaustion. In November 1980, a Los Angeles immunologist examined a young man who had diseases linked to immune system malfunctions. The doctor had a T-cell count taken of the patient's blood. T-cells are a type of white blood cell that plays a key role in immune responses. The patient had no helper T-cells.

By the end of 1980, 55 Americans were diagnosed with infections related to immune system breakdown; four had died. A year later the death toll was 74. Intravenous drug users had T-cell abnormalities. People who had received blood transfusions showed symptoms of immune system breakdown. By July 1982, 471 cases of the disease, now called Acquired Immune Deficiency Syndrome (AIDS), had been reported; 184 people had died.

In April 1984, American virologist Dr. Robert Gallo isolated the pathogen, or disease producer, responsible for AIDS. He called it HTLV-III. In Paris, Dr. Luc Montagnier identified a virus he called LAV. An international panel of scientists determined that both men had found the same virus. It became known as Human Immunodeficiency Virus (HIV). Blood banks began screening for HIV in 1985, but by then about 29,000 people had been infected through blood transfusions. Some 12,000 hemophiliacs had contracted HIV through blood-clotting products. By 1995, 477,900 Americans had AIDS; 295,500 had died.

In 1996, researchers announced drugs that reduced HIV in infected people. Today scientists are testing vaccines and believe that if HIV can be suppressed, then perhaps it can be <u>eradicated</u>, but it is still a race against time.

Main Idea   1

	Answer	Score
Mark the *main idea*	**M**	15
Mark the statement that is *too broad*	**B**	5
Mark the statement that is *too narrow*	**N**	5

a. Drugs seem able to suppress HIV.	☐	_____
b. The history of HIV spans 20 years.	☐	_____
c. A virus can be deadly.	☐	_____

Score 15 points for each correct answer.　　　　**Score**

Subject Matter　　**2**　This passage is mainly about
　　　　☐ a. the spreading of the disease known as HIV.
　　　　☐ b. the work of Dr. Robert Gallo.
　　　　☐ c. infectious diseases.
　　　　☐ d. the symptoms of HIV.　　　　_____

Supporting Details　　**3**　A T-cell is a
　　　　☐ a. patient's blood.
　　　　☐ b. deadly strain of tuberculosis.
　　　　☐ c. white blood cell important in providing immunity to disease.
　　　　☐ d. red blood cell.　　　　_____

Conclusion　　**4**　The final paragraph leads the reader to see that scientists
　　　　☐ a. have no hope in ever finding a cure for HIV.
　　　　☐ b. have hope that a cure for HIV will be found.
　　　　☐ c. have run out of time to find a cure for HIV.
　　　　☐ d. are in a contest against each other to find a cure for HIV.　　　　_____

Clarifying Devices　　**5**　The basic pattern used to develop this passage is
　　　　☐ a. chronological order.
　　　　☐ b. personal narrative.
　　　　☐ c. comparison and contrast.
　　　　☐ d. question and answer.　　　　_____

Vocabulary in Context　　**6**　The word <u>eradicated</u> means
　　　　☐ a. made extreme.
　　　　☐ b. celebrated.
　　　　☐ c. remove by rubbing.
　　　　☐ d. gotten rid of entirely.　　　　_____

Add your scores for questions 1–6. Enter the total here and on the graph on page 215.　　**Total Score**　　_____

45 Playing Havoc with Generations

In 1999 Daniel Benjamin noticed his university professor chatting with an elderly gentleman. The professor presently introduced Harrison Ruffin Tyler, a descendant of the 10th U.S. president, John Tyler. Since John Tyler was born in 1790 (as a child he had met George Washington), Daniel speculated that Harrison was President Tyler's great-great-grandson. Daniel assumed that a generation is about 30 years long. He figured that if President Tyler had had a child when he was 30, that child (let's call him John 2) would have been born in 1820; if John 2 had had a child when *he* was 30, John 3, the President's grandson, would have been born in 1850. John 4, President Tyler's great-grandson, would have been born in 1880, and John 5, his great-great-grandson, would have come along in 1910.

Was Harrison Tyler "John 5"? To Daniel, Harrison looked about 65—not old enough to have been born in 1910. Daniel decided that Harrison might even be "John 6," the President's great-great-great-grandson. Imagine his surprise when Harrison Tyler began to speak of his *grandfather,* President John Tyler! Here's how this strange fluke occurred: after President Tyler's first wife, Letitia, died in 1842, he married again to a woman 30 years his junior, Julia Gardiner. In 1853 (when John was 63 years old) he and Julia had a son named Lyon Gardiner Tyler. Lyon, too, married twice. His second wife, Sue Ruffin, was 36 years younger than her husband. Lyon and Sue's son Harrison Ruffin Tyler was born in 1928, when Lyon was 75! Harrison was 71 in 1999.

So much time had <u>elapsed</u> between the births of John and Lyon and between those of Lyon and Harrison that Harrison ended up way out of line with his family's generations. For example, Harrison's first cousin Robert Tyler Jones was 85 years older than Harrison—old enough to be Harrison's great-grandfather!

Main Idea   1

	Answer	Score
Mark the *main idea*	M	15
Mark the statement that is *too broad*	B	5
Mark the statement that is *too narrow*	N	5

a. A generation can be short or long.	☐	_____
b. In Harrison Tyler's family, generations were unusually long.	☐	_____
c. Lyon Tyler was 75 when his son was born.	☐	_____

Subject Matter   2   This passage is mainly about
- [ ] a. John Tyler's presidency.
- [ ] b. second marriages to younger women.
- [ ] c. the unusual generations in Harrison Tyler's family.
- [ ] d. Harrison Tyler's affection for his late grandfather.

_____

Supporting Details   3   Lyon Gardiner Tyler was born
- [ ] a. in 1842.
- [ ] b. when his father was 63.
- [ ] c. when his father was 30.
- [ ] d. in 1928.

_____

Conclusion   4   Daniel made an error when he decided
- [ ] a. to subtract 1853 from 1928.
- [ ] b. that a generation must be 30 years.
- [ ] c. that John Tyler was older than Julia.
- [ ] d. to subtract 1790 from 1853.

_____

Clarifying Devices   5   The names "John 2," "John 3," and so on, stand for
- [ ] a. Harrison Tyler's first cousins.
- [ ] b. John Tyler's many sons.
- [ ] c. generations of the Tyler family.
- [ ] d. actual individuals that Daniel had read about.

_____

Vocabulary in Context   6   The word <u>elapsed</u> means
- [ ] a. collapsed.
- [ ] b. passed.
- [ ] c. argued.
- [ ] d. exclaimed.

_____

Add your scores for questions 1–6. Enter the total here and on the graph on page 215.   **Total Score**

_____

46 Thirteen Days in October

John F. Kennedy, President of the United States, peered at the photographs taken by a U-2 spy plane flying high over Cuba. Nikita Khrushchev, premier of the Soviet Union, was installing offensive nuclear weapons just 90 miles off the Florida coast. It was October 15, 1962.

Kennedy called his advisers together. Some favored an immediate air strike and an invasion of Cuba; some thought the United States should put up a naval blockade around Cuba to turn away Soviet ships carrying weapons. Finally Kennedy decided. The navy would put up a blockade.

Khrushchev issued two orders. The Soviets would speed up work on the nuclear missile bases, and Soviet ship captains would ignore the blockade. Then the first unexpected event took place. Soviet ships approaching the blockade stopped dead in the water. The Soviet special envoy to Cuba had overruled Khrushchev and ordered Soviet ships to stop. Then on October 26, Kennedy received a letter from Khrushchev proposing that the Soviets would remove the missiles in exchange for a U.S. pledge never to invade Cuba. Before Kennedy could reply, a second Khrushchev letter arrived proposing a different solution. Khrushchev wanted U.S. missiles in Turkey removed in exchange for the removal of the Cuban missiles.

From the U.S. point of view, this was unacceptable, but Kennedy had one more strategy in mind. The terms of Khrushchev's first letter were acceptable, but not the terms of the second. So Kennedy ignored the second letter. He answered the first letter instead. He replied on October 27th, and the next day a message came from Khrushchev. Yes, the Soviet Union would accept the terms as stated in the President's letter. Somehow during those 13 days in October 1962, a war was avoided.

Main Idea	1	Answer	Score
	Mark the *main idea*	M	15
	Mark the statement that is *too broad*	B	5
	Mark the statement that is *too narrow*	N	5
	a. Communication is important.	☐	____
	b. War between the Soviets and the U.S. was narrowly avoided in October 1962.	☐	____
	c. The U.S. navy blockaded Soviet ships.	☐	____

Score 15 points for each correct answer. Score

Subject Matter 2 This passage is mostly about
☐ a. how Khrushchev became the Soviet premier.
☐ b. the naval blockade of Cuba.
☐ c. what Kennedy's advisers recommended.
☐ d. how the United States and the Soviet Union avoided war in 1962. _____

Supporting Details 3 The most important people affecting the outcome of the event in this passage are
☐ a. the Soviet special envoy and Khrushchev.
☐ b. Khrushchev and Kennedy.
☐ c. Kennedy's advisers.
☐ d. Kennedy and the Soviet ship captains. _____

Conclusion 4 According to this passage, the main reason war was avoided was the
☐ a. blockade.
☐ b. advisers.
☐ c. letters.
☐ d. U-2 spy plane. _____

Clarifying Devices 5 The first paragraph of this passage
☐ a. establishes the who, when, and where of the incident.
☐ b. gives a brief history of U.S.-Soviet relations.
☐ c. moves from present time to past time.
☐ d. helps us understand Kennedy's character. _____

Vocabulary in Context 6 In this passage <u>proposing</u> means
☐ a. putting forth for discussion.
☐ b. pretending.
☐ c. making an offer of marriage.
☐ d. bringing before a court of law. _____

Add your scores for questions 1–6. Enter the total here and on the graph on page 215. Total Score _____

47 The Development of Ballet

Ballet is a dance form that has a long history. The fact that it survives to this day shows that it has adjusted as times have changed.

Ballet began in the royal courts during the Renaissance. At that time it became common for kings and queens, as well as other nobility, to participate in <u>pageants</u> that included music, poetry, and dance. As these entertainments moved from the Italian courts to the French ones, court ladies began participating in them. Though their long dresses prevented much movement, they were able to perform elaborate walking patterns. It was not until the 1600s that women dancers shortened their skirts, changed to flat shoes, and began doing some of the leaps and turns performed by men.

It was also in the 1600s that professional ballet began. King Louis XIV of France, himself a devoted dancer, founded the Royal Academy of Dance. The five basic feet positions from which all ballet steps begin were finalized. In the late 1700s another important change occurred. Ballet began to tell a story on its own. It was no longer simply dance to be performed between acts of plays. Elaborate wigs and costumes were eliminated. By the early 1800s dancers learned to rise on their toes to make it appear that they were floating.

Classical ballet as we know it today was influenced primarily by Russian dancing. The Russians remained interested in ballet when it declined in other European countries in the mid-1800s. One of the most influential figures of the early 20th century was Sergei Diaghilev. His dance company, the Ballets Russes, brought a new energy and excitement to ballet. One of his chief assistants, George Balanchine, went on to found the New York City Ballet in 1948 and to influence new generations of dancers.

Main Idea	1		Answer	Score
	Mark the _main idea_		**M**	15
	Mark the statement that is _too broad_		**B**	5
	Mark the statement that is _too narrow_		**N**	5

a.	Ballet began as a court amusement.	☐	_____
b.	Ballet began in the Renaissance and developed through the present time.	☐	_____
c.	Ballet is a type of dance.	☐	_____

Subject Matter   **2**   This passage deals mainly with
- ☐ a. famous names in ballet.
- ☐ b. French versus Russian ballet.
- ☐ c. the way ballet developed.
- ☐ d. why ballet is no longer popular.   _____

Supporting Details   **3**   An important influence in early ballet was
- ☐ a. Balanchine.
- ☐ b. Marie Antoinette.
- ☐ c. Diaghilev.
- ☐ d. Louis XIV.   _____

Conclusion   **4**   You can conclude from this passage that ballet
- ☐ a. is a dying art.
- ☐ b. will continue to change as new people and ideas influence it.
- ☐ c. is only currently performed in Russia and the United States.
- ☐ d. is often performed by dancers with little training.   _____

Clarifying Devices   **5**   The information in this passage is presented
- ☐ a. through the story of one dancer.
- ☐ b. by describing various positions and steps.
- ☐ c. by listing reasons why ballet has succeeded.
- ☐ d. in chronological order.   _____

Vocabulary in Context   **6**   The word <u>pageants</u> means
- ☐ a. dances.
- ☐ b. instructors.
- ☐ c. kings.
- ☐ d. elaborate shows.   _____

Add your scores for questions 1–6. Enter the total here and on the graph on page 215.   **Total Score**   _____

48 Chemical Compounds

All the matter in the universe is composed of the atoms of more than 100 different chemical elements. The atoms of each element are unique. A sample of any pure element has only atoms that are characteristic of that element. For example, the atoms that make up the element carbon are different from the atoms that make up the element iron, and those atoms are different from the atoms that make up the element gold. Each element has its own symbol consisting of one, two, or three letters. The letters come from either the current name of the element, such as C, H, and O for carbon, hydrogen, and oxygen, or from the original name of the element. The original name is often its Latin name; for example, Fe is the symbol for iron, which had an original Latin name of *ferrum*.

Elements also combine with other elements to make chemical compounds. The atoms of the elements are like letters of the alphabet. Just as letters can be combined to form words, the atoms of the elements can combine to form many different compounds. The <u>formula</u> of a compound tells the types and the ratios of the atoms present in the compound. For example, water is a chemical compound of the elements of hydrogen and oxygen. The atoms are in the ratio of two hydrogen atoms for every oxygen atom. The formula for water is written H_2O. Methane is a chemical compound formed from the elements carbon and hydrogen. There are four hydrogen atoms for each single carbon atom. The formula for methane is written CH_4.

There are millions of known chemical compounds, and there are many more millions that have not yet been discovered.

Main Idea   1

	Answer	Score
Mark the *main idea*	M	15
Mark the statement that is *too broad*	B	5
Mark the statement that is *too narrow*	N	5

a. There are more than 100 different chemical elements. ☐ _____

b. Chemical elements and compounds are named in specific ways. ☐ _____

c. Matter is made of elements. ☐ _____

Subject Matter   2   This passage deals mainly with
- [ ] a. the more than 100 different elements.
- [ ] b. atoms.
- [ ] c. how elements and compounds are named.
- [ ] d. the formula for water.   _____

Supporting Details   3   The formula for methane, CH4, stands for
- [ ] a. a total of four atoms.
- [ ] b. one carbon atom and four hydrogen atoms.
- [ ] c. four carbon atoms and one hydrogen atom.
- [ ] d. four carbon atoms and four hydrogen atoms.   _____

Conclusion   4   This passage leads the reader to conclude that
- [ ] a. all chemical compounds contain carbon.
- [ ] b. there are exactly one million chemical compounds.
- [ ] c. the search for chemical compounds is ongoing.
- [ ] d. all chemical compounds have been discovered.   _____

Clarifying Devices   5   In the second paragraph, the statement that "atoms . . . are like letters of the alphabet" is
- [ ] a. a simile.
- [ ] b. a metaphor.
- [ ] c. personification.
- [ ] d. an exaggeration.   _____

Vocabulary in Context   6   In this passage the word <u>formula</u> means
- [ ] a. a statement of religious belief.
- [ ] b. a mixture fed to babies.
- [ ] c. the symbols that express a compound.
- [ ] d. a plan or method.   _____

Add your scores for questions 1–6. Enter the total here and on the graph on page 215.   **Total Score**   _____

49 If This Is San Francisco, It Must Be Yesterday

Tony Montecito is a United States citizen residing in Tokyo. On Friday, March 3, he attends an important business conference that lasts until noon. The next day, Saturday, March 4, Tony's brother is to be married in San Francisco, and Tony is best man. There will be a rehearsal banquet at 6 P.M. on Friday evening. Though a nonstop flight from Tokyo to San Francisco takes about nine hours, Tony arrives in plenty of time to take a siesta and a <u>leisurely</u> shower before Friday's rehearsal dinner.

Here is how this seemingly impossible scenario works. Suppose you live in California and your parents reside in Hawaii. Because it is two hours earlier there, they try to avoid calling too late in the evening; 9 P.M. in Hawaii is 11 P.M. in California. However, if your folks live in Tokyo, and you call them at 9 in the evening on Saturday, California time, it will be 1 P.M. *Sunday* Tokyo time. The culprit is an imaginary north-south line called the International Dateline (IDL) that lies in the Pacific between Hawaii and Japan. If you cross the IDL traveling west, the time is 24 hours ahead. That is, if you approach the IDL at noon on Saturday, it will be Sunday noon as soon as you cross it. If you count the time zones between California and Tokyo, there are only seven. But you have to take that extra 24-hour day into account. Subtracting 7 hours from 24 hours gives you 17 hours, the difference between Tokyo and California time.

So Tony, his conference completed, departs from Tokyo at 4:30 P.M. on Friday. He is heading east. When he arrives in San Francisco after the nine-hour flight, it is 1:30 A.M. Saturday Tokyo time, but it is 8:30 A.M. *Friday* San Francisco time—or 17 hours earlier. Just as his plane crossed the IDL sometime Friday night, the time turned back 24 hours. It became Thursday night at the same time. That's why it's only Friday morning when he lands in San Francisco—Tony gets a second Friday free!

Main Idea 1

	Answer	Score
Mark the *main idea*	M	15
Mark the statement that is *too broad*	B	5
Mark the statement that is *too narrow*	N	5

a. The world has many time zones.	☐	_____
b. A traveler gains or loses a day crossing the International Date Line.	☐	_____
c. Tony left Tokyo at 4:30 P.M. Friday.	☐	

Subject Matter   **2**   Another good title for this passage would be
      ☐ a. With Time to Spare.
      ☐ b. A Family Wedding.
      ☐ c. Business Conference in Japan.
      ☐ d. In the Nick of Time.   _____

Supporting Details   **3**   It is 17 hours earlier in
      ☐ a. New York than it is in California.
      ☐ b. Hawaii than it is in San Francisco.
      ☐ c. San Francisco than it is in Tokyo.
      ☐ d. Tokyo than it is in San Francisco.   _____

Conclusion   **4**   When traveling across the Pacific, one needs to
      ☐ a. plan on a 17-hour flight.
      ☐ b. fly from San Francisco to Hawaii to Tokyo.
      ☐ c. figure the IDL into one's schedule.
      ☐ d. try to avoid crossing the IDL.   _____

Clarifying Devices   **5**   The story about Tony is told
      ☐ a. because it is true.
      ☐ b. as an example of how the IDL affects time.
      ☐ c. to show that weddings require careful
          planning.
      ☐ d. to interest the reader in how the wedding
          turns out.   _____

Vocabulary in Context   **6**   The word <u>leisurely</u> means
      ☐ a. frantic.
      ☐ b. quick.
      ☐ c. warm.
      ☐ d. unhurried.   _____

Add your scores for questions 1–6. Enter the total here   **Total**
and on the graph on page 215.   **Score**   _____

50 The Bones Tell Another Story

One field of applied anthropology is known as forensic anthropology. It specializes in the identification of human skeletal remains for legal purposes. Clyde C. Snow, forensic anthropologist, usually uses his science to identify victims of disasters and violent crimes. But sometimes Snow is asked to apply his skills to unusual cases.

In Montana, just west of the Black Hills of South Dakota, lies the Custer Battlefield. This is the location where the Battle of the Little Bighorn was fought on June 25, 1876. General George Custer and all his men died there, leaving no one to tell the U.S. cavalry's side of the story. That story could only be pieced together from evidence found at the site. When a brushfire burned off the prairie grass in 1983, previously undiscovered artifacts were uncovered. Among these were bones of Custer's soldiers, including one nearly intact skeleton. Archaeologists from the National Park Service asked Snow to examine these bones.

When the skeleton's bones were reassembled, only one of Custer's 267 men fit the description. It was Mitch Boyer, one of Custer's scouts. One telling clue <u>culled</u> from Snow's investigation came from the skull's teeth. The arched marks on the left incisor and canine were the marks of a pipe smoker, and Boyer was a pipe smoker. The marks came from his habit of clenching the pipe stem between his teeth.

Indians who had fought in the battle had said that Boyer's detachment of troops was killed at another location. This location was a long way from where Boyer's bones were found. But forensic anthropology had now established a different scenario. Snow's identification of Boyer meant that a part of American history had to be rewritten.

Main Idea	1	Answer	Score
	Mark the *main idea*	M	15
	Mark the statement that is *too broad*	B	5
	Mark the statement that is *too narrow*	N	5

a. Forensic anthropology helped to rewrite a piece of American history. ☐ _____

b. Clyde Snow studied the bones found at the Little Bighorn battle site. ☐ _____

c. Forensic anthropology is a field of applied anthropology. ☐ _____

Subject Matter   **2**   This passage deals mainly with the work of
☐ a. an archaeologist.
☐ b. a U.S. cavalry soldier.
☐ c. a National Park ranger.
☐ d. a forensic anthropologist.   _____

Supporting Details   **3**   The bones were not found until 1983 when
☐ a. the area of the battle was identified.
☐ b. a prairie fire burned away brush and uncovered hidden artifacts.
☐ c. people were celebrating the anniversary of the battle.
☐ d. an earthquake made the bones visible.   _____

Conclusion   **4**   The fact that Mitch Boyer's name was known suggests that
☐ a. this battle had been carefully studied.
☐ b. he rather than Custer had led the cavalry.
☐ c. the Indians thought he was the bravest white man.
☐ d. "Boyer" was a common last name in 1876.   _____

Clarifying Devices   **5**   The writer presents information in this passage by
☐ a. describing the battle.
☐ b. telling a story.
☐ c. proving that Custer had not been killed.
☐ d. presenting a series of questions and answers.   _____

Vocabulary in Context   **6**   The word <u>culled</u> means
☐ a. killed.
☐ b. selected.
☐ c. overlooked.
☐ d. thrown away.   _____

Add your scores for questions 1–6. Enter the total here and on the graph on page 215.   **Total Score**   _____

51 Shakespeare's Tragedies

Shakespeare wrote amusing comedies and insightful history plays. But most people, when they think of Shakespeare's greatest works, think of his tragedies.

By definition, a tragedy is any serious work with an unhappy ending. Most of Shakespeare's tragedies end very unhappily: one or more of the main characters is killed. In *Romeo and Juliet,* for example, both of the young lovers end up dead. So do Brutus and Cassius in *Julius Caesar.* In *Hamlet,* the main character is killed by a poisoned sword, and several other characters die at the same time.

Some scholars claim that the four greatest Shakespearean tragedies are *Hamlet, Othello, Macbeth,* and *King Lear.* The main character in each play causes his own downfall through a personal shortcoming or a series of bad decisions. Hamlet, informed by his dead father's ghost that his own brother has murdered him, cannot take the steps necessary to bring his uncle to justice. Othello, <u>goaded</u> on by his chief aide, cannot believe that his young and beautiful wife can be faithful to him. Macbeth's desire to become king of Scotland leads him to murder the reigning king and anyone else who stands in his way. Lear foolishly believes the flattery of his two older daughters, who cast him out of their castles to wander about, homeless and going mad.

What makes these plays great is the way the characters are developed. Each main character is fully rounded, with both strengths and weaknesses. A device Shakespeare often uses is soliloquies, speeches in which characters reveal their thoughts and feelings only to the audience. Through these we learn of Macbeth's terror before he murders the king and Hamlet's disgust with himself for his inaction. Other figures are also sharply drawn, from Othello's gentle, trusting wife to the Fool who accompanies Lear. The characters are as real as if they had been created today, not some 400 years ago.

Main Idea	1		Answer	Score
	Mark the *main idea*		M	15
	Mark the statement that is *too broad*		B	5
	Mark the statement that is *too narrow*		N	5
	a. Shakespeare wrote several tragedies.		☐	____
	b. Shakespeare's tragedies—and four in particular—are his greatest works.		☐	____
	c. In most Shakespearean tragedies the main character dies at the end.		☐	____

Subject Matter   2   This passage is mainly about
- ☐ a. *Romeo and Juliet.*
- ☐ b. Shakespeare the writer.
- ☐ c. Shakespeare's important tragedies.
- ☐ d. what the word *tragedy* means.   _____

Supporting Details   3   Macbeth
- ☐ a. wants to become king of Scotland.
- ☐ b. murders his wife.
- ☐ c. is thrown out by his daughters.
- ☐ d. commits suicide.   _____

Conclusion   4   It is fair to conclude from this passage that
- ☐ a. Shakespeare wrote only six tragedies.
- ☐ b. tragedies are rarely written today.
- ☐ c. all tragedies end with characters' deaths.
- ☐ d. soliloquies can help the audience understand characters' motivations.   _____

Clarifying Devices   5   A main device the writer uses to develop this passage is
- ☐ a. comparison and contrast.
- ☐ b. providing examples.
- ☐ c. using an argument to persuade the reader.
- ☐ d. providing a biography of Shakespeare.   _____

Vocabulary in Context   6   In this passage <u>goaded</u> means
- ☐ a. poked with a stick.
- ☐ b. fought with.
- ☐ c. urged on.
- ☐ d. made sad.   _____

Add your scores for questions 1–6. Enter the total here and on the graph on page 216.   **Total Score**   _____

52 Whatever Floats Your Boat

There is a story that cannot be proven about the Greek mathematician and inventor Archimedes. Supposedly Archimedes was in his bath way back in the third century B.C., when he noted the level of the bath water rising as he submerged himself. It is said that he leaped from his bath and ran naked through the streets crying "Eureka!" which in English means, "I have found it." What had gotten Archimedes so excited became known as Archimedes' principle. This law of physics states that any object floating upon or submerged in a fluid is <u>buoyed</u> upward by a force equal to the weight of the displaced fluid.

What does that mean in real-life terms? In fact, Archimedes' principle is the basis of naval architecture. A ship launched into the ocean will sink until the weight of the water it displaces, or pushes out of the way, is equal to the ship's own weight. A ship is designed to carry fuel, lubricating oil, crew, and crew supplies to operate. This weight is called deadweight. Added to the deadweight is the weight of the ship's structure and machinery. This is known as lightship weight. The sum of deadweight and lightship weight is displacement—that is, the weight that must be equaled by the weight of displaced water if the ship is to float. A cargo ship must also be designed to carry a specified weight of cargo, because as the ship is loaded with cargo, it will sink deeper, displacing more water.

Naval architects use formulas to approximate the various weights needed to be figured into a ship's design. These experience-based formulas usually produce accurate predictions of the ship's draft—that is, the depth of water in which the finished ship will float. Like Archimedes, the naval architect can cry "Eureka!" when he or she has found the size of the ship that the sum of all weights requires.

Main Idea	1	Answer	Score
	Mark the *main idea*	M	15
	Mark the statement that is *too broad*	B	5
	Mark the statement that is *too narrow*	N	5

a. Archimedes' principle about water displacement is vital to shipbuilding. ☐ _____

b. Archimedes supposedly cried "Eureka!" ☐ _____

c. All ships displace water. ☐ _____

Score 15 points for each correct answer.　　　　**Score**

Subject Matter　2　This passage is mainly about
- [ ] a. the life of Archimedes.
- [ ] b. cargo ships.
- [ ] c. the laws of physics.
- [ ] d. Archimedes' principle and its effects on naval architecture.

_____

Supporting Details　3　A ship will sink until
- [ ] a. fuel, oil, crew, and supplies are removed.
- [ ] b. the water covers its cargo.
- [ ] c. the weight of the water it displaces is equal to its own weight.
- [ ] d. a naval architect supervises its loading.

_____

Conclusion　4　Before Archimedes' principle, ship captains were
- [ ] a. never exactly sure how much weight they could safely carry.
- [ ] b. anxious to sail to faraway ports.
- [ ] c. interested only in sailing heavyweight boats.
- [ ] d. sure that sea monsters moved ocean waters.

_____

Clarifying Devices　5　Which phrase defines the draft of a ship?
- [ ] a. experience-based formulas
- [ ] b. depth of water in which the finished ship will float
- [ ] c. the size of the ship
- [ ] d. approximate the various weights

_____

Vocabulary in Context　6　In this passage buoyed means
- [ ] a. destroyed by water.
- [ ] b. built by a naval architect.
- [ ] c. held up or kept from sinking.
- [ ] d. made to feel excited or happy.

_____

Add your scores for questions 1–6. Enter the total here and on the graph on page 216.　　**Total Score**

_____

53 Working Through a Math Puzzle

If you are as <u>intrigued</u> by mathematical games and puzzles as Veronica Tervalon is, proceed through the steps below with Veronica and see how this puzzle works.

On Halloween afternoon, 1999, this forwarded e-mail message appeared on Veronica's computer:

Dearest Friends and Esteemed Colleagues—We sincerely hope you'll enjoy this intriguing little mathematical game, which we assure you is anything but time-consuming: it takes approximately 30 seconds to complete. However, don't delay—the formula it is based on will be invalid when the new millennium commences.

(1) Pick the number of evenings per week that you would prefer dining in restaurants. [Veronica, who usually preferred her husband's cooking, chose 1.]

(2) Multiply your number by 2, and add 5. [Veronica's total was 7.]

(3) Multiply that total by 50. [Veronica's product was 350.]

(4) If you have already celebrated your birthday this year, add 1749; however, if your birthday is still to come, add 1748. [Since Veronica's birthday fell on December 31, she added 1748 for a sum of 2098.]

(5) Now subtract the four-digit number representing the year of your birth. [Veronica subtracted 1964 for a difference of 134.]

(6) These computations should have resulted in a three-digit number. The digit in the hundreds column should be your original number (number of evenings per week that you'd prefer dining in restaurants). [Yes, Veronica's number was 1.] *The other two digits should be your age.* [YES, Veronica was 34 years old!]

If an acquaintance of yours is a sophisticated mathematician who can create puzzles with numbers that automatically cancel themselves out, see if that person can adapt the data in this puzzle to make it work in the new millennium.

Main Idea   1 ───────────────────────────────

	Answer	Score
Mark the *main idea*	M	15
Mark the statement that is *too broad*	B	5
Mark the statement that is *too narrow*	N	5

a. A well-designed math puzzle will come up with the results it promises. ☐ ____

b. Math puzzles are very interesting. ☐ ____

c. Veronica worked the puzzle using her own numbers. ☐ ____

Subject Matter   2   Another good title for this passage might be
- ☐ a. Getting E-mail Messages.
- ☐ b. Halloween 1999.
- ☐ c. Creating a Brain Teaser.
- ☐ d. Solve Before the Millennium!   _____

Supporting Details   3   Veronica was to add the number 1748
- ☐ a. if she hadn't yet had a birthday in 1999.
- ☐ b. if she had already had her birthday in 1999.
- ☐ c. to the number of evenings she preferred dining in restaurants.
- ☐ d. to her age.   _____

Conclusion   4   A reason that your own numbers might not work in this puzzle is that
- ☐ a. it is no longer 1999.
- ☐ b. your birthday has already occurred this year.
- ☐ c. the steps are not in correct order.
- ☐ d. your numbers are probably the same as Veronica's.   _____

Clarifying Devices   5   The writer uses italic type to
- ☐ a. show Veronica's calculations as she worked the puzzle.
- ☐ b. highlight the steps of the puzzle.
- ☐ c. show that certain words are important.
- ☐ d. convey how excited Veronica felt when the puzzle worked.   _____

Vocabulary in Context   6   In this passage <u>intrigued</u> means
- ☐ a. surprised.
- ☐ b. frightened.
- ☐ c. fascinated.
- ☐ d. bored.   _____

Add your scores for questions 1–6. Enter the total here and on the graph on page 216.   **Total Score**   _____

54 Port Chicago

On July 17, 1944, two munitions ships blew up at Port Chicago, 30 miles northeast of San Francisco, while being loaded with bombs, shells, and depth charges. Those on the pier and aboard the ships were instantly killed, leaving 320 men dead and 390 military personnel and civilians injured. It was the biggest disaster of World War II to take place in the United States. But the disaster had another disturbing figure: of the 320 men who died, 202 were African Americans. All the sailors performing the dangerous job of loading munitions were black.

A navy court of <u>inquiry</u> investigated the accident and placed no blame, saying "rough handling [of munitions] by an individual or individuals" may have been the cause. Traumatized by the explosion, 258 black loaders refused to return to work and were imprisoned by the navy for three days. Most of those men, except for 50 seamen, then returned to work. These 50 were court-martialed, convicted of mutiny, and imprisoned until the end of the war. A young lawyer named Thurgood Marshall was outraged. "This is not 50 men on trial for mutiny," Marshall said. "This is the navy on trial for its whole vicious policy towards Negroes. Negroes in the navy don't mind loading ammunition. They just want to know why they are the only ones doing the loading!"

After the war, with Thurgood Marshall's persistence, the sentences of the 50 black sailors were reduced, but not overturned. However, the actions of the black sailors did make a difference. Soon after, white sailors were put to work side by side with black sailors loading ammunition at Port Chicago. Later, the navy followed through on a desegregation policy. And in 1967, the outspoken Thurgood Marshall became the first African-American justice of the United States Supreme Court.

Main Idea	1		
		Answer	**Score**
Mark the *main idea*		M	15
Mark the statement that is *too broad*		B	5
Mark the statement that is *too narrow*		N	5

a. A disaster prompted changes in the navy's segregation policy. ☐ _____

b. Naval disasters were part of World War II. ☐ _____

c. Black sailors loaded ammunition at Port Chicago. ☐ _____

Score 15 points for each correct answer.   Score

Subject Matter   2   This passage deals mainly with
☐ a. the battlefields of World War II.
☐ b. an injustice against black sailors.
☐ c. the life of Thurgood Marshall.
☐ d. how the two ships exploded.   _____

Supporting Details   3   The 50 seamen were found guilty of
☐ a. conspiracy.
☐ b. talking to Thurgood Marshall.
☐ c. being absent without leave.
☐ d. mutiny.   _____

Conclusion   4   Words like *disturbing* in the first paragraph and *made a difference* in the third paragraph suggest that the writer
☐ a. is critical of the sailors.
☐ b. sympathizes with the sailors.
☐ c. has no opinion about the incident.
☐ d. does not choose words very carefully.   _____

Clarifying Devices   5   The information in this passage is presented
☐ a. through a fictitious story.
☐ b. starting in the present and going back into the past.
☐ c. in chronological order.
☐ d. through a series of descriptions.   _____

Vocabulary in Context   6   In this passage inquiry means
☐ a. a search for information and truth.
☐ b. curiosity.
☐ c. a question.
☐ d. an accident.   _____

Add your scores for questions 1–6. Enter the total here and on the graph on page 216.   Total Score   _____

55 A Malaria-Carrying Mosquito

First come the shakes, the fever, the burning throat. Next are the chills. Your pulse rate <u>plummets</u>, and a drenching sweat ices you from head to toe. Your face turns pale, and your nails turn blue. Then you either cough up thick, black blood and die—or you survive. If you survive, depression might hang on for months. Finally, there's the fear that it might strike you again. This is the tropical disease *malaria.*

In 1904, the United States began building a canal through the Isthmus of Panama, but canal workers were getting sick and many were dying. That was because conditions in Panama were ideal for breeding the female *Anopheles,* a malaria-carrying mosquito. The females lay eggs in standing water in rain barrels, storage jars, and thousands of puddles. Larvae, called *wrigglers,* hatch from the eggs and develop into adult mosquitoes. When the mosquitoes suck the blood of a person infected with malaria, the deadly parasites breed in the mosquitoes' stomachs and migrate to their salivary glands. After that every person the mosquitoes bite gets a dose of deadly parasites. Infected victims transmit parasites to other mosquitoes that bite them, and these mosquitoes in turn infect other people. Unchecked, cases of malaria rise to epidemic proportions.

To eliminate mosquito breeding grounds in Panama, swamps were filled with dirt or drained dry. Other watery areas were coated with oil and larvicide. Surface-feeding fish, spiders, and lizards were put into rivers and fields to eat adult mosquitoes. Even human mosquito-catchers were paid 10 cents an hour to swat the deadly insects.

Malaria was never entirely eradicated, but it was reduced from infecting 82 percent of canal workers in 1906 to infecting less than eight percent in 1913 when the Panama Canal was completed.

Main Idea   1 ───────────────────────────────

	Answer	Score
Mark the *main idea*	M	15
Mark the statement that is *too broad*	B	5
Mark the statement that is *too narrow*	N	5

a. Tropical diseases are found in Panama. ☐ ___

b. Controlling the *Anopheles* mosquito helped the builders of the Panama Canal. ☐ ___

c. Malaria causes the chills. ☐ ___

Subject Matter 2 This passage is mainly about
- [ ] a. the fight against a tropical disease.
- [ ] b. insects.
- [ ] c. building the Panama Canal.
- [ ] d. canal workers in Panama. _____

Supporting Details 3 To lay their eggs, female Anopheles need
- [ ] a. deadly parasites.
- [ ] b. wrigglers.
- [ ] c. standing water.
- [ ] d. larvicide. _____

Conclusion 4 Without the mosquito-control efforts,
- [ ] a. there would have been war in Panama.
- [ ] b. the Panama Canal may never have been completed.
- [ ] c. cities would have been built along the canal.
- [ ] d. spiders and lizards would have died. _____

Clarifying Devices 5 In the second paragraph, *Anopheles* is
- [ ] a. the name of a species of mosquito.
- [ ] b. the title of a book about mosquitoes.
- [ ] c. a Panamanian expression.
- [ ] d. an emphasized word. _____

Vocabulary in Context 6 The word <u>plummets</u> means
- [ ] a. drops rapidly.
- [ ] b. resembles a smallish purple fruit.
- [ ] c. heats up.
- [ ] d. resembles a hammer. _____

Add your scores for questions 1–6. Enter the total here and on the graph on page 216. **Total Score** _____

56 The Gothic Cathedral

When architects plan buildings, they usually try to consider the function of the building and come up with a design to accommodate that function. One of the earliest examples of this sort of planning can be seen in Gothic cathedrals.

A cathedral is a large church where thousands of people may come to worship. In the years between about 1150 and 1550 A.D., religion played an especially vital part in people's lives. And so houses of worship were built both to express people's religious sentiments and to inspire them as they prayed.

A cathedral built in the Gothic style has several distinctive characteristics. The first is the use of thin, pointed arches that allowed the building to be taller than ever before and that raised churchgoers' eyes heavenward. Another characteristic is the flying buttress. This was a supporting arm on the outside of the cathedral that permitted the inner walls to be less massive. Some cathedrals had as many as 20 of these roughly right-angled structures. Often the buttresses were topped with small, pointed towers that, like the arches, formed a strong vertical line.

The high arches and thinner walls helped make possible another noteworthy characteristic of the Gothic cathedral: stained glass windows. Generally these windows were tall and thin, to complement the shape of the arches. But most cathedrals had at least one rose window, a large circular device with many small glass panels set into it. These panels were separated by thin bars of stone. The windows frequently showed scenes from the life of Christ and the saints, and <u>contemplating</u> them as the outside light shone through was certainly a moving religious experience.

Many Gothic cathedrals remain standing in Europe. Some of the most famous are in France, including those in the cities of Paris, Chartres, and Rheims,

Main Idea	1		
		Answer	**Score**
Mark the *main idea*		M	15
Mark the statement that is *too broad*		B	5
Mark the statement that is *too narrow*		N	5

a. Thin, pointed arches made cathedral-goers look up. ☐ _____

b. Gothic cathedrals were designed to bring out worshippers' faith. ☐ _____

c. Cathedrals were built in Europe. ☐ _____

Subject Matter   2   Another good title for this passage would be
☐ a. Medieval Architects.
☐ b. Paris, Chartres, and Rheims.
☐ c. Steps in Building a Cathedral.
☐ d. Designed with Worship in Mind.   _____

**Supporting
Details**   3   A rose window was
☐ a. long and narrow.
☐ b. circular.
☐ c. made of roses.
☐ d. made of clear glass.   _____

Conclusion   4   Gothic cathedrals looked
☐ a. rounded.
☐ b. small.
☐ c. cheerful.
☐ d. impressive.   _____

**Clarifying
Devices**   5   A term in this passage that is explained through
a definition is
☐ a. flying buttress.
☐ b. arch.
☐ c. stained glass.
☐ d. tower.   _____

**Vocabulary
in Context**   6   Contemplating means
☐ a. counting panes of glass.
☐ b. looking at or studying quietly.
☐ c. figuring out how something is built.
☐ d. begging forgiveness.   _____

**Add your scores for questions 1–6. Enter the total here
and on the graph on page 216.**   **Total
Score**   _____

57 Happy 22nd Birthday, Great-Great-Uncle Mike!

It is February 29, 2088, and Mike Slutzker is celebrating his 22nd birthday. His married sister Shelby Slutzker Fresco has come to attend the festivities; so have Shelby's children, grandchildren, great-grandchildren, and great-great-grandchildren—one of these, Mike's great-great-niece, is 30. How, you might ask, is this possible?

The answer is that little Mikey Slutzker was born on February 29, 2000, a leap-year day. The following year, 2001, had no February 29, so Mikey's family decided to celebrate his birthday on February 28. But in 2004, when Mikey turned four, it was leap year again, and there was a February 29. His parents joked that Mikey was only one year old, since this was the first time since he was born that his actual birthday had come around again. After that, it became a family tradition to celebrate Mike's "fake birthdays" on February 28 of nonleap years and his "real birthdays" on February 29 of leap years, and to pretend that he aged only one year for every four. Since 88 divided by 4 is 22, in 2088, a leap year, the family celebrated Mike's "real" 22nd birthday as well as his "fake" (his actual) 88th birthday.

The reason leap years exist is that ever since people began creating calendars, they were <u>plagued</u> by the difficulty of precisely calculating the length of a year. Calendar makers finally determined that a year is 365 days long, plus about 6 hours (¹⁄₄ of a day). If the calendar establishes a year that lasts 365 days when it actually lasts 365.25, after four years the calendar will be out of synch with the earth's orbit by a day. To correct the error, we have a leap year, or 366-day year, every four years.

Leap years are years that are exactly divisible by 4; for example, 1996 was a leap year, as was 1992. However, century years are exceptions to this rule. They are leap years only if they are exactly divisible by 400, such as 1600 and 2000.

Main Idea   1

	Answer	Score
Mark the *main idea*	M	15
Mark the statement that is *too broad*	B	5
Mark the statement that is *too narrow*	N	5

	Answer	Score
a. Leap years were created because a year is a little longer than 365 days	☐	_____
b. Mike was born on a leap-year day.	☐	_____
c. Calendars need to be accurate.	☐	_____

Score 15 points for each correct answer.   Score

Subject Matter   2   The passage is primarily about
☐ a. Mike Slutzker and his family.
☐ b. leap years.
☐ c. calendars.
☐ d. birthday celebrations.   _____

Supporting   3   In 2088, Mike was actually
Details   ☐ a. 22 years old.
☐ b. 30 years old.
☐ c. 88 years old.
☐ d. 4 years old.   _____

Conclusion   4   We can conclude from reading the passage that
☐ a. 2400 will be a leap year.
☐ b. 2058 will be a leap year.
☐ c. 2100 will be a leap year.
☐ d. 1200 was not a leap year.   _____

Clarifying   5   The story of Mike's "real" and "fake" birthdays
Devices   is presented to demonstrate
☐ a. a bizarre fact about Mike's family.
☐ b. how often leap years occur.
☐ c. that 88 divided by 22 is 4.
☐ d. the silliness of Michael's parents.   _____

Vocabulary   6   The word <u>plagued</u> means
in Context   ☐ a. altered.
☐ b. assisted.
☐ c. brutalized.
☐ d. bothered.   _____

Add your scores for questions 1–6. Enter the total here   Total
and on the graph on page 216.   Score   _____

115

58 The Global Positioning System

In 1983 a Korean Airlines flight went off course over the Soviet Union and was shot down. All passengers, including several Americans, were killed. An investigation revealed that the pilots had set their starting point wrong, and the error was magnified as they flew. Today's technology ensures that this disaster could not happen again. That technology is the Global Positioning System (GPS), which is now used routinely for navigation on over-water flights. GPS is a great aid when the geography of an area is uncertain. It would have kept the Korean plane on course.

GPS is the network of 24 satellites launched and maintained by the U.S. military. The satellites are in continuous orbit 12,000 miles above the earth. Using geometry, the satellite signals precisely pinpoint a location. GPS was first used by the military to locate troops and tanks. It can tell where a missile or aircraft is. It can also tell how to get a weapon to a target. There are even hand-held, battery-operated GPS units for use by individual soldiers. In 1995 a U.S. Air Force pilot was shot down by a missile over Bosnia. He used a hand-held unit to find his exact position and radio it to his rescuers before he could be captured by the enemy.

What began as a military application is now finding a rapidly growing civilian market. Fishermen at sea, hikers on <u>remote</u> trails, and even rental cars are equipped with GPS. It is also being used in an increasing number of fire trucks, police cars, and ambulances. GPS can be used by farmers, too, to accurately guide a tractor in the field. Researchers have successfully used GPS to guide vehicles in fog, at night, and without drivers. Although its military use is vital, it is most likely that GPS will get its greatest application in the civilian world.

Main Idea	1	Answer	Score
	Mark the *main idea*	M	15
	Mark the statement that is *too broad*	B	5
	Mark the statement that is *too narrow*	N	5

a. A Korean Airlines flight went off course over the Soviet Union. ☐ _____

b. GPS is part of today's technology. ☐ _____

c. GPS has both military and civilian uses. ☐ _____

Score 15 points for each correct answer.   **Score**

Subject Matter   2   This passage deals mainly with
- ☐ a. geometry.
- ☐ b. military tactics during war.
- ☐ c. using the Global Positioning System.
- ☐ d. problems with commercial airlines.   _____

Supporting Details   3   The story of the pilot in Bosnia in paragraph two is an example of
- ☐ a. a military application of GPS.
- ☐ b. a civilian application of GPS.
- ☐ c. missile technology.
- ☐ d. the superiority of the U.S. military.   _____

Conclusion Devices   4   GPS could help you most if you
- ☐ a. were trying to learn all the state capitals.
- ☐ b. bought a new car that featured computerized maps.
- ☐ c. already knew your latitude and longitude.
- ☐ d. had a car breakdown on a country road.   _____

Clarifying   5   This passage begins with an example of
- ☐ a. an event that would have benefited from GPS.
- ☐ b. GPS technology in use.
- ☐ c. a war caused by technology.
- ☐ d. Soviet technology.   _____

Vocabulary in Context   6   In this passage <u>remote</u> means
- ☐ a. able to be operated from a distance.
- ☐ b. isolated.
- ☐ c. crowded.
- ☐ d. unwilling to be friendly.   _____

Add your scores for questions 1–6. Enter the total here and on the graph on page 216.   **Total Score**   _____

117

59 Images of Migration

In the early years of the 20th century, particularly after World War I ended in 1918, African Americans began moving into the cities. They left their small towns and farms, mostly in the South, and went to places like New York City and Chicago. They were looking for freedom and opportunity, but life was often hard.

One African-American painter, Jacob Lawrence, decided to tell the story of this migration through art. It was a story he knew almost firsthand, for his own parents had been part of the migration. Beginning in 1940, when he was only 23 years old, Lawrence worked on this project for more than a year. The result was a series of paintings called *The Migration of the Negro.* It consists of 60 panels, beginning with the excited migrants at the train station gates and tracing all aspects of their experience. Some of these were joyful, but many were sad. One panel, for example, shows young girls learning in school. One simply shows a dark stairway in a tenement building, where the migrants were often forced to live and work. Yet another shows the coffin of a migrant, dead from the cramped conditions of city life.

Lawrence used a simple but <u>graphic</u> painting style to tell his story. Most of the human figures in the panels look flat and two-dimensional, their shapes appearing angular and simple. Many of the paintings are bathed in bright color, though the blackness of individual figures is always strongly emphasized.

The Migration of the Negro is probably Lawrence's most famous work, but he has created other series about the African-American experience as well. One, for example, chronicles Harriet Tubman's life and work. Others portray the lives of Frederick Douglass and the white abolitionist John Brown.

Main Idea	1		Answer	Score
	Mark the *main idea*		M	15
	Mark the statement that is *too broad*		B	5
	Mark the statement that is *too narrow*		N	5

a. Jacob Lawrence painted a series of paintings about African-American migration to the cities. ☐ _____

b. Jacob Lawrence is an African-American painter. ☐ _____

c. Some paintings in the series are sad. ☐ _____

Score 15 points for each correct answer.   **Score**

Subject Matter **2** Another good title for this passage would be
    ☐ a. Jacob Lawrence and African-American Migration.
    ☐ b. A Painter's Use of Color.
    ☐ c. Why Blacks Migrated Northward.
    ☐ d. Life in the Northern Cities.
                        _____

Supporting Details **3** *The Migration of the Negro* consists of
    ☐ a. 23 small drawings.
    ☐ b. 60 colored panels.
    ☐ c. 60 black and white sketches.
    ☐ d. 30 panels and 30 sketches.
                        _____

Conclusion **4** Which of the following was probably *not* a topic of the migration series?
    ☐ a. looking for housing
    ☐ b. looking for jobs
    ☐ c. taking vacations in the South
    ☐ d. feeling both crowded and lonely
                        _____

Clarifying Devices **5** The first paragraph of the passage is intended to
    ☐ a. show why Lawrence is a great painter.
    ☐ b. show what small-town life was like.
    ☐ c. describe U.S. cities after World War I.
    ☐ d. establish the background for Lawrence's work.
                        _____

Vocabulary in Context **6** In this passage <u>graphic</u> means
    ☐ a. drawn with a pencil.
    ☐ b. looking like a photograph.
    ☐ c. vivid and colorful.
    ☐ d. using figures and numbers.
                        _____

Add your scores for questions 1–6. Enter the total here and on the graph on page 216.   **Total Score**   _____

60 Carbon Is Everywhere

Carbon is the major component of many minerals. Carbon compounds form the common minerals magnesite, dolomite, marble, and limestone. Coral and the shells of oysters and clams are mainly calcium carbonate. Carbon is also in coal and in the organic compounds that make up petroleum, natural gas, and all plant and animal tissue.

Diamond, the hardest known natural substance, is pure carbon. The word *diamond* comes from the Greek word *adamas*, meaning "the invincible," a term that accurately describes a diamond's permanence. The properties of a diamond are derived from its crystal structure of interlocking four-sided carbon atoms. Each carbon atom is linked to four <u>equidistant</u> neighbors throughout the crystal. The hardness, brilliance, and sparkle of diamond makes it unsurpassed as a gemstone. Diamond is also ideal for industrial applications, such as drilling oil wells and boring tunnels in solid rock.

Graphite, a very different substance, is the other crystal form of carbon. Its name is derived from the Greek verb *graphein*, which means "to write." This name refers to graphite's property of leaving a dark mark when it is rubbed on a surface. Graphite is a black, lustrous substance that easily crumbles or flakes. Its slippery feel is caused by its breaking from the crystal in thin layers. Graphite is composed entirely of planes of three-sided carbon atoms joined in a honeycomb pattern. Each carbon molecule is bonded to three others. One of the main uses for graphite is as a lubricant. A familiar use is as the "lead" in pencils.

Carbon, the sixth most abundant element in the universe, also deserves the title of the most versatile known element.

Main Idea	1	Answer	Score
	Mark the *main idea*	M	15
	Mark the statement that is *too broad*	B	5
	Mark the statement that is *too narrow*	N	5

a. Carbon is an abundant, versatile element found in many substances. ☐ _____

b. Carbon is a chemical element. ☐ _____

c. Graphite is one of the crystal forms of carbon. ☐ _____

Subject Matter 2 This passage is mainly about
    ☐ a. the properties of graphite.
    ☐ b. familiar minerals and compounds in which carbon is found.
    ☐ c. the properties of minerals.
    ☐ d. crystal structures.   _____

Supporting Details 3 Calcium carbonate is present in
    ☐ a. coral.
    ☐ b. natural gas.
    ☐ c. marble.
    ☐ d. lead.   _____

Conclusion 4 Diamond is used in industrial applications because of its
    ☐ a. availability.
    ☐ b. sparkle.
    ☐ c. brilliance.
    ☐ d. hardness.   _____

Clarifying Devices 5 The phrases in quotations, "the invincible" and "to write," are
    ☐ a. Greek words.
    ☐ b. definitions of Greek words.
    ☐ c. key words in this passage.
    ☐ d. quoted words from Greek scientists.   _____

Vocabulary in Context 6 The word <u>equidistant</u> means
    ☐ a. equally separated.
    ☐ b. interlocking.
    ☐ c. not close together.
    ☐ d. on the equator.   _____

Add your scores for questions 1–6. Enter the total here and on the graph on page 216. **Total Score** _____

61 Riding the Stock Market Roller Coaster

The table below shows the performance over the course of a single week of Fosphorescent Multimedia International, an affluent conglomerate of which Illeana Ionesco owns 1,000 shares. The columns labeled **High** and **Low** record the stock's price fluctuations each day; **Close** indicates Fosphorescent's closing price as the stock exchange stopped trading each afternoon; **Net Change** shows the day's gain or loss.

Date	Stock	High	Low	Close	Net Change
Mon 9/27	Fospho	$19^7/_{16}$	$19^3/_{16}$	$19^5/_{16}$	$+ ^1/_8$
Tues 9/28	Fospho	$19^7/_8$	$19^1/_8$	$19^3/_8$	$+ ^1/_{16}$
Wed 9/29	Fospho	$18^9/_{16}$	$18^5/_{16}$	$18^5/_{16}$	$- 1^1/_{16}$
Thur 9/30	Fospho	$17^7/_8$	$17^5/_8$	$17^3/_4$	$- ^9/_{16}$
Fri 10/1	Fospho	$17^7/_8$	$16^7/_8$	$17^1/_8$	$- ^5/_8$

To indicate <u>minuscule</u> fluctuations of lower value than a dollar, stock prices are designated with fractions. The value of these fractions may be calculated by dividing the numerator by the denominator. Thus $^1/_8$ equals $0.125, or $12^1/_2$ cents; $^9/_{16}$ equals $0.5625, or $56^1/_4$ cents; and so on. When the market's final bell rang on September 27, Fosphorescent's price was $19^5/_{16}$, or $19.3125; the $+ ^1/_8$ net change shows that the price had risen $12^1/_2$ cents from its last, or closing, price on the previous Friday.

By market close on Friday, October 1, Fosphorescent's price had dropped to $17.125; thus between Monday and Friday a share's value had decreased by $2.1875. Since Illeana owned 1,000 shares, her stock's value plunged $2,187.50 in one week (1,000 × $2.1875). However, the market is notoriously unpredictable: imagine that on Monday, October 4, Fosphorescent announces a merger with a fantastically successful multinational company. The price skyrockets to a new annual high of $21^3/_4$, and this gain of $4^5/_8$, or $4.625 per share, increases Illeana's holdings an astonishing $4,625!

Main Idea 1

	Answer	Score
Mark the *main idea*	M	15
Mark the statement that is *too broad*	B	5
Mark the statement that is *too narrow*	N	5

a. Many people buy stock. ☐ _____

b. Illeana has stock in Fosphorescent. ☐ _____

c. Understanding stock tables can help you see how a stock's value changes. ☐ _____

Subject Matter **2** This passage's main purpose is to teach readers
- [ ] a. that it is unwise to purchase stock.
- [ ] b. how to divide using a calculator.
- [ ] c. about stock market crashes.
- [ ] d. how to read stock tables.

_____

Supporting Details **3** The closing price of Fosphorescent on Tuesday, 9/28 was
- [ ] a. $19^7/_8$.
- [ ] b. $19^1/_8$.
- [ ] c. $19^3/_8$.
- [ ] d. $^1/_{16}$.

_____

Conclusion **4** The best day to sell Fosphorescent would have been
- [ ] a. Friday, 10/1.
- [ ] b. Thursday, 9/30.
- [ ] c. Wednesday, 9/29.
- [ ] d. Tuesday, 9/28.

_____

Clarifying Devices **5** The table in this passage is useful for
- [ ] a. finding the price of Fosphorescent stock at exactly noon on 9/27.
- [ ] b. getting an overview of what the stock did in one week.
- [ ] c. figuring out how much Illeana has earned so far in dividends.
- [ ] d. learning Fosphorescent's price on Thursday, 9/23.

_____

Vocabulary in Context **6** <u>Minuscule</u> means
- [ ] a. tiny.
- [ ] b. moderate.
- [ ] c. unpredictable.
- [ ] d. crablike.

_____

Add your scores for questions 1–6. Enter the total here   **Total**
and on the graph on page 216.   **Score**

_____

62 An Independent Woman

In the Puritan settlement of Newtown, Massachusetts, across the river from Boston, Anne Hutchinson, age 45, wife and mother of 13 children, stood before Governor John Winthrop and the Great and General Court of Massachusetts. She was the first colonial woman who had dared to publicly challenge the authority of the church and state. It was November 1637.

Eight years before, Winthrop and his band of Puritans sailed to the New World to establish a society where everyone observed the will of God. Now he read the charges against Anne Hutchinson. She led women in prayer, and she analyzed the various strengths and weaknesses of the colony's ministers. The Puritans believed that no woman should teach. Certainly no woman should criticize a minister.

The court unanimously decided against Anne Hutchinson. She was excommunicated from the Puritan church and banished from the Bay Colony. She and her family left Massachusetts to settle in Rhode Island.

News came back to Winthrop that Hutchinson's next child had been born dead. He instructed the colony's ministers to make this the subject of their sermons. Congregations were told that the dead child had been born a monster and that this was a fitting punishment from God. In 1643 Anne Hutchinson was again the subject of Bay Colony sermons. She had been murdered by Indians. It was fitting, the ministers announced, that this be the final blow in Mistress Hutchinson's earthly punishment.

For years the story of Anne Hutchinson was held up as a lesson to any who might put their own personal wishes above the laws of Puritan society. For Anne Hutchinson, her rebellion against <u>restrictive</u> Puritan society had cost her everything.

Main Idea	1	Answer	Score
Mark the *main idea*		M	15
Mark the statement that is *too broad*		B	5
Mark the statement that is *too narrow*		N	5

		Answer	Score
a.	Puritan society was unforgiving.	☐	_____
b.	Anne Hutchinson's story was the subject of Puritan sermons.	☐	_____
c.	Anne Hutchinson risked everything to speak her beliefs in colonial Massachusetts.	☐	_____

Score 15 points for each correct answer.   Score

Subject Matter   **2**   Another good title for this passage would be
- [ ] a. Governor Winthrop and His Wife.
- [ ] b. The "Sins" of Anne Hutchinson.
- [ ] c. A Child Is Born Dead.
- [ ] d. Life in the 1600s.   _____

Supporting Details   **3**   Authority to banish Hutchinson was held by the
- [ ] a. male citizens in the region.
- [ ] b. ministers she was accused of criticizing.
- [ ] c. Great and General Court of Massachusetts.
- [ ] d. Bay Colony.   _____

Conclusion   **4**   The Puritans
- [ ] a. wanted religious freedom, but only for the views they agreed with.
- [ ] b. were tolerant of all churchgoers.
- [ ] c. wanted to settle in Rhode Island.
- [ ] d. were quick to forgive any wrongdoers.   _____

Clarifying Devices   **5**   Which sentence helps clarify the word *banished*?
- [ ] a. The court unanimously decided against Anne Hutchinson.
- [ ] b. She was excommunicated from the Puritan church.
- [ ] c. She and her family left Massachusetts to settle in Rhode Island.
- [ ] d. This was a fitting punishment from God.   _____

Vocabulary in Context   **6**   The word restrictive means
- [ ] a. early American.
- [ ] b. respectable.
- [ ] c. permissive.
- [ ] d. confining.   _____

Add your scores for questions 1–6. Enter the total here and on the graph on page 216.   Total Score   _____

63 Telling Tales About People

One of the most common types of nonfiction, and one that many people enjoy reading, is stories about people's lives. These stories fall into three general categories: autobiography, memoir, and biography.

An autobiography is the story of a person's life written by himself or herself. Often it begins with the person's earliest recollections and ends in the present. Autobiography writers may not be entirely objective in the way they present themselves. However, they offer the reader a good look at the way they are and what makes them that way. People as <u>diverse</u> as Benjamin Franklin and Helen Keller have written autobiographies. Other writers, such as James Joyce, have written thinly fictionalized accounts of their lives. These are not autobiographies, but they are very close to it.

Memoirs, strictly speaking, are autobiographical accounts that focus as much on the events of the times as on the life of the author. Memoir writers typically use these events as backdrops for their lives. They describe them in detail and discuss their importance. Recently, though, the term *memoir* seems to be becoming interchangeable with *autobiography*. A memoir nowadays may or may not deal with the outside world.

Biographies are factual accounts of someone else's life. In many senses, these may be the hardest of the three types to write. Autobiography writers know the events they write about because they lived them. But biography writers have to gather information from as many different sources as possible. Then they have to decide which facts to include. Their goal is to present a balanced picture of a person, not one that is overly positive or too critical. A fair, well-presented biography may take years to research and write.

Main Idea	1			Answer	Score
		Mark the *main idea*		M	15
		Mark the statement that is *too broad*		B	5
		Mark the statement that is *too narrow*		N	5
		a. People like reading about people.		☐	_____
		b. Nowadays memoirs are frequently little different from autobiographies.		☐	_____
		c. There are three basic categories of writing about people's lives.		☐	_____

Score 15 points for each correct answer.   **Score**

Subject Matter   **2**   This passage is mostly about
☐ a. the characteristics of autobiographies, memoirs, and biographies.
☐ b. famous autobiographies.
☐ c. why biography can be difficult to write.
☐ d. differences between autobiographies and memoirs.   _____

Supporting Details   **3**   Helen Keller wrote
☐ a. a memoir.
☐ b. an autobiography.
☐ c. a work of fiction.
☐ d. a biography.   _____

Conclusion   **4**   Autobiography writers are not always objective because they
☐ a. feel they have to make up details to make their books sell.
☐ b. constantly compete with biography writers.
☐ c. want to present themselves in a good light.
☐ d. have trouble remembering the good times.   _____

Clarifying Devices   **5**   The writer introduces each category in the passage by
☐ a. defining it.
☐ b. giving an example.
☐ c. explaining why it is hard to write.
☐ d. telling when people first began writing it.   _____

Vocabulary in Context   **6**   Diverse means
☐ a. able to swim in deep water.
☐ b. similar or alike.
☐ c. varied or different.
☐ d. enjoying poetry.   _____

Add your scores for questions 1–6. Enter the total here and on the graph on page 216.   **Total Score**   _____

64 Newton's Laws of Motion

Isaac Newton, while a student at Cambridge, showed no particular scientific talent. When the plague closed the university in 1665, Newton returned home to Lincolnshire, England. There he continued his studies on his own, and there his genius emerged. Within 18 months after leaving Cambridge, he made <u>revolutionary</u> advances in mathematics, optics, physics, and astronomy. He began a lifetime of scientific work that had tremendous influence on modern science. His three laws of motion form the foundation for all interactions of force, matter, and motion. He published these laws in 1686 in his book *Principia Mathematica.*

Newton's first law is that if a body (anything with mass) is at rest or moving at a constant speed in a straight line, it will remain at rest or keep moving in a straight line at constant speed unless it is acted upon by a force. This is the law of inertia. Prior to the 17th century, it was thought that bodies could move only as long as a force acted on them; they would remain at rest if no force moved them. Newton's first law helped scientists realize that no force was needed to keep the planets moving in their orbits.

Newton's second law states that the larger the force, the larger the acceleration; and the larger the mass, the smaller the acceleration. This law helps explain why if the same force is exerted on two objects, the lighter object will accelerate more quickly.

Newton's third law postulates that the actions of two bodies upon each other are always equal and directly opposite; that is, reaction is always equal and opposite to action. For example, the downward force of a book lying on a table is equal to the upward force of the table on the book. This law of motion is particularly relevant when considering gravitational forces—a flying airplane pulls up on the earth with the same force that the earth pulls down on the airplane.

Main Idea   1

	Answer	Score
Mark the *main idea*	M	15
Mark the statement that is *too broad*	B	5
Mark the statement that is *too narrow*	N	5

a. Isaac Newton was a student at Cambridge University. ☐ _____

b. Isaac Newton contributed to science. ☐ _____

c. Isaac Newton formulated the three laws of motion. ☐ _____

Score 15 points for each correct answer.　　　　**Score**

Subject Matter　**2**　The passage is mostly about
　　□ a. Newton's laws of motion.
　　□ b. Newton's education.
　　□ c. the work habits of scientists.
　　□ d. why planets stay in their orbits.　　　_____

Supporting Details　**3**　Newton's first law of motion helped 17th-century scientists understand
　　□ a. velocity.
　　□ b. the orbits of planets.
　　□ c. acceleration.
　　□ d. inertia.　　　_____

Conclusion　**4**　From reading about Newton's early life, one can conclude that he
　　□ a. learned more in school than on his own.
　　□ b. was most successful when working independently.
　　□ c. thought he had great teachers at Cambridge.
　　□ d. wanted to start his own school.　　　_____

Clarifying Devices　**5**　The second through fourth paragraphs
　　□ a. explain each of Newton's laws.
　　□ b. give a brief biography of Newton.
　　□ c. sum up Newton's lifetime of work.
　　□ d. explain mathematics, optics, and physics.　　　_____

Vocabulary in Context　**6**　In this passage <u>revolutionary</u> means
　　□ a. having to do with wars for freedom.
　　□ b. spinning in a circle.
　　□ c. new and surprising.
　　□ d. orbiting around the sun.　　　_____

Add your scores for questions 1–6. Enter the total here and on the graph on page 216.　　**Total Score**　_____

65 The Binary Number System

Looking at the numeral 1111111, you probably assume it has a value of one million, one hundred and eleven thousand, one hundred and eleven. But in the binary number system, the one used in computers, 1111111 represents a value of 127.

The decimal system—the system most commonly used today—got its name from the Latin word *decem,* which means "ten." In this system, every position in a number is the result of multiplying by 10. For example, there is a ones place (1 × 10), a tens place (1 × 10), a hundreds place (10 × 10), a thousands place (10 × 10 × 10), and so on. According to the decimal system, the 1 on the far right of 1111111 represents 1, the 1 to the left of that represents 10, the 1 to the left of *that* represents 100, and so on.

In the binary system (*bi*- means "two" in Latin), every position in a number is the result of multiplying by 2. Like the decimal system, the binary system begins with a ones place; however, the place to the left of the ones place is the twos place (1 × 2), the place to the left of that is the fours place (2 × 2), the place to its left is the eights place (2 × 2 × 2), and so on. By adding all numbers in the top row of this diagram that represent 1's in the bottom row, you could figure out what 1111111 "translates" to.

64	32	16	8	4	2	1
1	1	1	1	1	1	1

Binary 1111111 is decimal 127; it equals 64 + 32 + 16 + 8 + 4 + 2 + 1.

Though binary numbers can be <u>entertaining</u> to look at, they are difficult for the average person to work with. Because only two digits are used, numbers quickly become very lengthy: if 100110011 in binary is only 407 in decimals, can you imagine how many digits are needed to "translate" a decimal number like 10,000? And adding or dividing such numbers is complicated indeed—a task best left to a computer!

Main Idea 1

	Answer	Score
Mark the *main idea*	**M**	15
Mark the statement that is *too broad*	**B**	5
Mark the statement that is *too narrow*	**N**	5

a. There are several number systems. ☐ _____

b. The binary number system is best used in computers. ☐ _____

c. The binary number 1111111 represents decimal 127. ☐ _____

Subject Matter   **2**   This passage is mostly about
- ☐ a. how the decimal system works.
- ☐ b. adding and dividing large numbers.
- ☐ c. how the binary system works.
- ☐ d. how computers are programmed.   _____

Supporting Details   **3**   The binary system first has a ones place, then a
- ☐ a. tens place, a hundreds place, and so on.
- ☐ b. hundreds place, a tens place, and so on.
- ☐ c. twos place, a threes place, and so on.
- ☐ d. twos place, a fours place, and so on.   _____

Conclusion   **4**   We can conclude from reading the passage that the binary system uses the digits
- ☐ a. 1 through 9.
- ☐ b. 0 through 9.
- ☐ c. 0, 1, and 2.
- ☐ d. 0 and 1.   _____

Clarifying Devices   **5**   The second and third paragraphs are developed mainly through
- ☐ a. listing events in time order.
- ☐ b. relating an anecdote.
- ☐ c. giving reasons to prove a point.
- ☐ d. showing similarities and differences.   _____

Vocabulary in Context   **6**   In this passage <u>entertaining</u> means
- ☐ a. fun or amusing.
- ☐ b. serving food and drink to guests.
- ☐ c. complicated.
- ☐ d. singing and dancing.   _____

Add your scores for questions 1–6. Enter the total here and on the graph on page 216.   **Total Score**   _____

66 Separate No More

The "separate but equal" law in the United States allowed segregation to flourish. The first test of this law was in 1892, when a black man named Homer Plessy boarded a train on the East Louisiana Railroad. Plessy took a seat in a white coach and refused to move. He was arrested and charged with <u>violating</u> the law of segregation on public transportation. Plessy's case, *Plessy* v. *Ferguson,* was appealed to the U.S. Supreme Court. (The *v.* designation in court cases is an abbreviation for the word *versus*, which means "against.") In May 1896, the Court ruled against Plessy and upheld the separate but equal law, in spite of its being a violation of the equal protection clause of the 14th Amendment of the U.S. Constitution.

The separate but equal laws continued to be upheld until they were again challenged in the early 1950s by Oliver Brown. Brown, a minister in Topeka, Kansas, sued the local school board for the right to permit his daughter, Linda, to attend an all-white elementary school. Linda had been denied admission because she was black. *Brown* v. *Board of Education of Topeka* was taken to the Supreme Court. This time, in May 1954, the Supreme Court struck down "separate but equal" as unconstitutional. The Court stated:

> School segregation by state law causes a feeling of inferiority in black children that inflicts damage to their hearts and minds that may never be undone. Public school segregation by state law, therefore, violates the equal protection clause of the Fourteenth Amendment. . . . The old Plessy "separate but equal" rule is herewith formally overruled.

The Court's unanimous opinion influenced future civil rights legislation and launched the civil rights movement of the 1960s.

Main Idea 1

	Answer	Score
Mark the *main idea*	M	15
Mark the statement that is *too broad*	B	5
Mark the statement that is *too narrow*	N	5

a. "Separate but equal" laws were struck down by the Supreme Court. ☐ _____

b. Some laws are unconstitutional. ☐ _____

c. *Brown* v. *Board of Education* launched the civil rights movement. ☐ _____

Subject Matter   **2**   This passage deals mainly with
    ☐ a. important civil rights cases.
    ☐ b. the Constitution of the United States.
    ☐ c. public transportation in the United States.
    ☐ d. education in the United States.   _____

Supporting   **3**   *Brown* v. *Board of Education* was decided in
Details   ☐ a. 1892.
    ☐ b. May 1896.
    ☐ c. May 1954.
    ☐ d. the 1960s.   _____

Conclusion   **4**   Prior to the Brown decision, separate but equal
under the law meant that Linda Brown could not
    ☐ a. ride on the Louisiana Railroad.
    ☐ b. go to school.
    ☐ c. attend an all-white school.
    ☐ d. attend a school board meeting.   _____

Clarifying   **5**   The information within the parentheses in the
Devices   first paragraph
    ☐ a. is the topic sentence of the paragraph.
    ☐ b. is the writer's conclusion.
    ☐ c. is quoted material.
    ☐ d. clarifies information in the previous sentence.   _____

Vocabulary   **6**   In this passage <u>violating</u> means
in Context   ☐ a. stealing.
    ☐ b. breaking.
    ☐ c. upholding.
    ☐ d. harming.   _____

Add your scores for questions 1–6. Enter the total here   **Total**
and on the graph on page 216.   **Score**   _____

67 Tales from Ovid

No doubt you know the story of Midas. This king had a daughter who was transformed into a golden statue as a result of the king's own greed. Midas's tale, as well as many others involving some great and sudden change, is found in a long poem called *Metamorphoses*. Collected and told by the Roman poet Ovid around the time of Christ, many of these tales remain popular even today.

Ovid was not the <u>originator</u> of many of the tales he included. A majority of them come from Greek and Roman mythology. But what Ovid did is pick stories that fit his theme. Ovid thought that passion—love, anger, revenge—could so strongly affect individuals that they would be physically changed. A man might turn into a woman, or a nymph (a lesser goddess of nature) might turn into a fountain. All together, Ovid told about 250 such tales, many in very brief form.

Here are some of Ovid's tales that you may know. In the story of Pyramus and Thisbe, an elderly couple are repaid for their hospitality to the gods by being changed into interlocking trees, together eternally. In the story of Echo and Narcissus, the goddess Hera punishes the too-talkative nymph Echo by transforming her into just a voice that can only repeat what others say. Narcissus, for his vanity, is made to fall in love with his own reflection and to pine away until he turns into a flower. The story of Arachne has a woman who boasts too often of her weaving ability turn into a spider that must weave forever.

Why have Ovid's stories stayed so popular down through the centuries? Perhaps it is because all people recognize the transforming power of love—and because they desire the changes that anger or revenge makes them imagine.

Main Idea	1		
		Answer	**Score**
	Mark the *main idea*	M	15
	Mark the statement that is *too broad*	B	5
	Mark the statement that is *too narrow*	N	5
	a. Ancient stories can be entertaining.	☐	_____
	b. The stories in Ovid's *Metamorphoses* involve physical changes.	☐	_____
	c. A woman may be changed into a tree or a spider.	☐	_____

Subject Matter 2 This passage is mainly about
☐ a. Ovid's life.
☐ b. what Ovid wrote about in *Metamorphoses*.
☐ c. Greek and Roman myths.
☐ d. what the word *change* meant to Ovid. _____

Supporting Details 3 Pyramus was changed into
☐ a. a bird.
☐ b. an echo.
☐ c. a tree.
☐ d. a flower. _____

Conclusion 4 It seems true that often the changes that Ovid's characters undergo
☐ a. relate closely to what they have done.
☐ b. make them look foolish.
☐ c. make men into women and women into men.
☐ d. are so slight that they are hardly noticeable. _____

Clarifying Devices 5 The expression *pine away* in the third paragraph means to
☐ a. turn into a tree.
☐ b. become sad.
☐ c. be planted in the ground.
☐ d. fight with others. _____

Vocabulary in Context 6 The word <u>originator</u> means
☐ a. source.
☐ b. collector.
☐ c. buyer.
☐ d. controller. _____

Add your scores for questions 1–6. Enter the total here and on the graph on page 216.

Total Score _____

68 Mr. Jefferson's Moose

Thomas Jefferson—author of the Declaration of Independence, statesman, architect, inventor, and scientist—was offended when he read the inaccurate reporting of a French naturalist, Count Georges de Buffon. Buffon had written in *Histoire Naturelle* (*Natural History*) that America was one big gloomy swamp inhabited by weak and tiny animals. Jefferson, who was both a dedicated naturalist and a patriotic American, vowed to set the French count straight. Jefferson's opportunity came in 1784, when the U.S. Congress asked him to serve as a diplomat in Paris.

When in Paris, Jefferson asked to meet Buffon. They were introduced at a party. Jefferson began to tell him about the very large animals in America. One he mentioned was the American moose, so huge that a European reindeer could walk under it without its antlers touching the moose's belly. Jefferson's story was rudely interrupted by laughter. Buffon thought this was the silliest thing he had ever heard. Jefferson decided to provide proof. He wrote to his friend, Governor John Sullivan of New Hampshire, and asked him to ship him the biggest moose in the North Woods. Eagerly Sullivan and a group of men <u>trekked</u> deep into the woods until they found, trapped, and killed a giant seven-foot moose. Sullivan had the moose stuffed, packed in a crate, and shipped to France.

Everyone gathered around as the crate was opened in Paris. Inside was the biggest moose any of them had ever seen! It was not exactly pretty, as most of its hair had fallen out. But with the hairless moose towering over him, Buffon admitted his error. He promised that in his next book he would revise his statements about animal life in North America.

Main Idea	1			
			Answer	**Score**
	Mark the *main idea*		M	15
	Mark the statement that is *too broad*		B	5
	Mark the statement that is *too narrow*		N	5
	a.	Thomas Jefferson knew about nature.	☐	_____
	b.	Thomas Jefferson's stuffed moose proved a scientific point.	☐	_____
	c.	Thomas Jefferson had a moose shipped to him in Paris.	☐	_____

Subject Matter   **2**   This passage is mostly about
        ☐ a. the animals of North America.
        ☐ b. French scientific studies.
        ☐ c. hunting in New Hampshire.
        ☐ d. how Thomas Jefferson made his case
            about American animals.   _____

Supporting   **3**   At a party in Paris, Jefferson described
Details
        ☐ a. the silliest thing he had ever seen.
        ☐ b. a French reindeer.
        ☐ c. the size of an American moose.
        ☐ d. a moose's belly.   _____

Conclusion   **4**   The moose sent to Jefferson in Paris provided
        ☐ a. visual scientific evidence.
        ☐ b. oral scientific evidence.
        ☐ c. a scientific theory.
        ☐ d. a lot of laughs for the French scientists.   _____

Clarifying   **5**   In the first paragraph, *Histoire Naturelle*
Devices
        ☐ a. is the name of a naturalist.
        ☐ b. is the title of a book.
        ☐ c. is an old French expression.
        ☐ d. was Buffon's name for America.   _____

Vocabulary   **6**   The word <u>trekked</u> means
in Context
        ☐ a. hid.
        ☐ b. illegally walked on someone else's land.
        ☐ c. knocked down trees.
        ☐ d. traveled.   _____

**Add your scores for questions 1–6. Enter the total here   Total
and on the graph on page 216.   Score**   _____

69 Buying and Maintaining an Economy Car

If you've ever been curious about how much it actually costs to own and operate a car, the following story demonstrates a way to figure out these expenses.

In 1994 Kimberly Ridgemont bought an economy car known as a Hedgehog. The total price, including sales tax and license, was $8,856.92. Kimberly paid $1,000 <u>down</u> and borrowed the rest, $7,856.92, from the National Automobile Corporation, the manufacturer of the Hedgehog, at an annual interest rate of 7.25 percent. Kim bought the car on July 31, 1994, and on September 1, her first payment of $156.50 was due. When she finished paying for the car in 1999, she was curious to determine what her total purchase price actually came to. Since it had taken her 60 months to repay the loan, the total she had spent to purchase the car was $10,390 ($156.50 × 60 months + $1,000 down payment). Her calculations showed that she had paid an additional $1,533.08 in interest above the purchase price.

Soon after that, Kimberly decided to sell her Hedgehog and wanted to see how much it had cost her per month to own it. During the five years it had taken to pay off the loan, she had paid about $70 per month for car insurance, or $4,200 total. She had also spent about $30 per month for gas, for a total of $1,800, and about $380 per year in maintenance ($1,900 total). Adding these numbers to her total purchase cost of $10,390, Kimberly found that she had spent about $18,290 on her Hedgehog. Those were her expenses—but she also had made money on the car when she sold it for $3,640. Subtracting $3,640 from $18,290 lowered her expenses to $14,650. Dividing that number by 60 months, Kimberly calculated that her Hedgehog had cost her about $244.17 per month.

Main Idea	1		
		Answer	**Score**
Mark the *main idea*		M	15
Mark the statement that is *too broad*		B	5
Mark the statement that is *too narrow*		N	5
a. Kimberly got a car loan at 7.25 percent.		☐	
b. To figure total car costs, interest and maintenance expenses must be included.		☐	
c. Some cars can be bought and run cheaply.		☐	

Score 15 points for each correct answer. **Score**

Subject Matter 2 Another good title for this passage might be
  ☐ a. What Does It Cost to Own a Hedgehog?
  ☐ b. The Magnificent Hedgehog.
  ☐ c. Buying on Credit.
  ☐ d. Getting a Good Used Car. _____

Supporting Details 3 Kimberly's total purchase price for the car was
  ☐ a. $7,856.92.
  ☐ b. $10,390.
  ☐ c. $3,640.
  ☐ d. $1,533.08. _____

Conclusion 4 Kimberly paid a total of $1,900 in maintenance because
  ☐ a. she paid $380 a year for five years.
  ☐ b. she paid $380 a month for 60 months.
  ☐ c. the interest rate on her loan was 7.25 percent.
  ☐ d. she had a down payment of $1,000. _____

Clarifying Devices 5 The writer tells the story of Kimberly to
  ☐ a. show how frugal young women can be.
  ☐ b. present an example that sounds like real life.
  ☐ c. make you wonder what her next car will be.
  ☐ d. make you want to get as good an interest rate as she did. _____

Vocabulary in Context 6 In this passage <u>down</u> means
  ☐ a. in cash at the time of purchase.
  ☐ b. below.
  ☐ c. sad or unhappy.
  ☐ d. soft feathers or hair. _____

Add your scores for questions 1–6. Enter the total here and on the graph on page 216. **Total Score** _____

70 The Changing Middle Class

The United States perceives itself to be a middle-class nation. However, middle class is not a real designation, nor does it carry privileges. It is more of a perception, which probably was as true as it ever could be right after World War II. The economy was growing, more and more people owned their own homes, workers had solid contracts with the companies that employed them, and nearly everyone who wanted a higher education could have one. Successful people enjoyed upward social mobility. They may have started out poor, but they could become rich. Successful people also found that they had greater geographic mobility. In other words, they found themselves moving to and living in a variety of places.

The middle class <u>collectively</u> holds several values and principles. One strong value is the need to earn enough money to feel that one can determine one's own economic fate. In addition, middle-class morality embraces principles of individual responsibility, importance of family, obligations to others, and believing in something outside oneself.

But in the 1990s those in the middle class found that there was a price for success. A *U.S. News & World Report* survey in 1994 indicated that 75 percent of Americans believed that middle-class families could no longer make ends meet. Both spouses now worked, as did some of the children; long commutes became routine; the need for child care put strains on the family; and public schools were not as good as they once were. Members of the middle class were no longer financing their lifestyles through earnings but were using credit to stay afloat. The understanding of just what *middle class* meant was changing.

Main Idea	1	Answer	Score
	Mark the *main idea*	M	15
	Mark the statement that is *too broad*	B	5
	Mark the statement that is *too narrow*	N	5

		Answer	Score
a.	Being middle class involves believing in individual responsibility.	☐	_____
b.	People categorize themselves into classes.	☐	_____
c.	The middle class is held together by values its members have in common.	☐	_____

Subject Matter   **2**   The information in this passage deals with
- ☐ a. an individual.
- ☐ b. a social and economic group.
- ☐ c. a political organization.
- ☐ d. government.

_____

Supporting Details   **3**   A common middle class value is that
- ☐ a. people should always have fun.
- ☐ b. children should be seen and not heard.
- ☐ c. debt is nothing to worry about.
- ☐ d. the family is very important.

_____

Conclusion   **4**   In the years after World War II, the middle class could be defined as
- ☐ a. overburdened and in debt.
- ☐ b. hard working and suspicious.
- ☐ c. prosperous and optimistic.
- ☐ d. young and foolish.

_____

Clarifying Devices   **5**   The phrase "In other words" in the first paragraph means that the following statement is
- ☐ a. an exception to the previous idea.
- ☐ b. a denial of the previous idea.
- ☐ c. a restatement of the previous idea.
- ☐ d. a contrasting idea.

_____

Vocabulary in Context   **6**   The word <u>collectively</u> means
- ☐ a. as a group.
- ☐ b. hesitatingly.
- ☐ c. unknowingly.
- ☐ d. weakly.

_____

Add your scores for questions 1–6. Enter the total here and on the graph on page 216.

Total Score

_____

71 The Photography of Manuel Alvarez Bravo

Some photographers work to record events, such as those who choose, or are assigned, to cover wars. Others try to create artistic representations of the world around them. Many photographers fall into this second category, including Mexican photographer Manuel Alvarez Bravo. This talented artist's work spans most of the 20th century.

Alvarez Bravo was born in 1902 and thus came of age during the years after the Mexican Revolution. This was a time when art was flourishing in Mexico City. Some of the first professional photographs that he took were for a magazine called *Mexican Folkways,* which focused on the country's native scenes and culture. These topics would always remain part of Alvarez Bravo's work, but as he grew and developed as a photographer the way he presented them changed.

Through the 1920s and 1930s Alvarez Bravo took many pictures on the streets of Mexico City—of store windows, of people sitting in restaurants and cafes, of laundry hanging beside buildings. But he wanted to endow these photos with deeper meaning. He wanted the viewer to stop and think. So a store window might feature fashion <u>mannequins</u> that seem to be laughing at the viewer. The people in a cafe might be photographed in such a way that they appear to be headless. Alvarez Bravo made it clear that he wanted people to think about his photos by insisting early on that they all have titles. What might a photo called "The Evangelist" mean? It is up to the viewer to look at the photo, consider the title, and decide how the two fit together.

In the 1940s Alvarez Bravo expanded his subject matter to include many shots of the Mexican countryside. But throughout this work, and even in the filmmaking he later did, a quality of timelessness persists.

Main Idea   1

	Answer	Score
Mark the *main idea*	M	15
Mark the statement that is *too broad*	B	5
Mark the statement that is *too narrow*	N	5

a. Manuel Alvarez Bravo photographed landscapes. ☐ _____

b. Some photographers are very artistic. ☐ _____

c. Manuel Alvarez Bravo took photos with more than surface meanings. ☐ _____

Score 15 points for each correct answer.   **Score**

Subject Matter   **2** This passage is mostly about
- ☐ a. war photographers.
- ☐ b. tricks photographers use.
- ☐ c. the kinds of photos Alvarez Bravo took.
- ☐ d. how Alvarez Bravo got started in photography.   _____

Supporting Details   **3** Alvarez Bravo believed that all his photos
- ☐ a. should be in color.
- ☐ b. should have titles.
- ☐ c. deserved to be famous.
- ☐ d. should feature the countryside.   _____

Conclusion   **4** Alvarez Bravo believed that
- ☐ a. the Mexican Revolution had no bearing on his life.
- ☐ b. city scenes could be made to show deep meanings.
- ☐ c. it was better to photograph the countryside than the city.
- ☐ d. love was the only important emotion.   _____

Clarifying Devices   **5** The information in this passage is presented mostly
- ☐ a. in chronological order.
- ☐ b. through questions and answers.
- ☐ c. through spatial descriptions.
- ☐ d. through persuasive statements.   _____

Vocabulary in Context   **6** In this passage <u>mannequins</u> are
- ☐ a. statues on which clothing is displayed.
- ☐ b. people who always wear outrageous clothes.
- ☐ c. children who beg in the streets.
- ☐ d. old men.   _____

Add your scores for questions 1–6. Enter the total here   **Total**
and on the graph on page 216.   **Score**   _____

72 Cryosurgery

Have you ever heard of cryosurgery? It is a procedure in which abnormal body tissues (sometimes referred to as *lesions*) are destroyed by exposing them to extremely cold temperatures. The temperatures used range from −150°C (−238°F) to absolute zero (−273°C or −460°F). The surgical procedure freezes unhealthy tissue, and the freezing destroys the cells. For external lesions, liquid nitrogen. which has a temperature of −196°C (−320.8°F), is applied directly to the cells. For internal tumors, liquid nitrogen is circulated through an instrument called a *cryoprobe,* a low-temperature scalpel or probe cooled by liquid nitrogen.

How does cryosurgery destroy cells? The intracellular ice created by the liquid nitrogen will destroy nearly all cells it comes in contact with. As ice forms around a cell, the free water inside the cell is drawn off. This causes the cell to shrink and the walls or membranes inside the cell to collapse. Toxic proteins or chemicals within the cell are released. Finally, as the ice around shrunken cells begins to thaw, large amounts of free water rush back inside the cells, causing them to burst. The dead cells are then removed through normal bodily processes.

How well does cryosurgery work? The procedure has proved successful in removing tonsils, hemorrhoids, warts, cataracts, and some tumors. Cryosurgery may be used as well to remove freckles (for cosmetic reasons) and to treat some skin cancers. It is also used as a treatment of internal bone <u>cavities</u>, including bone cancer. Cryosurgery has evolved from the first attempts to freeze tissue with a salt-ice mixture in the 1850s to the sophisticated cryoprobe method used today.

Main Idea	1		
		Answer	**Score**
	Mark the *main idea*	M	15
	Mark the statement that is *too broad*	B	5
	Mark the statement that is *too narrow*	N	5
	a. Cryosurgery is used to treat patients.	☐	_____
	b. Cryosurgery is used in the treatment of some skin cancers.	☐	_____
	c. Cryosurgery is used in the treatment of abnormal tissue.	☐	_____

Subject Matter   **2**   This passage is mainly about
- ☐ a. the medical procedure of cryosurgery.
- ☐ b. the structure of unhealthy cells.
- ☐ c. the advantages and disadvantages of cryosurgery.
- ☐ d. cancer treatments.

_____

Supporting Details   **3**   The temperatures used in cryosurgery range from
- ☐ a. $-196°C$ to $-320.8°F$.
- ☐ b. $-150°C$ to absolute zero $(-273°C)$.
- ☐ c. the intracellular to the intercellular.
- ☐ d. $-150°C$ to $-238°F$.

_____

Conclusion   **4**   Medical interest in cryosurgery began
- ☐ a. thousands of years ago.
- ☐ b. in the last 20 years.
- ☐ c. more than a century ago.
- ☐ d. in the 1990s.

_____

Clarifying Devices   **5**   The overall structure of this passage is
- ☐ a. a personal narrative.
- ☐ b. cause and effect.
- ☐ c. steps in a process.
- ☐ d. question and answer.

_____

Vocabulary in Context   **6**   As used in this passage, <u>cavities</u> are
- ☐ a. holes in teeth.
- ☐ b. taking place between the stars.
- ☐ c. hollow places.
- ☐ d. happening outside the walls of a cell.

_____

Add your scores for questions 1–6. Enter the total here and on the graph on page 216.   **Total Score**

_____

73 Adding 100 Numbers in Minutes

As an adult Carl Friedrich Gauss became a renowned mathematician, but as a young student in the Duchy of Brunswick (now a region of Germany), no one was yet aware of his amazing facility for discerning mathematical patterns. Apparently Carl (like many precocious children) was difficult for his teachers to control. One legend claims that, perhaps hoping to distract him for a time, a teacher ordered him to sit silently and add the numbers from 1 to 100. The teacher probably assumed that Carl would be challenged for hours, but minutes later the boy had the correct response.

Carl did what most trained mathematicians would have done: look for a pattern. Recently, Annabelle Leigh, an adult student of average mathematical aptitude, reasoned this way: If you add the numbers from 1 to 10, you get 55. If you add the numbers from 11 to 20, you get 155; the numbers from 21 to 30 total up to 255. Following this pattern, Annabelle added 55 + 155 + 255 + 355 + 455 + 555 + 655 + 755 + 855 + 955 = 5050. Annabelle determined the solution in about 15 minutes, but she was using a calculator. The young Carl Friedrich, who grew up in the late 1700s, obviously did not have access to this tool. Carl calculated his amazingly quick response by identifying this pattern:

1	2	3	4	5	6	7	8	9	and so on to 50
100	99	98	97	96	95	94	93	92	and so on to 51
101	101	101	101	101	101	101	101	101	and so on.

Once Carl had determined that the sum of each number pair is 101, all he needed to do was multiply 101 by 50, the number of addition problems needed to total up all the numbers, to arrive at the answer, 5050. Throughout his lifetime Gauss created many more complex mathematical formulae, but perhaps none was quite as rewarding as this early challenge.

Main Idea 1

	Answer	Score
Mark the *main idea*	M	15
Mark the statement that is *too broad*	B	5
Mark the statement that is *too narrow*	N	5

a. Gauss was a brilliant mathematician.	☐	_____
b. Young Carl used 50 × 101 = 5050.	☐	_____
c. Carl Gauss showed his talent by quickly solving a difficult problem.	☐	_____

Score 15 points for each correct answer.　　　**Score**

Subject Matter　**2**　Another good title for this passage might be

☐ a. A Simple, Brilliant Solution.

☐ b. Practice Makes Perfect.

☐ c. The Duchy of Brunswick.

☐ d. School Days in the 1700s.　　＿＿＿

Supporting　**3**　Carl's solution involved

Details

☐ a. adding multiples of 10 (10, 20, 30, etc.).

☐ b. working out a pattern.

☐ c. adding the numbers from 1 to 10, 11 to 20, and so on.

☐ d. adding 1 + 2 + 3 + 4, and so on.　　＿＿＿

Conclusion　**4**　We can conclude from the passage that

☐ a. some people are born with an extremely high level of mathematical aptitude.

☐ b. Carl had been studying math since age two.

☐ c. most bright kids can reason as well as Carl.

☐ d. the teacher disapproved of Carl's solution.　　＿＿＿

Clarifying　**5**　Annabelle Leigh's solution is mentioned to show

Devices

☐ a. how a present-day adult with a calculator might solve the problem.

☐ b. that women are just as smart as young boys.

☐ c. that calculators make all math easy.

☐ d. that some problems have several answers.　　＿＿＿

Vocabulary　**6**　The word <u>precocious</u> means

in Context

☐ a. adorable.

☐ b. developed earlier than usual.

☐ c. ill-mannered.

☐ d. slow to adapt to strict rules.　　＿＿＿

Add your scores for questions 1–6. Enter the total here　**Total**

and on the graph on page 216.　**Score**　＿＿＿

74 The Seneca Falls Convention

In 1848, Seneca Falls was a rural town in a remote corner of upstate New York. One small notice in the local *Seneca County Courier* announced that public meetings would be held at the Wesleyan Chapel on the subject of women's rights. A few dozen people were expected to attend, but to the astonishment of the organizers, hundreds of women showed up.

Elizabeth Cady Stanton (1815–1902) had never before spoken in public; few women in America had. As Stanton began, however, she discovered that she was a natural-born speaker. "Resolved," she read from the *Declaration of Sentiments and Resolutions*, "that it is the duty of the women of this country to secure to themselves their sacred right to the elective franchise." As expected, there was opposition to the resolution, but to Stanton's great relief and joy, it passed. Elizabeth Cady Stanton learned that she was not the only one in America who believed women deserved the right to vote.

The public expressed outrage and disgust. Newspapers reacted as if the women had set out to tear down the nation. One paper accused them of trying to "upheave existing institutions and overturn all the social relations of life." The clergy was outraged too. The women were accused of <u>undermining</u> organized religion and blaspheming God.

But something had been set in motion. More women's rights meetings were held, and two years later the first National Women's Rights Convention was held in Wooster, Massachusetts. When women finally gained the right to vote in a national election, in 1920, only one woman who had attended the Seneca Falls convention was still alive to cast her vote—72 years after Elizabeth Cady Stanton's act of monumental daring.

Main Idea 1

	Answer	Score
Mark the *main idea*	M	15
Mark the statement that is *too broad*	B	5
Mark the statement that is *too narrow*	N	5

a. Elizabeth Cady Stanton was an effective public speaker. ☐ _____

b. Women met about their rights. ☐ _____

c. The Seneca Falls convention paved the way for women's right to vote. ☐ _____

Subject Matter   **2**   The best newspaper headline about the event
in this passage would be

☐ a. Seneca Falls—Home to Conventions.

☐ b. Women Want the Right to Vote.

☐ c. Stanton Speaks to Women.

☐ d. Wesleyan Chapel Site of Meeting.   _____

Supporting Details   **3**   The resolution read by Elizabeth Cady Stanton
was part of the

☐ a. *Seneca County Courier.*

☐ b. *Declaration of Independence.*

☐ c. *Declaration of Sentiments and Resolutions.*

☐ d. *Seneca Falls Convention Report.*   _____

Conclusion   **4**   It seems likely that

☐ a. women easily won the right to vote.

☐ b. Elizabeth Cady Stanton made many
more public speeches.

☐ c. the majority of women at the convention
disapproved of Stanton.

☐ d. Stanton later voted in a national election.   _____

Clarifying Devices   **5**   In the third paragraph, the phrase "the public"
refers specifically to

☐ a. the women's husbands.

☐ b. newspaper writers and clergy.

☐ c. politicians and office-seekers.

☐ d. the voting public.   _____

Vocabulary in Context   **6**   <u>Undermining</u> means

☐ a. planting bombs beneath.

☐ b. dressing in a scandalous manner.

☐ c. showing strong support for.

☐ d. weakening or destroying.   _____

**Add your scores for questions 1–6. Enter the total here
and on the graph on page 216.**   **Total
Score**   _____

75 Tap Dancing

Most of the arts in America are a combination of ideas and influences from many sources. Tap dancing certainly fits in this category. It is truly an American art, but it has been influenced by English and Irish dance steps as well as steps from Africa.

Some historians contend that tap dancing was first done by slaves on Southern plantations, and that originally steps were done wearing soft-soled shoes. Irish step dancing, which also involves intricate foot patterns, contributed the movement of the free leg to one side and the swing of the elbows outward. Wooden clog shoes were worn as tap dancing evolved, but for a long time the steps were done flat-footed.

Tap dancing developed into the form we recognize today in the early 20th century. Metal taps were added to dance shoes, and a number of new techniques were perfected. One of the most important was the change from the flat-footed step to dancing on the balls of the feet. This is commonly <u>attributed</u> to dancer Bill Robinson. Another was the "cramp roll," in which the dancer would rapidly move from the ball of the right foot to the ball of the left, and then to the heel of each foot. This separation of the steps into distinct areas of the foot, an innovation by dancer John Bubbles, allowed dancers to improvise even more new patterns. Slides across the floor and movements up and down stairs further enlivened tap. So did relaxed arm and shoulder movements. Challenges became a common part of dance routines, with dancers vying to outperform each other with new and difficult steps.

Many dancers excelled at tap and contributed to its development. Besides Bill Robinson and John Bubbles, well-known tappers have included Sammy Davis, Jr., Fred Astaire, Eleanor Powell, Gregory Hines, and Savion Glover.

Main Idea	1	Answer	Score
Mark the *main idea*		**M**	15
Mark the statement that is *too broad*		**B**	5
Mark the statement that is *too narrow*		**N**	5
a. Tap dancing is an American art.		☐	_____
b. Tap dancing changed as it developed.		☐	_____
c. Tappers changed their shoe style in the 20th century.		☐	_____

Score 15 points for each correct answer.   Score

Subject Matter   **2**   This passage is mostly about
    ☐ a. famous tap dancers.
    ☐ b. tap dancing on Southern plantations.
    ☐ c. tap shoes.
    ☐ d. the development of tap dancing.   _____

Supporting Details   **3**   Credit for the "cramp roll" is usually given to
    ☐ a. Fred Astaire.
    ☐ b. Bill Robinson.
    ☐ c. Savion Glover.
    ☐ d. John Bubbles.   _____

Conclusion   **4**   One of the most important elements of tap dancing is
    ☐ a. intricate footwork.
    ☐ b. smooth, flowing motions.
    ☐ c. dancing in rhythm with a partner.
    ☐ d. wearing wooden shoes.   _____

Clarifying Devices   **5**   Names are mentioned in this passage in order to
    ☐ a. tell about the lives of famous tap dancers.
    ☐ b. connect tap with jazz music.
    ☐ c. show the influence of women on tap dance.
    ☐ d. give credit to famous tap dancers.   _____

Vocabulary in Context   **6**   The word <u>attributed</u> means
    ☐ a. given credit for.
    ☐ b. described.
    ☐ c. notified.
    ☐ d. stated as a question.   _____

Add your scores for questions 1–6. Enter the total here and on the graph on page 216.   Total Score   _____

76 George Washington and the Gregorian Calendar

George Washington was born on February 11, 1731. On February 11, 1752, he celebrated his 21st birthday—or did he? Actually, Washington's 21st birthday fell on February 22, 1753, and he had no birthday at all during 1752! The person indirectly responsible for this was Gregory XIII, a pope during the late 1500s. The calendar we use today, the Gregorian calendar, was named for him.

The Julian calendar, commonly used till Gregory's time, included a leap year every four years. This calendar was, however, slightly out of <u>synchrony</u> with the solar year: approximately every 131 years it was too long by a day. To remedy this, Pope Gregory decreed that October 4, 1582, would be followed by October 15, 1582. This eliminated 10 days, the extra days accumulated since the Julian calendar had been used. To make datekeeping still more accurate, Gregory dropped three leap years from every four centuries by specifying that only century years exactly divisible by 400 would be leap years (1600 and 2000 for example).

England and its American colonies did not switch to the Gregorian calendar until September 1752. By then the old calendar was 11 days behind the new one. Washington's date of birth couldn't simply be changed from February 11, 1731, to February 22, 1731 because in the colonies New Year's Day had been March 25 rather than January 1. When the colonies switched over to the new calendar, they had to start celebrating New Year's Day on January 1. That meant that 1752 lasted from March 25 to December 31 only. George's birthday month, February, was deleted from 1752, as was January and most of March. To avoid skipping from age 20 to 22 on the new calendar, George had to count his birth year as 1732, not 1731.

Main Idea	1		Answer	Score
	Mark the *main idea*		**M**	15
	Mark the statement that is *too broad*		**B**	5
	Mark the statement that is *too narrow*		**N**	5

a.	George Washington was born on February 11, 1731.	☐ ___
b.	People have used various calendars over the centuries.	☐ ___
c.	Washington's birth date changed because of the Gregorian calendar.	☐ ___

Score 15 points for each correct answer.   **Score**

Subject Matter **2** Another good title for this passage might be
- [ ] a. Switching to the Gregorian Calendar.
- [ ] b. Switching to the Julian Calendar.
- [ ] c. Pope Gregory XIII.
- [ ] d. The American Colonies.   _____

Supporting Details **3** Washington changed his birth year from
- [ ] a. 1582 to 1731.
- [ ] b. 1731 to 1732.
- [ ] c. 1732 to 1731.
- [ ] d. 1600 to 2000.   _____

Conclusion **4** It is likely that the American colonies switched to the Gregorian calendar in 1752 because
- [ ] a. England switched then.
- [ ] b. the Romans switched then.
- [ ] c. they were at war with England.
- [ ] d. George Washington recommended it.   _____

Clarifying Devices **5** The writer uses the story of George Washington
- [ ] a. to give a specific example of how the Gregorian calendar caused changes.
- [ ] b. because he was our first president.
- [ ] c. because no one is sure what year he died.
- [ ] d. to explain why the Julian calendar was used for so long.   _____

Vocabulary in Context **6** Synchrony is the state of
- [ ] a. occurring in an oval pattern.
- [ ] b. occurring together.
- [ ] c. being completely separate.
- [ ] d. being enemies.   _____

Add your scores for questions 1–6. Enter the total here and on the graph on page 217.   **Total Score**   _____

77 Hurricanes

Hurricanes were named long ago by a Caribbean island people who blamed the devastating storms on Huracan, their god of evil. In Australia, hurricanes are called *cyclones* or *willy-willies;* in India they are *typhoons;* in parts of Mexico, they are called *cordonazo,* "lash of a whip."

Hurricanes form over tropical oceans when high surface water temperatures (about 80°F) cause the evaporation of massive quantities of water. This provides the tropical atmosphere with a rich supply of water vapor. The moist air is carried aloft where it condenses and releases latent heat. This warming strengthens the updraft, creating a low-pressure area in the lower atmosphere. Surrounding air moves into this low-pressure region, which in turn provides more energy from the condensation of even more lifted water vapor. Another ingredient in the formation of hurricanes is the <u>convergence</u> of winds blowing from different directions. These winds collide and create a pileup of air. The air at the center of the collision moves upward, becoming an updraft.

Rising air and convergence create ordinary thunderstorms, but as more hot updrafts rise into the storms, the clouds grow larger. Several thunderstorms might cluster together to become a tropical disturbance, the first stage in hurricane formation. The next stage occurs when the developing thunderstorm cluster begins to swirl, a movement caused by the rotation of the earth. When swirling winds reach sustained speeds of 23 miles per hour, the circulating vortex is called a tropical depression. When wind speeds reach 40 miles per hour, it is called a tropical storm. At 74 miles per hour, it is a hurricane. Hurricanes last approximately five to seven days. When they cross land or cool ocean water, losing their oceanic moisture source, their energy-providing latent heat decreases. The storm loses intensity and dies out.

Main Idea   1

	Answer	Score
Mark the *main idea*	**M**	15
Mark the statement that is *too broad*	**B**	5
Mark the statement that is *too narrow*	**N**	5

a. Hurricanes form over warm oceans.	☐	_____
b. Many storms form over warm oceans.	☐	_____
c. Moist air rises over warm oceans.	☐	_____

Subject Matter   2   This passage is mainly about
- ☐ a. how hurricanes got their names.
- ☐ b. the dangers of hurricanes.
- ☐ c. storm safety.
- ☐ d. the formation of hurricanes.   _____

Supporting Details   3   When wind speeds of a circulating vortex reach 74 miles an hour, the storm is called
- ☐ a. an ordinary thunderstorm.
- ☐ b. a tropical storm.
- ☐ c. a hurricane.
- ☐ d. a tropical depression.   _____

Conclusion   4   Over which of the following would a hurricane most likely *not* lose strength?
- ☐ a. Mexico
- ☐ b. a tropical sea
- ☐ c. the east coast of the United States
- ☐ d. the cold north Atlantic Ocean   _____

Clarifying Devices   5   The information in this passage is mainly presented through
- ☐ a. a historical perspective.
- ☐ b. a personal narrative.
- ☐ c. an explanation of a process.
- ☐ d. a descriptive account.   _____

Vocabulary in Context   6   The word <u>convergence</u> means
- ☐ a. the act of coming together.
- ☐ b. clouds that produce rain and thunder.
- ☐ c. the process of water vapor changing into liquid.
- ☐ d. an updraft.   _____

Add your scores for questions 1–6. Enter the total here and on the graph on page 217.   **Total Score**   _____

78 Brazil's Favelas

In recent years, more than six million people have migrated to Brazilian cities from the rural areas. Many people are looking for a better life. They live in temporary shelters while they collect materials to build a house or because there is nowhere else to live. Their settlements are called *favelas*. Many are in the hills surrounding cities.

Building temporary shelters is one thing, but providing the necessary urban infrastructure is another. Roads, water, electricity, sanitation, schools, and health clinics in the favelas are inadequate.

Andarai, one of the smaller, oldest favelas, may look well-kept and permanent, but it is crowded. Through the self-help community association's efforts, Andarai has electricity and other improvements. But as you move up the hill, conditions <u>deteriorate</u>. Some of the housing is about to collapse. Some children are kept locked inside while their mothers are at work. Open sewers run down gullies. The people are destroying the forest near the top of the hill to get wood for fuel and building materials. They know this increases the chance of flood and landslides, but they have no alternative.

Most favela residents want to upgrade their houses, provide clean water and electricity, and improve the roads. They need day-care centers, preschool programs, a community center, and health clinics. They also want to participate in decisions about the favela.

Many people do improve their property, or they move to better areas. Self-help community associations organize to improve conditions. The successes of the community associations show that when people work together progress is possible.

Main Idea	1			
			Answer	**Score**
	Mark the *main idea*		M	15
	Mark the statement that is *too broad*		B	5
	Mark the statement that is *too narrow*		N	5
	a. People in Andarai need improvements.		☐	_____
	b. People have migrated to Brazil's cities.		☐	_____
	c. Brazil's favelas may provide housing, but they lack infrastructure.		☐	_____

Score 15 points for each correct answer.　　　　Score

Subject Matter　**2**　This passage deals mostly with
　　　　　　☐ a. the history of the favelas.
　　　　　　☐ b. why Brazil is a poor country.
　　　　　　☐ c. life in the favelas.
　　　　　　☐ d. community organizations.　　　_____

Supporting　**3**　Destroying the hillside forests may lead to
Details　　　☐ a. floods and landslides.
　　　　　　☐ b. jobs.
　　　　　　☐ c. a decrease in annual rainfall.
　　　　　　☐ d. a rise in population.　　　_____

Conclusion　**4**　You can conclude from this passage that many
　　　　　　Brazilian cities are
　　　　　　☐ a. located near the ocean.
　　　　　　☐ b. beautiful.
　　　　　　☐ c. overcrowded.
　　　　　　☐ d. decreasing in population.　　　_____

Clarifying　**5**　The writer discusses conditions in favelas through
Devices　　　☐ a. cause and effect.
　　　　　　☐ b. a specific example.
　　　　　　☐ c. a personal narrative.
　　　　　　☐ d. a list of reasons.　　　_____

Vocabulary　**6**　The word <u>deteriorate</u> means
in Context　　☐ a. have limits.
　　　　　　☐ b. improve.
　　　　　　☐ c. are steeper.
　　　　　　☐ d. become worse.　　　_____

Add your scores for questions 1–6. Enter the total here　**Total**
and on the graph on page 217.　　　　**Score**　_____

79 Caribbean Writers

During the 1990s a number of writers whose origins were in the Caribbean became popular in the United States. Most of these writers had either been born in the United States of immigrant parents or brought here at a very young age. Their writing, in English, deals both with their family's place of origin and with their own take on life in America.

Julia Alvarez, whose family <u>emigrated</u> from the Dominican Republic when she was 10, has written both poetry and novels. One of her novels, *How the García Girls Lost Their Accents,* deals with the problems of young girls getting used to a new culture in much the same way she had to. Alvarez, who is now a college instructor, continues to write and publish.

Oscar Hijuelos was born in the United States, but his parents were immigrants from Cuba. Hijuelos has written fanciful tales of Cuban/Irish/American families such as *The Fourteen Sisters of Emilio Montez O'Brien.* In his best-known book, *The Mambo Kings Play Songs of Love,* Hijuelos depicts the struggles of two Cuban brothers as they try to become successful musicians in the United States.

Edwidge Danticat, whose country of origin is Haiti, writes both of the hardships of life there and of coping with life here. One of her most recent works, *The Farming of Bones,* is a historical novel about a massacre that took place in Haiti in the 1930s. An earlier novel, *Breath, Eyes, Memory,* tells of Haitians who have come to New York.

Rosario Ferré is Puerto Rican and continues to live in Puerto Rico. Her first novel, published in English in 1995, was *The House on the Lagoon.* This novel and much of her other work reflects the great influence of the mainland United States on Puerto Rican island life.

Main Idea	1			
			Answer	**Score**
	Mark the *main idea*		M	15
	Mark the statement that is *too broad*		B	5
	Mark the statement that is *too narrow*		N	5
	a. Edwidge Danticat is from Haiti.		☐	_____
	b. Many writers have Caribbean backgrounds.		☐	_____
	c. Caribbean authors in the U.S. often write of both their old and new countries.		☐	_____

Subject Matter   **2**   This passage is mostly about
- ☐ a. writers who live in Caribbean countries.
- ☐ b. Caribbean writers who live in the United States.
- ☐ c. Caribbean writers of nonfiction.
- ☐ d. writing about one's native country.   _____

Supporting Details   **3**   Oscar Hijuelos
- ☐ a. often writes about massacres.
- ☐ b. has written 14 novels.
- ☐ c. was born in Cuba.
- ☐ d. was born in the United States.   _____

Conclusion   **4**   Rosario Ferré is different from the other writers because she
- ☐ a. is a woman.
- ☐ b. is not from the Caribbean.
- ☐ c. doesn't live in the mainland United States.
- ☐ d. writes poetry as well as novels.   _____

Clarifying Devices   **5**   The first paragraph of the passage summarizes
- ☐ a. characteristics of the writers that the passage will discuss.
- ☐ b. plots of several of the novels.
- ☐ c. the lives of several of the writers.
- ☐ d. why Caribbean writers are popular.   _____

Vocabulary in Context   **6**   Emigrated means
- ☐ a. journeyed across the seas.
- ☐ b. learned a new language.
- ☐ c. went to a country.
- ☐ d. left a country.   _____

Add your scores for questions 1–6. Enter the total here and on the graph on page 217.   **Total Score**   _____

80 Who Drinks Mineral Water?

The following puzzle is a variation of a brain-strainer entitled "Who Owns the Zebra?" It begins with this premise: *In San Francisco three Victorian mansions stand in a row, each painted a different color and inhabited by a homeowner of a different nationality. Each householder owns a different exotic pet and drinks a different beverage.*

Here are the clues and the puzzle to be solved. (1) The Brazilian resides in the vermilion mansion. (2) The Vietnamese coddles the kangaroo. (3) Cappuccino is elegantly sipped in the magenta mansion. (4) The Vietnamese drinks pomegranate nectar. (5) The chartreuse mansion stands immediately to the right of the vermilion one. (6) The Dalmatian owner <u>imbibes</u> cappuccino. (7) The chimpanzee owner resides in the splendid vermilion edifice. (8) Pomegranate nectar is drunk in the mansion on the far right. Now: *Who drinks mineral water, and in which house does the Ukrainian live?*

Two essentials for working out a puzzle such as this include charting information into categories and discarding clues that are irrelevant. A careful reading of the puzzle's original premise reveals the categories below.

nationality   house   color   pet   drink

Once these categories are established, it is a fairly simple matter to chart the information provided by the clues and discover unfilled spots in the puzzle, which would reveal the answers. But you also need to recognize the unnecessary clues, those about positions of houses, that the puzzle does not ask about. By identifying those clues, numbers 5 and 8, and then discarding them, you should be able to quickly come up with a solution.

Main Idea   1 —————————————————————————————

	Answer	Score
Mark the *main idea*	M	15
Mark the statement that is *too broad*	B	5
Mark the statement that is *too narrow*	N	5

a. Solving logic puzzles requires categorizing information and eliminating irrelevant details. ☐ _____

b. The Brazilian lives in the vermilion mansion. ☐ _____

c. Logic puzzles can be entertaining to solve. ☐ _____

Subject Matter   **2**   Another good title for this passage might be
- ☐ a. Owning an Exotic Pet.
- ☐ b. Solving a Logic Puzzle.
- ☐ c. A List of Facts and Details.
- ☐ d. Splendid Victorian Mansions.

_____

Supporting Details   **3**   The Vietnamese homeowner
- ☐ a. lives in an elegant magenta mansion.
- ☐ b. owns a chimpanzee.
- ☐ c. drinks pomegranate nectar.
- ☐ d. does not live near the Ukrainian.

_____

Conclusion   **4**   The blanks in a completed diagram would reveal
- ☐ a. where *Ukrainian* and *mineral water* belong.
- ☐ b. that the puzzle cannot be solved.
- ☐ c. the positions of the various houses.
- ☐ d. how many chimpanzees there were.

_____

Clarifying Devices   **5**   The last sentence of the passage is intended to
- ☐ a. challenge you to solve the puzzle yourself.
- ☐ b. confuse you.
- ☐ c. tell you what the solution is.
- ☐ d. prove that the puzzle is difficult.

_____

Vocabulary in Context   **6**   <u>Imbibes</u> means
- ☐ a. buys.
- ☐ b. sells.
- ☐ c. drinks.
- ☐ d. hates.

_____

Add your scores for questions 1–6. Enter the total here and on the graph on page 217.

Total Score

_____

81 Kinds of Rock

Rock, the hard, solid part of the earth, can be grouped by its mineral content, by its appearance, and even by the way it is used. But the most common way to classify rocks is to group them by the way they are formed. Using this method of classification, there are three main kinds of rocks.

Igneous. The word *igneous* means "having to do with fire." Igneous rocks form from magma—molten material—that reaches the earth's surface as lava or that cools and solidifies within the earth's crust before reaching the surface. Examples of igneous rocks are glassy obsidian, porous pumice, the finely crystalline rocks of basalt and felsite, and the coarsely crystalline rocks of granite and gabbros.

Sedimentary. Sedimentary rocks form when particles that have eroded from other rocks of all kinds are buried. Sedimentary rocks also come from other rocks and minerals that have dissolved in ocean water. The particles, or sediments, become hard and <u>compact</u>. Over long periods of time they turn into sedimentary rocks. The size, shape, and chemical nature of the particles determine the kind of rock the particles become. Examples of sedimentary rocks are sandstone, shale, and limestone.

Metamorphic. These rocks get their name from the Greek words *meta* and *morphe,* which together mean "change of form." Metamorphic rocks are igneous or sedimentary rocks that have been altered by great pressure or temperature. In some metamorphic rocks, new minerals are formed and the appearance of the rock changes greatly. This happens when the calcite in limestone recrystallizes to form marble, and when the quartz grains in sandstone grow larger to form the connecting crystals of quartzite.

Main Idea 1

	Answer	Score
Mark the *main idea*	M	15
Mark the statement that is *too broad*	B	5
Mark the statement that is *too narrow*	N	5

a. Rocks are the solid part of the earth. ☐ _____

b. Rocks can be classified by the way they are formed. ☐ _____

c. Metamorphic rocks may be igneous rocks that have been altered. ☐ _____

Score 15 points for each correct answer.　　　　　**Score**

Subject Matter　**2**　This passage is mostly about
- ☐ a. why rock is categorized in different ways.
- ☐ b. Greek words meaning "rock."
- ☐ c. characteristics of the three main kinds of rocks.
- ☐ d. grouping rocks by their mineral content. _____

Supporting Details　**3**　Igneous rocks come from
- ☐ a. cooled magma.
- ☐ b. layers of sediment at the bottom of the oceans.
- ☐ c. rocks under great pressure.
- ☐ d. sandstone crystals. _____

Conclusion　**4**　It seems likely that rock formation happens
- ☐ a. only on land.
- ☐ b. only in water.
- ☐ c. over a long period of time.
- ☐ d. quite quickly. _____

Clarifying Devices　**5**　The subheads in bold type are the three kinds of
- ☐ a. rock.
- ☐ b. crystals.
- ☐ c. Greek words.
- ☐ d. minerals. _____

Vocabulary in Context　**6**　In this passage <u>compact</u> means
- ☐ a. small or miniature.
- ☐ b. a contract or agreement.
- ☐ c. of a beautiful and high quality.
- ☐ d. firmly packed together. _____

Add your scores for questions 1–6. Enter the total here and on the graph on page 217.　**Total Score** _____

82 "Don't Ride the Buses"

"We are asking every Negro to stay off the buses on Monday in protest of the arrest and trial. Don't ride the buses to work, to town, to school, or anywhere on Monday." Within 48 hours of the December 1955 arrest of Rosa Parks, 5,000 <u>leaflets</u> with this statement were distributed to black churches throughout Montgomery, Alabama. The leaflets told of Rosa Parks's arrest due to her refusal to move to the so-called "colored section" in the back of a public bus. A young pastor, Reverend Martin Luther King, Jr., was elected to lead the boycott.

On the first day, African Americans traveled by cars, taxis, horse-drawn carts, mules, bicycles, and foot. They did not ride the buses. Through the winter months, organized car pools of about 300 vehicles and black-owned taxi companies carried passengers to their destinations. Churches bought station wagons and ran taxi services. The bus company's losses mounted, but the owners refused to give in.

Meanwhile, lawyers representing the boycott leaders petitioned the federal court to declare Alabama's bus segregation laws unconstitutional—and won. Alabama appealed to the U.S. Supreme Court, but no one knew when the case would be settled.

But another legal battle was closer to resolution. In November 1956 Montgomery city leaders petitioned the state circuit court to outlaw the black car pools, claiming they were a business operating without city permission. Without the car pools, the boycott would be defeated. Martin Luther King, Jr., was at the Montgomery County courthouse waiting for the car pool decision when he heard this news: The U.S. Supreme Court had declared Alabama's bus segregation laws unconstitutional. After a year of boycotting, the estimated 50,000 African-American citizens of Montgomery had prevailed.

Main Idea	1			
			Answer	Score
	Mark the *main idea*		M	15
	Mark the statement that is *too broad*		B	5
	Mark the statement that is *too narrow*		N	5

a. Segregation was a problem in Montgomery.   ☐   _____

b. Rosa Parks was arrested in late 1955.   ☐   _____

c. The 1955 bus boycott helped end segregation in Montgomery.   ☐   _____

Subject Matter   **2**   This passage is mostly about
     ☐ a. Rosa Parks's life.
     ☐ b. the people who rode buses in Montgomery.
     ☐ c. the end of bus segregation in Montgomery.
     ☐ d. Dr. Martin Luther King, Jr.'s life.   _____

Supporting Details   **3**   City leaders claimed that the black car pools
     ☐ a. were operating without city permission.
     ☐ b. should be carrying white people.
     ☐ c. were no threat to the bus system.
     ☐ d. operated unsafe vehicles.   _____

Conclusion   **4**   The phrase "African-American citizens of Montgomery had prevailed" suggests that
     ☐ a. the citizens' actions were misguided.
     ☐ b. the boycott was a failure.
     ☐ c. a civil rights lawyer began the boycott.
     ☐ d. the boycott was a success.   _____

Clarifying Devices   **5**   Which sentence clarifies the true reason why the city was against black car pools?
     ☐ a. Churches . . . ran taxi services.
     ☐ b. The car pools were a business operating without city permission.
     ☐ c. Without the car pools, the boycott would be defeated.
     ☐ d. The bus company's losses were mounting.   _____

Vocabulary in Context   **6**   In this passage <u>leaflets</u> are
     ☐ a. small hymn books.
     ☐ b. parts of a tree.
     ☐ c. sheets of printed material.
     ☐ d. receipts.   _____

Add your scores for questions 1–6. Enter the total here and on the graph on page 217.   **Total Score**   _____

83 Art Deco

During the 1920s in both Europe and America, the speed and sophistication of modern life fascinated many people. And so when it came to developing new architectural and design styles, it seemed logical to capture that sophistication and streamlined quality. The result was a style known today as Art Deco. This name comes from a 1925 exhibition in Paris known as the *Exposition Internationale des Arts Decoratifs Industriels et Modernes.*

Art Deco style was applied to many objects. It was found in furniture, jewelry, and ships, as well as in architecture. It was basically a simple style, using geometric shapes such as circles and strong vertical and horizontal lines. Decorative sunbursts and lightning bolts were common. The skyscraper of the time, with its strong vertical emphasis, is a good symbol of Art Deco. (The Chrysler Building in New York, topped with sunbursts leading to a spire, is one famous example.) Sleek, silver-covered passenger trains, their horizontal lines <u>epitomizing</u> speed, were also classic Art Deco.

There are Art Deco buildings in almost every large city in America. The largest group of them today, however, is in Miami Beach, Florida. Built roughly between 1930 and 1940, these structures, nearly all hotels and apartment buildings, line the waterfront and the nearby streets. Most of the buildings are no more than three or four stories high. They often have curved corners, long, sweeping ledges, and horizontal trim. Some are decorated with Egyptian designs, another characteristic of Art Deco. Many have round windows resembling portholes, which accentuate their similarity to ocean liners that may be sailing nearby. Most of these buildings have been restored in the last 10 or 15 years. Their pastel colors, painted to match the tropical scenery, suggest the era of simple beachfront pleasures for which they were built.

Main Idea 1		Answer	Score
Mark the *main idea*		M	15
Mark the statement that is *too broad*		B	5
Mark the statement that is *too narrow*		N	5
a. Miami Beach has a lot of Art Deco buildings.		☐	_____
b. Architecture represents the era it is built in.		☐	_____
c. Art Deco style uses simple lines to represent speed and sophistication.		☐	_____

Subject Matter   2   This passage deals mostly with
- ☐ a. characteristics and examples of Art Deco.
- ☐ b. life in Miami Beach in the 1930s.
- ☐ c. how Art Deco developed in Paris.
- ☐ d. the Chrysler Building and other skyscrapers.   _____

Supporting Details   3   Art Deco developed in the
- ☐ a. 1910s.
- ☐ b. 1920s.
- ☐ c. 1930s.
- ☐ d. 1940s.   _____

Conclusion   4   Many of the Art Deco buildings in Miami Beach were
- ☐ a. high rises.
- ☐ b. covered with intricate ornamental patterns.
- ☐ c. torn down to make way for newer buildings.
- ☐ d. built to harmonize with their setting.   _____

Clarifying Devices   5   The first paragraph of the passage
- ☐ a. provides some background about Art Deco.
- ☐ b. discusses the style that came before Art Deco.
- ☐ c. tells a brief story to make a point.
- ☐ d. tells how to recognize Art Deco buildings.   _____

Vocabulary in Context   6   Epitomizing means
- ☐ a. painting.
- ☐ b. building.
- ☐ c. destroying.
- ☐ d. being a strong example of.   _____

Add your scores for questions 1–6. Enter the total here and on the graph on page 217.   Total Score   _____

84 Getting Out of Credit Card Debt

Geraldine Ghirardelli was $2,500 in debt to a company called BicentennialCard when she received an introductory offer from MillenniumCard Corporation of a six-month 3.9 percent payment rate on balance transfers. In February Gerri transferred her balance to MillenniumCard, and MillenniumCard paid BicentennialCard $2,500 on March 1. Gerri's intent was to pay off her debt during the six-month period of MillenniumCard's special rate. Fortunately, she had just obtained a <u>lucrative</u> position in a telecommunications firm that enabled her to make substantial monthly payments.

Gerri correctly estimated that as long as she didn't make any additional charges on the card, six payments of $425, or a total payment of $2,550, would get her out of debt in time. Gerri arrived at her estimate this way. She multiplied the amount of the debt times the percentage rate for the loan ($2,500 × .039), for a total of $97.50, then divided that amount by 2 (because she was only paying for half of the year). Rounding her total of $48.75 up to $50, Gerri paid that amount in interest over the six months and was able to retire her debt.

It was worth it for Gerri to stretch a little to pay off what she owed, and getting that low interest rate was a particularly lucky break. A more typical rate is about 17.5 percent. If Gerri tried to pay off her debt in six months at that level, she could have estimated her total interest payments to be $218.75. Though estimates like these are a little higher than you would actually pay, they give a good idea of how quickly interest on a debt piles up. And remember, the estimate of $218.75 would hold only if you didn't make any more purchases on the card. With every new purchase, the credit card company, through complicated formulas, adds additional interest to your debt. It is a good idea to follow Gerri's lead and pay off those credit cards.

Main Idea   1

	Answer	Score
Mark the *main idea*	M	15
Mark the statement that is *too broad*	B	5
Mark the statement that is *too narrow*	N	5

a. Gerri owed $2,500 to a credit card company. ☐ _____

b. It is wise to get out of credit card debt as Gerri did. ☐ _____

c. Many people owe on credit cards. ☐ _____

Score 15 points for each correct answer.   **Score**

Subject Matter   **2**   Another good title for this passage might be
- [ ] a. Looking Closely at Credit Card Bills.
- [ ] b. Working in Telecommunications.
- [ ] c. The BicentennialCard Company.
- [ ] d. The MillenniumCard Corporation.   _____

Supporting Details   **3**   The $50 interest charge that Gerri estimated was
- [ ] a. at a 17.5 percent interest rate.
- [ ] b. at a 3.9 percent interest rate.
- [ ] c. for a loan she would pay off in one year.
- [ ] d. for a $2,550 debt.   _____

Conclusion   **4**   If $218.75 was the interest on a loan for six months, for one year the interest would be
- [ ] a. the same.
- [ ] b. half that much.
- [ ] c. three times that much.
- [ ] d. twice that much.   _____

Clarifying Devices   **5**   BicentennialCard and MillenniumCard are
- [ ] a. new credit card companies.
- [ ] b. credit card companies that have been forced out of business.
- [ ] c. names made up for the sake of the story.
- [ ] d. credit card companies with no membership charges.   _____

Vocabulary in Context   **6**   In this passage <u>lucrative</u> means
- [ ] a. creative.
- [ ] b. secretarial.
- [ ] c. well-paying.
- [ ] d. stressful.   _____

Add your scores for questions 1–6. Enter the total here and on the graph on page 217.   **Total Score**   _____

85 Endangered Amphibians

Amphibians are the only group of animals on the earth that spend part of their lives on land and part in the water. Worldwide the amphibian populations—that is, the numbers of creatures such as frogs, toads, and salamanders—are <u>declining</u>. Among the possible causes for this phenomenon is pollution. Scientific data strongly suggest that certain kinds of pollution are at least partially responsible. One of the sources of pollution is acid precipitation.

Acid rain and snow can affect amphibians in remote places that seem free of human activity. Precipitation in the air mixes with pollutants, such as sulfur and nitrate from automobile exhaust and coal-burning factories, to produce sulfuric acid and nitric acid. Acid precipitation can be devastating to life.

The acid from precipitation accumulates in and around lakes and ponds where amphibians live. Concentrations of acid are highest in early spring, which puts newly laid amphibian eggs at risk. Melting acid snow can produce an acid pulse, which is a sudden release of acid into the water. It acts like a dose of poison. Studies show that even slightly acidic water can kill the eggs of frogs and toads or cause deformed tadpoles. Acid precipitation has been blamed for the disappearance of tiger salamanders from parts of the Colorado Rockies.

Some amphibian species, such as the New Jersey Pine Barrens frog, thrive in water with high acid content. Scientists offer an explanation for this exception: because the level of acid has been the same for many years, the frogs have managed to adapt to conditions that would kill other species. Amphibians are highly adaptable, but they need time to adapt to new conditions. Human-made changes, such as acid pulses, can be deadly.

Main Idea	1		
		Answer	**Score**
	Mark the *main idea*	M	15
	Mark the statement that is *too broad*	B	5
	Mark the statement that is *too narrow*	N	5
	a. Acid rain can cause deformed tadpoles.	☐	_____
	b. There are fewer amphibians around.	☐	_____
	c. Acid rain may be causing the amphibian population to decrease.	☐	_____

Subject Matter   **2**   This passage is mainly about
- ☐ a. how amphibians grow.
- ☐ b. precipitation.
- ☐ c. pollution's effect on lakes and ponds.
- ☐ d. pollution's effect on amphibians.

_____

Supporting Details   **3**   Acidic water can
- ☐ a. melt snow.
- ☐ b. cause rain to fall.
- ☐ c. kill amphibian eggs.
- ☐ d. accelerate the pulse of a frog.

_____

Conclusion   **4**   Which statement is probably true about amphibians?
- ☐ a. They may adapt to certain kinds of pollutants.
- ☐ b. They need acid rain to survive.
- ☐ c. They are found only in isolated areas.
- ☐ d. They lay their eggs in late summer.

_____

Clarifying Devices   **5**   The structure of this passage is
- ☐ a. chronological.
- ☐ b. narrative.
- ☐ c. cause and effect.
- ☐ d. question and answer.

_____

Vocabulary in Context   **6**   In this passage <u>declining</u> means
- ☐ a. arguing.
- ☐ b. absorbing.
- ☐ c. lessening.
- ☐ d. increasing.

_____

Add your scores for questions 1–6. Enter the total here and on the graph on page 217.   **Total Score**

_____

86 Antarctica: Is There Something There?

Is there anything to do in Antarctica, the earth's fifth-largest and southernmost continent? There is if you want to experience the coldest climate on the earth with the lowest temperature ever recorded ($-126.9°F$), where annual precipitation varies from two inches of snowfall in the interior to 40 inches on the coast. There is if you think that three-mile-thick ice, mountain peaks, sea-washed coastlines, and a frozen waterfall bigger than Niagara Falls are scenic. There is if you study frozen lakes or are intrigued by one with a water temperature of 77°F underneath 10-foot-thick ice. Would you enjoy a three-month-long summer day? Would you like to live with a summer population of only several thousand people? Would you prefer wintering with a few hundred scientists and support personnel in extreme conditions?

Antarctica is more than one and one-half times the size of the United States. It covers about 5,500,000 square miles and is surrounded by the Antarctic Ocean. Some 98 percent of the continent is covered with ice, but there are some 1,500 square miles of windswept bare ground in the Dry Valleys area. Here, where ice does not hide the secrets of the earth, there are exposed pale brown and black layers of rock and blue-green algae-covered hillsides.

Algae, fungi, and bacteria that are insensitive to repeated freezing and thawing live between grains of sandstone. Bacteria-eating nematodes (<u>microscopic</u> worms) in the Dry Valleys go into a dry, lifeless state called anhydrobiosis when no moisture is present. But just a little bit of moisture from snow or a melt causes the nematodes to emerge from their freeze-dried state. Do you still think there is nothing to do or experience in Antarctica?

Main Idea	1	Answer	Score
	Mark the *main idea*	M	15
	Mark the statement that is *too broad*	B	5
	Mark the statement that is *too narrow*	N	5

a. Antarctica has frozen lakes and a frozen waterfall.	☐	____
b. Antarctica is a place to see.	☐	____
c. Antarctica is a varied and interesting continent.	☐	____

Score 15 points for each correct answer.   Score

Subject Matter   2   This passage is mostly about
☐ a. sights and conditions of Antarctica.
☐ b. explorers of Antarctica.
☐ c. tours to Antarctica.
☐ d. animals of Antarctica.   _____

Supporting   3   Antarctica has
Details   ☐ a. trees.
☐ b. polar bears.
☐ c. no solid surfaces.
☐ d. a lake with a water temperature of 77°F.   _____

Conclusion   4   The question at the end of the passage is
intended to make the reader
☐ a. think about the information in the passage.
☐ b. want to travel to Antarctica.
☐ c. conclude that there is nothing to see in
Antarctica.
☐ d. write a response to the passage.   _____

Clarifying   5   The phrase "more than one and one-half times
Devices   the size of the United States" tells the size of the
☐ a. Dry Valleys.
☐ b. continent of Antarctica.
☐ c. Antarctic Ocean.
☐ d. population of Antarctica.   _____

Vocabulary   6   <u>Microscopic</u> means
in Context   ☐ a. looking like a microscope.
☐ b. very nearsighted.
☐ c. very tiny.
☐ d. slightly smaller than a telescope.   _____

Add your scores for questions 1–6. Enter the total here   **Total**
and on the graph on page 217.   **Score**   _____

87 Thinking in the Metric System

Although the units and relationships of the metric system have been taught in U.S. schools since the mid-1970s, most people in the United States have little or no "feeling" for metric units. They have no immediate answers for such questions as How many grams does a small dog weigh? or How many centimeters wide is a standard kitchen countertop? or Is 100 liters of water enough to fill a bathtub?

To develop a feeling for metric units, you can choose what are called *benchmarks*. These are known quantities that you memorize and then use to estimate other lengths, weights, and capacities. Common objects make good choices for benchmarks since they are things that people are familiar with. For example, one centimeter measures about the width of a fingernail. A meter is about the height of a desk or filing cabinet and the width of a normal door, so the desk height or door width can be selected as benchmarks to remember the size of one meter. For a benchmark to be helpful, clearly it must be something that is familiar to *you*. For instance, if you like track and field events, you might pace off 100 meters, get a mental sense of how long this measurement is, and use it in estimating longer distances.

Centimeters and meters, as well as kilometers, measure length or distance. You'll also need benchmarks for capacity and weight, measured in metrics by liters or milliliters (capacity) and grams or kilograms (weight). Plastic soft drink bottles that hold two liters have become extremely common. Couple that knowledge with the fact that two liters equals 2,000 milliliters and you have one benchmark for liquid capacity; another might be the 200–300 milliliters of liquid in a water glass or coffee cup. And for estimating weights? A cordless phone handset is about 25 grams, and 100 pounds is about 45 kilograms—either of these facts can help you choose a weight benchmark.

Main Idea   1 —————————————————————————————————————

	Answer	Score
Mark the *main idea*	M	15
Mark the statement that is *too broad*	B	5
Mark the statement that is *too narrow*	N	5

a. Choosing personal benchmarks can help you understand the metric system. ☐ _____

b. You need benchmarks for capacity and weight. ☐ _____

c. Many systems of measurement exist. ☐ _____

Subject Matter   2   This passage is mostly concerned with
- ☐ a. adding and subtracting in the metric system.
- ☐ b. ways of getting more familiar with metrics.
- ☐ c. finding out how much certain objects weigh.
- ☐ d. why yards and pounds are easier than meters and kilograms.

_____

Supporting Details   3   The width of a door is a good benchmark for a
- ☐ a. gram.
- ☐ b. centimeter.
- ☐ c. meter.
- ☐ d. kilometer.

_____

Conclusion   4   The author of this passages believes that
- ☐ a. metrics are a waste of time.
- ☐ b. if you use benchmarks you'll never have to measure.
- ☐ c. metrics are commonly used by Americans.
- ☐ d. people should have some knowledge of the metric system.

_____

Clarifying Devices   5   The examples in the first paragraph show that most people
- ☐ a. have never heard of the metric system.
- ☐ b. have trouble estimating with metrics.
- ☐ c. think length and distance are different things.
- ☐ d. think weight and capacity are the same thing.

_____

Vocabulary in Context   6   In this passage the word <u>couple</u> means
- ☐ a. a man and woman who are dating.
- ☐ b. to link together or connect.
- ☐ c. a piece that holds two train cars together.
- ☐ d. a few.

_____

Add your scores for questions 1–6. Enter the total here and on the graph on page 217.   **Total Score**

_____

88 A New Vision of Nature

She died in 1986, when she was 98 years old. In her later years, when she lived in New Mexico and her eyesight was getting bad, she turned from painting to making pottery. Her name was Georgia O'Keeffe, and she is considered one of the most important American artists of the 20th century.

O'Keeffe began painting in the early years of the century, and at first her work was not terribly original. But beginning in 1912, O'Keeffe moved away from the Midwest where she had grown up and began teaching in the South and Southwest. The vast open spaces and desert landscapes that she encountered in Texas were an inspiration to her painting. Her style and subject matter began to change and develop.

An important influence in O'Keeffe's life was photographer Alfred Stieglitz, who discovered her work and exhibited it in New York City in 1916. Other exhibits followed, and soon O'Keeffe's artistic talents were widely recognized.

Two significant qualities that make O'Keeffe so important as a painter are her subject matter and her originality. O'Keeffe retained a lifetime interest in the Southwest, spending much of her time in New Mexico from 1929 on, and much of her painting focuses on the landscape there. Skulls, whitewashed bones, peasant churches: all are presented in a simple, greatly enlarged style. Another favorite subject area was flowers such as lilies and irises, all painted very large—sometimes with a clear, vibrant <u>palette</u>, other times with a pale, subtle one. No other painter saw or portrayed images from the American landscape from quite the same perspective; certainly no other painter has shown the same ability to present simple, natural objects in a mysterious, sometimes even exotic, manner.

Main Idea 1

	Answer	Score
Mark the *main idea*	M	15
Mark the statement that is *too broad*	B	5
Mark the statement that is *too narrow*	N	5

a. Georgia O'Keeffe was an American artist. ☐ _____

b. Georgia O'Keeffe developed into a painter of unusual, original works. ☐ _____

c. Georgia O'Keeffe often painted flowers. ☐ _____

Subject Matter   **2**   This passage is mostly about
  ☐ a. landscape painting.
  ☐ b. Georgia O'Keeffe's life and work.
  ☐ c. O'Keeffe's relationship with Alfred Stieglitz.
  ☐ d. American women painters.   _____

Supporting Details   **3**   O'Keeffe spent most of her life in
  ☐ a. New York City.
  ☐ b. Texas.
  ☐ c. the Midwest.
  ☐ d. New Mexico.   _____

Conclusion   **4**   A subject O'Keeffe would be likely to paint is
  ☐ a. a young married couple.
  ☐ b. the moon high above a sand dune.
  ☐ c. a late-model car.
  ☐ d. a motorboat on a river.   _____

Clarifying Devices   **5**   The first paragraph is written to
  ☐ a. briefly summarize O'Keeffe's life.
  ☐ b. introduce O'Keeffe's best paintings.
  ☐ c. compare O'Keeffe with other painters.
  ☐ d. give a physical description of O'Keeffe.   _____

Vocabulary in Context   **6**   In this passage palette means
  ☐ a. ability to taste food.
  ☐ b. a small, cotlike bed.
  ☐ c. thin board to mix paints on.
  ☐ d. set of colors used by a painter.   _____

Add your scores for questions 1–6. Enter the total here and on the graph on page 217.   **Total Score**   _____

89 Come In. It's COOL Inside!

It may be difficult to imagine a movie theater today that wouldn't be cool on a hot day, but air-conditioned comfort was once a big bonus for your ticket price. In fact circulating conditioned air, fed into the theater from the ceiling and taken out from the floor level, was first installed in 1922 at Graumann's Metropolitan Theater in Los Angeles, California.

Willis Carrier invented a mechanical air conditioner in 1911. With the development of Freons in the early 1930s, air-conditioning systems began to be installed in office buildings, hospitals, apartments, trains, and buses. Freons are highly efficient refrigerant gases that are carbon compounds containing fluorine and chlorine or bromine. The refrigerant becomes a liquid and gives off heat when it is <u>compressed</u>. When the pressure is removed, it becomes a gas and absorbs heat.

In the air-cooling cycle, warm, humid air is drawn from the room and over the cooling coil that contains the refrigerant. The warm air gives up its heat to the refrigerant. The refrigerant fluid vaporizes as it absorbs the heat in the air. The moisture in the cooled air condenses on fins over the coils, and the water runs down the fins and drains. The cooled, dehumidified air is blown back into the room.

Meanwhile, the vaporized and now much warmer refrigerant moves to the compressor. The compressor pumps it under pressure to the condenser coils. Here the heat in the refrigerant is transferred outside by fan. The refrigerant is recirculated to the cooling coil as a liquid to continue the cooling process. A thermostat controls the compressor motor, turning it off when the room temperature is cool enough and restarting it as temperatures begin to rise. As for the movie-going audience, all they have to do is enjoy the movie as the air conditioner keeps them cool.

Main Idea 1

	Answer	Score
Mark the *main idea*	M	15
Mark the statement that is *too broad*	B	5
Mark the statement that is *too narrow*	N	5

a. Air conditioning keeps people cool.	☐	_____
b. Freons are refrigerants.	☐	_____
c. The air conditioning process uses refrigerant gases to remove heat from the air.	☐	_____

Score 15 points for each correct answer. 　　　　**Score**

Subject Matter　**2**　This passage is mainly about
　　　　□ a. movie theaters.
　　　　□ b. the development of Freons.
　　　　□ c. how air conditioners work.
　　　　□ d. compressors and thermostats.　　　_____

Supporting　**3**　Air conditioners began to be installed in office
Details　　　buildings in the
　　　　□ a. 1920s.
　　　　□ b. 1910s.
　　　　□ c. 1950s.
　　　　□ d. 1930s.　　　_____

Conclusion　**4**　The development of Freons was important
　　　　to the development of
　　　　□ a. large-scale air conditioning.
　　　　□ b. office buildings.
　　　　□ c. carbon compounds.
　　　　□ d. movie theaters.　　　_____

Clarifying　**5**　In the fourth paragraph, the word *meanwhile*
Devices　　　indicates that the process is happening
　　　　□ a. at the same time the cooled air is blown
　　　　　　　into the room.
　　　　□ b. after the cooled air is blown into the room.
　　　　□ c. before the cooled air is blown into the room.
　　　　□ d. in another series of machines.　　　_____

Vocabulary　**6**　In this passage <u>compressed</u> means
in Context　　□ a. frozen.
　　　　□ b. squeezed together by pressure.
　　　　□ c. exploded.
　　　　□ d. complicated.　　　_____

Add your scores for questions 1–6. Enter the total here　**Total**
and on the graph on page 217.　**Score**　_____

90 Evacuation from Saigon

April 28, 1975. The South Vietnamese government surrendered, and the North Vietnamese army was about to invade the capital city of Saigon. Ever since the early 1960s, U.S. presidents Kennedy, Johnson, and Nixon had dispatched military advisors and troops to fight for the noncommunist government of South Vietnam. But for all the millions of dollars committed and the thousands of lives lost, the U.S. military failed to prevent South Vietnam from falling to the forces of communism. As a result, any Vietnamese who had opposed the communists was in <u>grave</u> danger.

Nine-year-old Hoang Nhu Tran and his family were among the thousands of Vietnamese forced to flee their homeland. Hoang's father was a major in the South Vietnamese air force. The Trans drove to Tan Son Nhut airport, where refugees were being evacuated on U.S. transport planes. By the time the Trans arrived, however, heavy rocket fire from oncoming tanks made takeoffs impossible. The airport was closed. The Trans had one final hope as they made their way back into the city and headed for the main dock on the Saigon River. The U.S. Navy had cargo ships and amphibious landing craft to evacuate the refugees, but there were more refugees than the boats could handle. Thousands pushed frantically up against the high wire fence that ran along the dock. Hoang's family forced its way into the hysterical crowd, somehow getting to the gate, where their military credentials got them into a boat.

The landing craft lumbered down the Saigon River and out into the South China Sea, as Hoang looked up at the rockets shooting across the sky. There was no turning back. The Tran family headed eastward, away from the fallen city, having no idea of what might lie ahead. They only knew that Vietnam was no longer their home.

Main Idea	1		
		Answer	**Score**
	Mark the *main idea*	M	15
	Mark the statement that is *too broad*	B	5
	Mark the statement that is *too narrow*	N	5

a.	The fall of Saigon forced the evacuation of thousands of refugees.	☐ ____
b.	Refugees escaped Saigon by boat.	☐ ____
c.	South Vietnam surrendered to North Vietnam.	☐ ____

Score 15 points for each correct answer.   Score

Subject Matter   2   This passage looks mainly at
☐ a. military maneuvers in Vietnam.
☐ b. the aftermath of the Vietnam war.
☐ c. Vietnamese in the United States.
☐ d. causes of war in Vietnam.

_____

Supporting Details   3   The Tan Son Nhut airport was closed because
☐ a. it was overcrowded with refugees.
☐ b. there were tanks on the runways.
☐ c. the invading North Vietnamese were firing rockets at it.
☐ d. bad weather reduced visibility.

_____

Conclusion   4   The Tran family's main reason for leaving Saigon was that
☐ a. their home had been bombed.
☐ b. they were in danger because Hoang's father had opposed the communists.
☐ c. they wanted to live in America.
☐ d. a war-torn country was no place to raise a child.

_____

Clarifying Devices   5   Which phrase helps clarify the meaning of _Saigon_ in the first sentence?
☐ a. the capital city
☐ b. flee their homeland
☐ c. about to invade
☐ d. The South Vietnamese government

_____

Vocabulary in Context   6   In this passage the word <u>grave</u> means
☐ a. burial place.
☐ b. life-threatening.
☐ c. dignified.
☐ d. important.

_____

Add your scores for questions 1–6. Enter the total here and on the graph on page 217.   Total Score

_____

91 Winning Combinations

Francisca Rodrigues was a fast runner. She considered entering the 100-meter race in the local Teenage Olympics. She learned that 45 people had applied to compete in the race. Francisca wondered how many possible ways there were for this <u>substantial</u> group of runners to win first-, second-, and third-place medals.

Francisca's teacher explained that she could find the number of possible winning arrangements by multiplying. For example, suppose there were just three runners—A, B, and C—in a race. Any of the three would be a possible first-place winner. Once the first-place winner was determined, the two remaining runners would be possible second-place winners. That would leave just one possible third-place winner. So three runners could finish in one of the following ways:

A B C	B C A	C B A
A C B	B A C	C A B

The multiplication equation for this problem is $3 \times 2 \times 1 = 6$.

Since there were 45 entrants in the 100-meter race, there were 45 possibilities for first place. That left 44 second-place possibilities and 43 third-place possibilities. To find out the total number of ways 45 runners could finish first, second, and third Francisca did the following multiplication: $45 \times 44 \times 43$. To her surprise, there were 85,140 possible combinations of first-, second-, and third-place winners.

After qualifying rounds were held, only 10 runners were actually entered in the 100-meter race. Francisca was one of them. To find out the number of possibilities for first-, second-, and third-place combinations of 10 runners, she multiplied $10 \times 9 \times 8$. There were 720 possibilities.

Main Idea   1

	Answer	Score
Mark the *main idea*	**M**	15
Mark the statement that is *too broad*	**B**	5
Mark the statement that is *too narrow*	**N**	5

a. The number of possible arrangements of first-, second-, and third-place winners in a race depends on the number of runners. ☐ _____

b. Francisca was interested in running. ☐ _____

c. With 45 runners, there were 85,140 possible combinations of winners. ☐ _____

182

Subject Matter   2   Another good title for this passage might be
- [ ] a. The 10 Runners.
- [ ] b. The Teenage Olympics.
- [ ] c. Winning Possibilities.
- [ ] d. Winning a Medal.

_____

Supporting Details   3   With 10 runners competing in the 100-meter-race
- [ ] a. there would be more than 85,000 possible arrangements of first-, second-, and third-place winners.
- [ ] b. the field was very crowded.
- [ ] c. there would be 720 possible arrangements of first-, second-, and third-place winners.
- [ ] d. more than three runners are guaranteed to win medals.

_____

Conclusion   4   You could determine the number of ways that a group of 20 runners could place first, second, or third place in a race by
- [ ] a. adding 20 + 19 + 18.
- [ ] b. dividing the number of runners by the number of places.
- [ ] c. multiplying 20 $\times$ 3.
- [ ] d. multiplying 20 $\times$ 19 $\times$ 18.

_____

Clarifying Devices   5   The term _qualifying rounds_ means
- [ ] a. preliminary races run to eliminate contestants.
- [ ] b. the length of time before a race.
- [ ] c. races run in a circle.
- [ ] d. the length and shape of the course.

_____

Vocabulary   6   <u>Substantial</u> means
- [ ] a. superior.
- [ ] b. athletic.
- [ ] c. very large.
- [ ] d. differing from one to another.

_____

Add your scores for questions 1–6. Enter the total here and on the graph on page 217.   **Total Score**

_____

92 Native American Literature

When Europeans began to settle in North America, they brought their language, customs, and literature with them. As a result, some people think of American literature as beginning in the 17th century, not long after the Pilgrims landed at Plymouth Rock. This belief is a serious <u>misconception</u>, however. By that time a thriving literature existed among many of the native peoples of North America.

One of the reasons that Native American literature may not have been noticed immediately is that it was primarily oral, handed down by word of mouth through the generations. Another is that there were more than 200 different groups and languages spread throughout the land.

Many early Native American stories dealt with the origins of the earth. The Huron people, for example, told the tale of a woman falling through a hole in the sky and how the water animals built up a vast island for her to live on. The Iroquois tell a similar story. In the Cherokee creation story, the earth is attached to the sky by four cords, and under the earth is another world that can be approached through mountain springs. There are also stories recounting how specific natural phenomena, such as the Little Dipper constellation in the sky, came to be.

Stories of tricksters were common among some groups. These were clever, sometimes deceitful animals who also performed good works. For example, it was believed that tricksters had brought order to a chaotic world by killing monsters or by bringing the sun or fire to humans. Coyote was the trickster in many stories from the Southwest; Raven was often the trickster in tales from the Pacific Northwest.

Poems and songs were also part of Native American literature. These were used for many purposes, including celebrating, mourning, and worshipping.

Main Idea	1		Answer	Score
	Mark the *main idea*		M	15
	Mark the statement that is *too broad*		B	5
	Mark the statement that is *too narrow*		N	5

a.	Many Native American stories were creation myths.	☐	_____
b.	Native Americans had tales and poems of many types and purposes.	☐	_____
c.	Native Americans told many stories.	☐	_____

Score 15 points for each correct answer. Score

Subject Matter 2 This passage is primarily about
- [ ] a. kinds of early Native American literature.
- [ ] b. tales of tricksters.
- [ ] c. kinds of stories told in different regions.
- [ ] d. why Native American literature was not noticed.

_____

Supporting Details 3 Stories about Raven are frequently found in the
- [ ] a. Midwest.
- [ ] b. Southwest.
- [ ] c. Southeast.
- [ ] d. Northwest.

_____

Conclusion 4 Many Native American stories had to do with
- [ ] a. why the world is as it is.
- [ ] b. war.
- [ ] c. love and romance.
- [ ] d. wicked people.

_____

Clarifying Devices 5 The last three paragraphs present
- [ ] a. lists of important works.
- [ ] b. three basic types of literature.
- [ ] c. stories from three different Native American groups.
- [ ] d. descriptions of Native American life.

_____

Vocabulary in Context 6 A <u>misconception</u> is a
- [ ] a. premature birth.
- [ ] b. mistaken idea.
- [ ] c. missing part or piece.
- [ ] d. large collection of something.

_____

Add your scores for questions 1–6. Enter the total here and on the graph on page 217. Total Score _____

93 Can You Hear This?

When something creates a sound wave in a room or an auditorium, listeners hear the sound wave directly from the source. They also hear the reflections as the sound bounces off the walls, floor, and ceiling. These sounds are called the *reflected wave* or *reverberant sound,* which can be heard even after the sound is no longer coming from the source.

The reverberation time of an auditorium is determined by the volume or interior size of the auditorium. It is also determined by how well or how poorly the walls, ceiling, floor, and contents of the room (including the people) absorb sound. There is no ideal reverberation time, because each use of an auditorium calls for different reverberation. Speech needs to be understood clearly; therefore rooms used for talking must have a short reverberation time. The full-sound performance of music such as Wagner operas or Mahler symphonies should have a long reverberation time. The light, rapid musical passages of Bach or Mozart need a reverberation time somewhere between.

<u>Acoustic</u> problems often are caused by poor auditorium design. Smooth, curved reflecting surfaces, such as domes and curved walls, create large echoes. Parallel walls reflect sound back and forth, creating a rapid, repetitive pulsing effect. Large pillars, corners, and low balconies can cause acoustic shadows as the sound waves try to pass around the object. Some of these problems can be lessened by using absorbers and reflectors to change the reverberation time of a room. For example, hanging large reflectors, called clouds, over the performers will allow some sound frequencies to reflect and others to pass to achieve a pleasing mixture of sound.

Main Idea	1		Answer	Score
	Mark the *main idea*		**M**	15
	Mark the statement that is *too broad*		**B**	5
	Mark the statement that is *too narrow*		**N**	5
	a. Listeners hear sound waves.		☐	_____
	b. Various factors must be considered to get good sound in auditoriums.		☐	_____
	c. Parallel walls make sound bounce back and forth.		☐	_____

Score 15 points for each correct answer.   **Score**

Subject Matter 2 This passage is mainly about
- ☐ a. how the sound of speech differs from the sound of music.
- ☐ b. the types of music orchestras play.
- ☐ c. why auditoriums shouldn't have curved walls.
- ☐ d. how auditoriums should be designed to account for sound waves.

_____

Supporting Details 3 Opera music sounds fuller in an auditorium with
- ☐ a. long reverberation time.
- ☐ b. short reverberation time.
- ☐ c. intermediate reverberation time.
- ☐ d. no reverberation time.

_____

Conclusion 4 This passage suggests that the goal of good auditorium design is to
- ☐ a. achieve a pleasing mixture of sound.
- ☐ b. get rid of all echoes.
- ☐ c. make sure sound is not too loud.
- ☐ d. make auditoriums larger.

_____

Clarifying Devices 5 Large pillars and low balconies
- ☐ a. make sound rich and full.
- ☐ b. are cures for sound problems.
- ☐ c. are sources of sound problems.
- ☐ d. work the same as clouds.

_____

Vocabulary in Context 6 Acoustic means
- ☐ a. located in a large, open room.
- ☐ b. having to do with music.
- ☐ c. having to do with sound.
- ☐ d. overwhelming.

_____

Add your scores for questions 1–6. Enter the total here and on the graph on page 217.   Total Score

_____

94 Resurrecting a Spanish Galleon

Pensacola Bay in the Gulf of Mexico was a landing site for Spanish colonists during the 16th century. Underwater archaeologists were looking for evidence of this fact when in October 1992 they discovered a mound of ballast stones lying on a sandbar. Months of exploration and artifact analysis between 1992 and 1995 led to the conclusion that the wreck was one of the larger vessels in a Spanish fleet led by Captain Tristán de Luna y Arellano.

In 1559 the Luna expedition of 11 ships, loaded with supplies, weapons, 540 soldiers, and 240 horses, left Veracruz, Mexico. It also included more than 1,000 colonists and servants. The expedition's mission was to establish a military colony in what is now the state of Florida. On August 15, the fleet anchored in Pensacola Bay. The colonists went ashore to build a town. On September 19, a hurricane sank eight of the vessels, <u>dooming</u> the young colony.

Evidence of the lives of the unfortunate colonists had been sealed beneath a thick layer of oyster, clam, and mussel shells for nearly 450 years. Archaeologists uncovered leather shoes, butchered animal bones, and a small carved piece of wood in the shape of a 16th-century Spanish galleon. The discovery of a large metal pitcher, copper cooking cauldron, and copper skillet told the archaeologists that they had located the ship's galley. Rat bones, remains of mice, and body parts of cockroaches were evidence of the animal life on board. But there was little evidence of cargo. This probably means that the colonists salvaged what they could after the hurricane.

The Spanish galleon is now listed on the National Register of Historic Places. It offers a historical look at Hispanic sea migration.

Main Idea	1		Answer	Score
	Mark the *main idea*		M	15
	Mark the statement that is *too broad*		B	5
	Mark the statement that is *too narrow*		N	5

a. Underwater archaeologists uncovered a Spanish galleon. ☐ _____

b. The galleon is listed on the National Register of Historic Places. ☐ _____

c. A Spanish galleon gives a look at the lives of 16th-century Hispanic colonists. ☐ _____

Subject Matter 2 This passage is mainly about
- [ ] a. what the wreck showed about the Spanish colonists.
- [ ] b. early settlements around Pensacola.
- [ ] c. the work of underwater archaeologists.
- [ ] d. Captain Tristán de Luna y Arellano.

_____

Supporting Details 3 Archaeologists knew they had found the ship's galley when they uncovered
- [ ] a. a leather shoe.
- [ ] b. a cooking cauldron and skillet.
- [ ] c. mussel shells.
- [ ] d. a map carved in wood.

_____

Conclusion 4 This passage suggests the idea that for early colonists, life was
- [ ] a. easy.
- [ ] b. violent.
- [ ] c. social.
- [ ] d. uncertain.

_____

Clarifying Devices 5 The second paragraph mainly presents
- [ ] a. a personal narrative of the shipwreck.
- [ ] b. a description of the setting.
- [ ] c. events in chronological order.
- [ ] d. comparison and contrast.

_____

Vocabulary in Context 6 <u>Dooming</u> means
- [ ] a. sinking.
- [ ] b. constructing.
- [ ] c. causing a bad outcome.
- [ ] d. arguing to make a point.

_____

Add your scores for questions 1–6. Enter the total here and on the graph on page 217. **Total Score**

_____

95 What a Coincidence!

Janella Molina, a veterinarian, was on a flight from Minneapolis to Albuquerque. Her seatmate was Stephanie Watanabe, a kindergarten teacher who had grown up in Honolulu and now worked in San Diego. The two women were strangers; however, they were about the same age and both were nervous flyers, so they struck up a conversation. When the pilot pointed out a mountain range below, they began talking about Yosemite National Park. Janella's cousin Carmina and her husband Santiago had recently gone camping there with another couple, Santiago's brother and his wife. Stephanie remarked that a first-grade teacher from her school had also recently visited Yosemite and had told Stephanie about a park ranger she had met there named Danielle Boone. Janella was <u>flabbergasted</u> when she heard this, but not just because the ranger's name was humorous. "That's amazing—I think my cousin ran into the same ranger!" she exclaimed. Soon Janella and Stephanie figured out something even more incredible: Stephanie's co-worker was none other than Carmina's sister-in-law (she was married to Janella's cousin's husband's brother)!

It's likely that this story reminds you of a similar occurrence in your own life. In fact, everyone you know probably has a comparable anecdote to relate. This is because of the simple mathematics behind such coincidences, which really aren't so remarkable after all. Let's say you know about 1,500 people who are somewhat spread out around the United States. You meet a stranger and discover that one of the people you know knows one of the people he or she knows. If the stranger, like you, knows about 1,500 people, then there are $1,500 \times 1,500$ (or 2,250,000) opportunities for connections among your friends, family members, and acquaintances and those of the stranger. It is likely that at least one connection will exist.

Main Idea	1			
			Answer	**Score**
	Mark the *main idea*		M	15
	Mark the statement that is *too broad*		B	5
	Mark the statement that is *too narrow*		N	5

a. Janella's cousin and Stephanie's co-worker were at Yosemite together. ☐ ____

b. It is likely that two strangers will find people they know in common. ☐ ____

c. Coincidences occur quite often. ☐ ____

Subject Matter   **2** This passage is primarily about
- [ ] a. making friends on airline flights.
- [ ] b. multiplying large numbers.
- [ ] c. the likelihood of connections between strangers.
- [ ] d. how amazing it is that Janella had a connection to Stephanie.

_____

Supporting Details   **3** Janella and Stephanie were connected because
- [ ] a. one's cousin had married the other's brother.
- [ ] b. they both knew Danielle Boone.
- [ ] c. they had each visited Yosemite.
- [ ] d. they knew people who visited Yosemite at the same time.

_____

Conclusion   **4** The writer wants us to conclude that
- [ ] a. coincidences are not as amazing as we think.
- [ ] b. coincidences are even more remarkable than we think.
- [ ] c. Janella and Stephanie had met before.
- [ ] d. Danielle Boone was from Kentucky.

_____

Clarifying Devices   **5** The first paragraph is developed mainly through
- [ ] a. comparing and contrasting.
- [ ] b. listing the steps in a process.
- [ ] c. relating an anecdote.
- [ ] d. providing details to support a main idea.

_____

Vocabulary in Context   **6** The word <u>flabbergasted</u> means
- [ ] a. obese.
- [ ] b. surprised.
- [ ] c. amused.
- [ ] d. frightened.

_____

Add your scores for questions 1–6. Enter the total here and on the graph on page 217.   **Total Score**   _____

96 Dance, Medieval Style

Movies set in the Middle Ages frequently take place in elegant castles, with characters typically wearing elaborate embroidered or brocade costumes. For entertainment these characters often attend formal dances or masked balls, where they flirt <u>covertly</u>. In fact, these portrayals of upper-class amusement are fairly close to reality.

At a typical 16th-century formal dance in England, France, or Italy, you might hear recognizable instruments such as the flute, but you might also encounter less familiar instruments such as the lute or clavichord. A lute is a pear-shaped stringed instrument similar to a guitar; a clavichord resembles a piano. Both instruments emit a narrower, "tinnier" sound than their present-day counterparts.

At certain points during the evening a singer might entertain, singing either unaccompanied or with a lute played in the background. A sweet, melancholy love song was often the music of choice.

For the actual dancing, a common practice at the time was to group two dances together—one slow and dignified, the other quicker. Two frequently paired dances were the *pavane* and the *galliard,* both of which might look a little strange to a modern audience. In the slow, stately pavane, lines of couples circulated around a dance floor taking steps forward and backward, swaying from side to side as they moved. The lively galliard, which might be done by either singles or couples, was composed of four hopping steps followed by a high leap.

Generally in these formal dances partners danced side by side; if they faced each other, they did not touch. The introduction of a dance called *la volta,* a variation of the galliard, scandalized some people because the couple moved in a close embrace.

Main Idea	1		Answer	Score
		Mark the *main idea*	M	15
		Mark the statement that is *too broad*	B	5
		Mark the statement that is *too narrow*	N	5
	a.	People have always liked to dance.	☐	_____
	b.	Sixteenth-century music and dance might seem unfamiliar today.	☐	_____
	c.	Slow dances were frequently paired with livelier ones.	☐	_____

Subject Matter   **2**   Another good title for this passage might be
☐ a. The Lute and the Clavichord.
☐ b. The *Pavane* and the *Galliard*.
☐ c. A Formal Dance in the Middle Ages.
☐ d. Singing and Dancing in Everyday Life.   _____

Supporting Details   **3**   The pavane was a
☐ a. musical instrument.
☐ b. type of song.
☐ c. quick dance.
☐ d. slow dance.   _____

Conclusion   **4**   The galliard was probably danced mostly by
☐ a. old people.
☐ b. couples in a close embrace.
☐ c. little girls.
☐ d. energetic young people.   _____

Clarifying Devices   **5**   A term that is *not* defined in this passage is
☐ a. pavane.
☐ b. flute.
☐ c. lute.
☐ d. galliard.   _____

Vocabulary in Context   **6**   The word <u>covertly</u> means
☐ a. secretly.
☐ b. noisily.
☐ c. sadly.
☐ d. angrily.   _____

Add your scores for questions 1–6. Enter the total here and on the graph on page 217.   **Total Score**   _____

97 Genetic Engineering

Genetic engineering began when the DNA molecule, the most basic unit of life, was first described in 1953 by James Watson and Francis Crick. An understanding of DNA led to the altering of normal cell reproduction. Experiments with altering human cells began in 1970. In one of the first experiments, patients were injected with a virus that would produce a life-saving enzyme, but their bodies would not accept it. In 1980 patients with a rare but fatal blood disease were injected with a purified gene that was cloned through DNA technology. Another failure.

Genetic engineering got a legal boost in 1980. The U.S. Supreme Court said that a patent could be granted on a genetically engineered "oil-eating" bacterium. This bacterium would help clean up oil spills. The ruling encouraged companies to invent new life forms, and three important medical products were quickly developed.

- **Human interferon**—a possible solution to some cancers and viral diseases. A newly engineered bacterium produced human interferon as a by-product. This new product reduced the cost of interferon.
- **Human growth hormone**—for children whose bodies do not grow to normal height. An expensive growth hormone was previously produced from human cadavers, but by changing the genetic make-up of the single-cell bacterium *E. coli,* an affordable growth hormone could be produced.
- **Human insulin**—for the treatment of diabetes. People with diabetes used to rely on a beef- or pork-based product until 1982. Now insulin can be manufactured by genetically altered bacteria.

Advances in genetic engineering have continued, though these constantly must be <u>weighed</u> against the safety of procedures. There is clearly much more to discover.

Main Idea   1

	Answer	Score
Mark the *main idea*	M	15
Mark the statement that is *too broad*	B	5
Mark the statement that is *too narrow*	N	5

a. Despite failures, genetic engineering has produced some useful products. ☐ _____

b. DNA knowledge keeps growing. ☐ _____

c. Interferon was developed as a result of genetic engineering. ☐ _____

Score 15 points for each correct answer. Score

Subject Matter 2 This passage is mainly about
☐ a. the human growth hormone.
☐ b. the effects of altering cells.
☐ c. insulin.
☐ d. U.S. Supreme Court rulings. _____

Supporting Details 3 Interferon
☐ a. is a hormone.
☐ b. has been used in the treatment of cancer.
☐ c. is a disease.
☐ d. has been cured. _____

Conclusion 4 Genetic engineering may be defined as
☐ a. the altering of normal cell reproduction.
☐ b. the production of all medicine.
☐ c. a procedure that holds little promise.
☐ d. life-saving enzymes. _____

Clarifying Devices 5 In this passage, the genetically engineered medical products are presented
☐ a. as a process.
☐ b. from earliest to latest.
☐ c. in a simple list.
☐ d. in a personal narrative. _____

Vocabulary in Context 6 In this passage <u>weighed</u> means
☐ a. had great influence.
☐ b. became a burden.
☐ c. determined the heaviness of.
☐ d. considered carefully. _____

Add your scores for questions 1–6. Enter the total here and on the graph on page 217. Total Score _____

98 Who Planned This Park?

Frederick Law Olmsted (1822–1903), a Connecticut farm boy, saw his first public park in Liverpool, England, as he accompanied his brother on a walking tour. He was impressed by the park's winding paths, open fields, lakes, and bridges. Perhaps the most wondrous thing of all was that the park was open to everyone.

A movement beginning in 1840 to set aside park land on New York City's Manhattan Island successfully culminated in 1856 with the purchase of 840 acres of rocky and swampy land, bought with about $5 million in state funds. Olmsted's chance meeting with a project organizer led to his applying for the job of park superintendent. In 1857 Olmsted was appointed superintendent of the proposed park, and the clearing of the site began. But a park needs a plan, so the park commissioners offered a $2,000 prize for a winning design.

Calvert Vaux, a British architect, asked Olmsted to <u>collaborate</u> with him on a park design, and Olmsted agreed. Vaux saw the park as a work of art, while Olmsted saw the park as a place for people to escape the bustle and noise of the city. Together they devised a plan that would give city dwellers a tranquil, green park and would also preserve and enhance the natural features of the land. The commissioners voted in favor of Vaux and Olmsted's plan, and in 1858, the two became the official designers of New York City's Central Park.

It took millions of cartloads of topsoil to build Central Park's gentle slopes, shady glens, and steep, rocky ravines. Five million trees and shrubs were planted, a water-supply system was laid, and bridges, arches, roads, and paths were constructed. The park officially opened in 1876, and today, well over a century later, people still escape the bustle and noise of the city in Olmsted and Vaux's great work of art.

Main Idea   1

	Answer	Score
Mark the *main idea*	M	15
Mark the statement that is *too broad*	B	5
Mark the statement that is *too narrow*	N	5

a. Olmstead and Vaux planned and designed Central Park. ☐ _____

b. Olmstead and Vaux built shady glens and rocky ravines. ☐ _____

c. New York City needed parks. ☐ _____

Score 15 points for each correct answer. **Score**

Subject Matter **2** This passage is mainly
☐ a. a biography of Frederick Law Olmsted.
☐ b. an engineering plan for Central Park.
☐ c. a history of the planning of Central Park.
☐ d. a guided walking tour of Central Park. _____

Supporting Details **3** Olmsted became superintendent of Central Park because of
☐ a. a chance meeting with one of the park's organizers.
☐ b. his winning a design competition.
☐ c. his friendship with Calvert Vaux.
☐ d. his hard work in clearing the land. _____

Conclusion **4** The phrase "great work of art" in the last sentence indicates that the writer thinks Central Park
☐ a. is only for people who can afford it.
☐ b. is a beautiful place.
☐ c. is like a museum.
☐ d. should be looked at but not touched. _____

Clarifying Devices **5** The basic organization of this passage is
☐ a. personal narrative.
☐ b. from latest event to earliest.
☐ c. from earliest event to latest.
☐ d. comparison and contrast. _____

Vocabulary in Context **6** The word <u>collaborate</u> means
☐ a. vote.
☐ b. comment.
☐ c. disagree.
☐ d. work together. _____

Add your scores for questions 1–6. Enter the total here and on the graph on page 217. **Total Score** _____

99 Avoiding Supermarket Booby Traps

On your next visit to your local supermarket, be aware that it has probably been booby trapped (by marketing experts) with ingenious features designed to lengthen your stay and entice you to spend your money freely.

What sights and smells greet you upon entering a supermarket? Chances are it's those of the bakery or floral section. Exquisitely displayed bouquets or freshly baked cinnamon rolls can send <u>subliminal</u> messages to customers: "This is a classy store! Go ahead and pamper yourself—you deserve a treat! Who cares about the cost?"

If parents are softhearted and their kids are drawn to bright packages decorated with zany cartoon characters, it's probably best to leave the kids at home. Many stores place "kid friendly" products such as sugary breakfast cereals where kids are most likely to see them—and begin clamoring for them. Don't be surprised if you have to stretch to reach the Health Farm High-Fiber Crunchies, while the Sugar-Sparkled Choco Krispies are right there at children's eye level.

Supermarkets profit when patrons linger longer. That's why you'll often see cartons of merchandise stacked artistically in the aisles, partially blocking your way and creating a warehouse atmosphere that whispers "This store is chock-full of bargains!" Impulse buys such as pricey gourmet salad dressing or expensive imported marmalade are usually prominently placed at the very beginning of an aisle or on an endcap, a special display area at the head or foot of an aisle.

If you're interested in saving money, practice dodging these marketing booby traps. One possible antidote to impulse buying is to eat heartily *before* you go grocery shopping. Just think how smug you'll feel when you outsmart the marketing experts!

Main Idea	1	Answer	Score
	Mark the *main idea*	M	15
	Mark the statement that is *too broad*	B	5
	Mark the statement that is *too narrow*	N	5
	a. Marketing makes people buy.	☐	___
	b. "Kid friendly" products are placed at kids' eye level.	☐	___
	c. Be aware of marketing methods used in supermarkets.	☐	___

Score 15 points for each correct answer.   **Score**

Subject Matter   2   This passage is mainly about
    ☐ a. marketing experts.
    ☐ b. flowers sold in supermarkets.
    ☐ c. supermarket architecture.
    ☐ d. supermarket marketing techniques.   _____

Supporting Details   3   An endcap is a display area located
    ☐ a. in front of a supermarket.
    ☐ b. in the middle of an aisle, at eye level.
    ☐ c. at children's eye level.
    ☐ d. at the head or foot of an aisle.   _____

Conclusion   4   The writer probably wants to help readers
    ☐ a. locate supermarkets that do not use marketing techniques.
    ☐ b. know the challenges of store design.
    ☐ c. avoid buying items they don't really need.
    ☐ d. learn how to become supermarket managers.   _____

Clarifying Devices   5   The writer uses the idea of booby traps to
    ☐ a. remind shoppers to avoid slipping on slick floors.
    ☐ b. represent marketing techniques.
    ☐ c. represent methods of saving money.
    ☐ d. suggest that supermarkets have poor safety records.   _____

Vocabulary in Context   6   In this passage <u>subliminal</u> means
    ☐ a. fragrant.
    ☐ b. unconscious.
    ☐ c. bright.
    ☐ d. garbled.   _____

Add your scores for questions 1–6. Enter the total here   **Total**
and on the graph on page 217.   **Score**   _____

100 A Play for Every Decade

For many writers, composing stories or plays is a part-time endeavor: to support themselves they take on other jobs such as teaching. It is one sign of August Wilson's success that for many years he has been able to make a living solely by writing plays.

Wilson was born in Pittsburgh and dropped out of school in the ninth grade. He was an avid reader, however, and continued his education by reading library books, learning about black nationalist movements of the time, and closely observing the lives of the inhabitants of the poor community in which he resided.

In the late 1960s Wilson collaborated in establishing a theater company called Black Horizons and began to think of ways to portray African-American life on the stage. He conceived of the idea of a cycle of plays, each set in a different decade of the 20th century, that demonstrate how African-American life has evolved.

The first successful play of this series was *Ma Rainey's Black Bottom.* Dealing with black musicians in Chicago in the 1920s, it demonstrates their frustration at being excluded from white society. Other plays in the series include *Joe Turner's Come and Gone,* about blacks in the 1910s who have migrated north to Pittsburgh in search of a new identity; *Fences,* which focuses on a father-son conflict in the 1950s; and *The Piano Lesson,* about a 1930s family that hesitates to sell the family's heirloom. For the last two of these plays Wilson was awarded Pulitzer Prizes.

Wilson has written eight plays in his cycle, the most recent being *King Hedley the Second,* a play set in the 1980s, written in 1999. The appeal of his plays is not limited to black audiences; with their strong undercurrents of blues, jazz, and black history and mythology, they <u>engage</u> anyone who is interested in the African-American experience.

Main Idea	1		
		Answer	**Score**
	Mark the *main idea*	M	15
	Mark the statement that is *too broad*	B	5
	Mark the statement that is *too narrow*	N	5
	a. August Wilson wrote many plays.	☐	____
	b. August Wilson planned a play for every decade of the 20th century.	☐	____
	c. August Wilson founded a theater company called Black Horizons.	☐	____

Score 15 points for each correct answer. Score

Subject Matter 2 Another good title for this passage is
☐ a. A Whole Series of Plays.
☐ b. Growing Up in Pittsburgh.
☐ c. A Part-Time Playwright.
☐ d. Plays for the New Century.
_____

Supporting Details 3 Wilson won Pulitzer Prizes for
☐ a. *Ma Rainey's Black Bottom* and *Fences.*
☐ b. *The Piano Lesson* and *Fences.*
☐ c. *The Piano Lesson* and *King Hedley the Second.*
☐ d. *King Hedley the Second* and *Joe Turner's Come and Gone.*
_____

Conclusion 4 It is likely that in his series of 20th-century plays Wilson plans to write
☐ a. no more.
☐ b. two more.
☐ c. three more.
☐ d. four more.
_____

Clarifying Devices 5 The writer explains Wilson's play cycle by
☐ a. telling why he decided to write it.
☐ b. presenting a list of its titles in order.
☐ c. telling which plays won prizes.
☐ d. naming some of the plays and telling what they are about.
_____

Vocabulary in Context 6 In this passage <u>engage</u> means
☐ a. plan to marry.
☐ b. keep busy.
☐ c. set a date for a meeting.
☐ d. cause interest in.
_____

Add your scores for questions 1–6. Enter the total here and on the graph on page 217. Total Score _____

Answer Keys

Answer Key: Passages 1–25

Passage 1:	1a. **B**	1b. **N**	1c. **M**	2. **b**	3. **b**	4. **a**	5. **a**	6. **c**
Passage 2:	1a. **M**	1b. **N**	1c. **B**	2. **b**	3. **d**	4. **a**	5. **b**	6. **c**
Passage 3:	1a. **M**	1b. **B**	1c. **N**	2. **d**	3. **b**	4. **a**	5. **c**	6. **c**
Passage 4:	1a. **M**	1b. **N**	1c. **B**	2. **c**	3. **c**	4. **c**	5. **d**	6. **a**
Passage 5:	1a. **M**	1b. **N**	1c. **B**	2. **a**	3. **d**	4. **a**	5. **d**	6. **c**
Passage 6:	1a. **N**	1b. **M**	1c. **B**	2. **d**	3. **b**	4. **d**	5. **b**	6. **d**
Passage 7:	1a. **N**	1b. **M**	1c. **B**	2. **c**	3. **c**	4. **b**	5. **a**	6. **d**
Passage 8:	1a. **N**	1b. **M**	1c. **B**	2. **d**	3. **a**	4. **b**	5. **a**	6. **b**
Passage 9:	1a. **N**	1b. **B**	1c. **M**	2. **c**	3. **d**	4. **a**	5. **a**	6. **b**
Passage 10:	1a. **M**	1b. **N**	1c. **B**	2. **a**	3. **d**	4. **a**	5. **a**	6. **b**
Passage 11:	1a. **N**	1b. **B**	1c. **M**	2. **a**	3. **c**	4. **b**	5. **d**	6. **c**
Passage 12:	1a. **B**	1b. **N**	1c. **M**	2. **c**	3. **b**	4. **d**	5. **b**	6. **d**
Passage 13:	1a. **B**	1b. **M**	1c. **N**	2. **b**	3. **b**	4. **b**	5. **a**	6. **d**
Passage 14:	1a. **M**	1b. **N**	1c. **B**	2. **a**	3. **c**	4. **a**	5. **c**	6. **d**
Passage 15:	1a. **M**	1b. **N**	1c. **B**	2. **d**	3. **c**	4. **c**	5. **a**	6. **b**
Passage 16:	1a. **M**	1b. **B**	1c. **N**	2. **d**	3. **a**	4. **a**	5. **d**	6. **c**
Passage 17:	1a. **N**	1b. **M**	1c. **B**	2. **b**	3. **d**	4. **a**	5. **b**	6. **c**
Passage 18:	1a. **M**	1b. **B**	1c. **N**	2. **b**	3. **d**	4. **a**	5. **c**	6. **b**
Passage 19:	1a. **M**	1b. **B**	1c. **N**	2. **a**	3. **c**	4. **d**	5. **c**	6. **c**
Passage 20:	1a. **B**	1b. **M**	1c. **N**	2. **b**	3. **a**	4. **c**	5. **d**	6. **a**
Passage 21:	1a. **B**	1b. **M**	1c. **N**	2. **a**	3. **a**	4. **d**	5. **c**	6. **c**
Passage 22:	1a. **N**	1b. **M**	1c. **B**	2. **b**	3. **c**	4. **b**	5. **a**	6. **d**
Passage 23:	1a. **N**	1b. **B**	1c. **M**	2. **c**	3. **d**	4. **a**	5. **c**	6. **b**
Passage 24:	1a. **B**	1b. **M**	1c. **N**	2. **b**	3. **b**	4. **c**	5. **a**	6. **c**
Passage 25:	1a. **N**	1b. **M**	1c. **B**	2. **c**	3. **c**	4. **b**	5. **c**	6. **a**

Answer Key: Passages 26–50

Passage 26:   1a. **M**   1b. **B**   1c. **N**   2. **b**   3. **c**   4. **a**   5. **b**   6. **d**

Passage 27:   1a. **N**   1b. **M**   1c. **B**   2. **d**   3. **b**   4. **b**   5. **a**   6. **c**

Passage 28:   1a. **B**   1b. **M**   1c. **N**   2. **a**   3. **a**   4. **a**   5. **c**   6. **b**

Passage 29:   1a. **B**   1b. **N**   1c. **M**   2. **c**   3. **a**   4. **c**   5. **a**   6. **d**

Passage 30:   1a. **B**   1b. **M**   1c. **N**   2. **c**   3. **a**   4. **c**   5. **a**   6. **b**

Passage 31:   1a. **N**   1b. **M**   1c. **B**   2. **c**   3. **a**   4. **b**   5. **b**   6. **a**

Passage 32:   1a. **B**   1b. **M**   1c. **N**   2. **c**   3. **b**   4. **a**   5. **c**   6. **a**

Passage 33:   1a. **B**   1b. **N**   1c. **M**   2. **a**   3. **a**   4. **c**   5. **b**   6. **a**

Passage 34:   1a. **B**   1b. **N**   1c. **M**   2. **d**   3. **a**   4. **b**   5. **a**   6. **b**

Passage 35:   1a. **B**   1b. **N**   1c. **M**   2. **b**   3. **d**   4. **b**   5. **a**   6. **c**

Passage 36:   1a. **N**   1b. **B**   1c. **M**   2. **b**   3. **d**   4. **c**   5. **a**   6. **a**

Passage 37:   1a. **B**   1b. **N**   1c. **M**   2. **a**   3. **b**   4. **b**   5. **c**   6. **b**

Passage 38:   1a. **M**   1b. **B**   1c. **N**   2. **b**   3. **c**   4. **c**   5. **a**   6. **b**

Passage 39:   1a. **N**   1b. **M**   1c. **B**   2. **b**   3. **d**   4. **b**   5. **b**   6. **b**

Passage 40:   1a. **M**   1b. **B**   1c. **N**   2. **c**   3. **d**   4. **a**   5. **b**   6. **c**

Passage 41:   1a. **N**   1b. **B**   1c. **M**   2. **d**   3. **c**   4. **c**   5. **b**   6. **a**

Passage 42:   1a. **B**   1b. **M**   1c. **N**   2. **a**   3. **c**   4. **b**   5. **b**   6. **d**

Passage 43:   1a. **M**   1b. **N**   1c. **B**   2. **c**   3. **d**   4. **b**   5. **b**   6. **a**

Passage 44:   1a. **N**   1b. **M**   1c. **B**   2. **a**   3. **c**   4. **b**   5. **a**   6. **d**

Passage 45:   1a. **B**   1b. **M**   1c. **N**   2. **c**   3. **b**   4. **b**   5. **c**   6. **b**

Passage 46:   1a. **B**   1b. **M**   1c. **N**   2. **d**   3. **b**   4. **c**   5. **a**   6. **a**

Passage 47:   1a. **N**   1b. **M**   1c. **B**   2. **c**   3. **d**   4. **b**   5. **d**   6. **d**

Passage 48:   1a. **N**   1b. **M**   1c. **B**   2. **c**   3. **b**   4. **c**   5. **a**   6. **c**

Passage 49:   1a. **B**   1b. **M**   1c. **N**   2. **a**   3. **c**   4. **c**   5. **b**   6. **d**

Passage 50:   1a. **M**   1b. **N**   1c. **B**   2. **d**   3. **b**   4. **a**   5. **b**   6. **b**

Answer Key: Passages 51–75

Passage 51:	1a. **B**	1b. **M**	1c. **N**	2. **c**	3. **a**	4. **d**	5. **b**	6. **c**
Passage 52:	1a. **M**	1b. **N**	1c. **B**	2. **d**	3. **c**	4. **a**	5. **b**	6. **c**
Passage 53:	1a. **M**	1b. **B**	1c. **N**	2. **d**	3. **a**	4. **a**	5. **b**	6. **c**
Passage 54:	1a. **M**	1b. **B**	1c. **N**	2. **b**	3. **d**	4. **b**	5. **c**	6. **a**
Passage 55:	1a. **B**	1b. **M**	1c. **N**	2. **a**	3. **c**	4. **b**	5. **a**	6. **a**
Passage 56:	1a. **N**	1b. **M**	1c. **B**	2. **d**	3. **b**	4. **d**	5. **a**	6. **b**
Passage 57:	1a. **M**	1b. **N**	1c. **B**	2. **b**	3. **c**	4. **a**	5. **b**	6. **d**
Passage 58:	1a. **N**	1b. **B**	1c. **M**	2. **c**	3. **a**	4. **d**	5. **a**	6. **b**
Passage 59:	1a. **M**	1b. **B**	1c. **N**	2. **a**	3. **b**	4. **c**	5. **d**	6. **c**
Passage 60:	1a. **M**	1b. **B**	1c. **N**	2. **b**	3. **a**	4. **d**	5. **b**	6. **a**
Passage 61:	1a. **B**	1b. **N**	1c. **M**	2. **d**	3. **c**	4. **d**	5. **b**	6. **a**
Passage 62:	1a. **B**	1b. **N**	1c. **M**	2. **b**	3. **c**	4. **a**	5. **c**	6. **d**
Passage 63:	1a. **B**	1b. **N**	1c. **M**	2. **a**	3. **b**	4. **c**	5. **a**	6. **c**
Passage 64:	1a. **N**	1b. **B**	1c. **M**	2. **a**	3. **b**	4. **b**	5. **a**	6. **c**
Passage 65:	1a. **B**	1b. **M**	1c. **N**	2. **c**	3. **d**	4. **d**	5. **d**	6. **a**
Passage 66:	1a. **M**	1b. **B**	1c. **N**	2. **a**	3. **c**	4. **c**	5. **d**	6. **b**
Passage 67:	1a. **B**	1b. **M**	1c. **N**	2. **b**	3. **c**	4. **a**	5. **b**	6. **a**
Passage 68:	1a. **B**	1b. **M**	1c. **N**	2. **d**	3. **c**	4. **a**	5. **b**	6. **d**
Passage 69:	1a. **N**	1b. **M**	1c. **B**	2. **a**	3. **b**	4. **a**	5. **b**	6. **a**
Passage 70:	1a. **N**	1b. **B**	1c. **M**	2. **b**	3. **d**	4. **c**	5. **c**	6. **a**
Passage 71:	1a. **N**	1b. **B**	1c. **M**	2. **c**	3. **b**	4. **b**	5. **a**	6. **a**
Passage 72:	1a. **B**	1b. **N**	1c. **M**	2. **a**	3. **b**	4. **c**	5. **d**	6. **c**
Passage 73:	1a. **B**	1b. **N**	1c. **M**	2. **a**	3. **b**	4. **a**	5. **a**	6. **b**
Passage 74:	1a. **N**	1b. **B**	1c. **M**	2. **b**	3. **c**	4. **b**	5. **b**	6. **d**
Passage 75:	1a. **B**	1b. **M**	1c. **N**	2. **d**	3. **d**	4. **a**	5. **d**	6. **a**

Answer Key: Passages 76–100

Passage 76:	1a. **N**	1b. **B**	1c. **M**	2. **a**	3. **b**	4. **a**	5. **a**	6. **b**
Passage 77:	1a. **M**	1b. **B**	1c. **N**	2. **d**	3. **c**	4. **b**	5. **c**	6. **a**
Passage 78:	1a. **N**	1b. **B**	1c. **M**	2. **c**	3. **a**	4. **c**	5. **b**	6. **d**
Passage 79:	1a. **N**	1b. **B**	1c. **M**	2. **b**	3. **d**	4. **c**	5. **a**	6. **d**
Passage 80:	1a. **M**	1b. **N**	1c. **B**	2. **b**	3. **c**	4. **a**	5. **a**	6. **c**
Passage 81:	1a. **B**	1b. **M**	1c. **N**	2. **c**	3. **a**	4. **c**	5. **a**	6. **d**
Passage 82:	1a. **B**	1b. **N**	1c. **M**	2. **c**	3. **a**	4. **d**	5. **c**	6. **c**
Passage 83:	1a. **N**	1b. **B**	1c. **M**	2. **a**	3. **b**	4. **d**	5. **a**	6. **d**
Passage 84:	1a. **N**	1b. **M**	1c. **B**	2. **a**	3. **b**	4. **d**	5. **c**	6. **c**
Passage 85:	1a. **N**	1b. **B**	1c. **M**	2. **d**	3. **c**	4. **a**	5. **c**	6. **c**
Passage 86:	1a. **N**	1b. **B**	1c. **M**	2. **a**	3. **d**	4. **a**	5. **b**	6. **c**
Passage 87:	1a. **M**	1b. **N**	1c. **B**	2. **b**	3. **c**	4. **d**	5. **b**	6. **b**
Passage 88:	1a. **B**	1b. **M**	1c. **N**	2. **b**	3. **d**	4. **b**	5. **a**	6. **d**
Passage 89:	1a. **B**	1b. **N**	1c. **M**	2. **c**	3. **d**	4. **a**	5. **a**	6. **b**
Passage 90:	1a. **M**	1b. **N**	1c. **B**	2. **b**	3. **c**	4. **b**	5. **a**	6. **b**
Passage 91:	1a. **M**	1b. **B**	1c. **N**	2. **c**	3. **c**	4. **d**	5. **a**	6. **c**
Passage 92:	1a. **N**	1b. **M**	1c. **B**	2. **a**	3. **d**	4. **a**	5. **b**	6. **b**
Passage 93:	1a. **B**	1b. **M**	1c. **N**	2. **d**	3. **a**	4. **a**	5. **c**	6. **c**
Passage 94:	1a. **B**	1b. **N**	1c. **M**	2. **a**	3. **b**	4. **d**	5. **c**	6. **c**
Passage 95:	1a. **N**	1b. **M**	1c. **B**	2. **c**	3. **d**	4. **a**	5. **c**	6. **b**
Passage 96:	1a. **B**	1b. **M**	1c. **N**	2. **c**	3. **d**	4. **d**	5. **b**	6. **a**
Passage 97:	1a. **M**	1b. **B**	1c. **N**	2. **b**	3. **b**	4. **a**	5. **c**	6. **d**
Passage 98:	1a. **M**	1b. **N**	1c. **B**	2. **c**	3. **a**	4. **b**	5. **c**	6. **d**
Passage 99:	1a. **B**	1b. **N**	1c. **M**	2. **d**	3. **d**	4. **c**	5. **b**	6. **b**
Passage 100:	1a. **B**	1b. **M**	1c. **N**	2. **a**	3. **b**	4. **b**	5. **d**	6. **d**

Diagnostic Charts
For Student Correction

Diagnostic Chart: Passages 1–25

Directions: For each passage, write your answers to the left of the dotted line in the blocks for each skill category. Then correct your answers using the Answer Key on page 204. If your answer is correct, do not make any more marks in the block. If your answer is incorrect, write the letter of the correct answer to the right of the dotted line.

	Categories of Comprehension Skills								
	1 Main Idea				**2**	**3**	**4**	**5**	**6**
	Statement a	Statement b	Statement c	Subject Matter	Supporting Details	Conclusion	Clarifying Devices	Vocabulary in Context	
Passage 1									
Passage 2									
Passage 3									
Passage 4									
Passage 5									
Passage 6									
Passage 7									
Passage 8									
Passage 9									
Passage 10									
Passage 11									
Passage 12									
Passage 13									
Passage 14									
Passage 15									
Passage 16									
Passage 17									
Passage 18									
Passage 19									
Passage 20									
Passage 21									
Passage 22									
Passage 23									
Passage 24									
Passage 25									

Diagnostic Chart: Passages 26–50

Directions: For each passage, write your answers to the left of the dotted line in the blocks for each skill category. Then correct your answers using the Answer Key on page 205. If your answer is correct, do not make any more marks in the block. If your answer is incorrect, write the letter of the correct answer to the right of the dotted line.

	Categories of Comprehension Skills								
	1 Main Idea				2	3	4	5	6
	Statement a	Statement b	Statement c	Subject Matter	Supporting Details	Conclusion	Clarifying Devices	Vocabulary in Context	
Passage 26									
Passage 27									
Passage 28									
Passage 29									
Passage 30									
Passage 31									
Passage 32									
Passage 33									
Passage 34									
Passage 35									
Passage 36									
Passage 37									
Passage 38									
Passage 39									
Passage 40									
Passage 41									
Passage 42									
Passage 43									
Passage 44									
Passage 45									
Passage 46									
Passage 47									
Passage 48									
Passage 49									
Passage 50									

Diagnostic Chart: Passages 51–75

Directions: For each passage, write your answers to the left of the dotted line in the blocks for each skill category. Then correct your answers using the Answer Key on page 206. If your answer is correct, do not make any more marks in the block. If your answer is incorrect, write the letter of the correct answer to the right of the dotted line.

	Categories of Comprehension Skills								
	1 Main Idea				2	3	4	5	6
	Statement a	Statement b	Statement c	Subject Matter	Supporting Details	Conclusion	Clarifying Devices	Vocabulary in Context	
Passage 51									
Passage 52									
Passage 53									
Passage 54									
Passage 55									
Passage 56									
Passage 57									
Passage 58									
Passage 59									
Passage 60									
Passage 61									
Passage 62									
Passage 63									
Passage 64									
Passage 65									
Passage 66									
Passage 67									
Passage 68									
Passage 69									
Passage 70									
Passage 71									
Passage 72									
Passage 73									
Passage 74									
Passage 75									

Diagnostic Chart: Passages 76–100

Directions: For each passage, write your answers to the left of the dotted line in the blocks for each skill category. Then correct your answers using the Answer Key on page 207. If your answer is correct, do not make any more marks in the block. If your answer is incorrect, write the letter of the correct answer to the right of the dotted line.

	Categories of Comprehension Skills								
	1 Main Idea				2	3	4	5	6
	Statement a	Statement b	Statement c	Subject Matter	Supporting Details	Conclusion	Clarifying Devices	Vocabulary in Context	
Passage 76									
Passage 77									
Passage 78									
Passage 79									
Passage 80									
Passage 81									
Passage 82									
Passage 83									
Passage 84									
Passage 85									
Passage 86									
Passage 87									
Passage 88									
Passage 89									
Passage 90									
Passage 91									
Passage 92									
Passage 93									
Passage 94									
Passage 95									
Passage 96									
Passage 97									
Passage 98									
Passage 99									
Passage 100									

Progress Graphs

Progress Graph: Passages 1–25

Directions: Write your Total Score for each passage in the comprehension score box under the number of the passage. Then plot your score on the graph itself by putting a small *x* on the line directly above the number of the passage, across from the score you got for that passage. As you mark your score for each passage, graph your progress by drawing a line to connect the *x*'s.

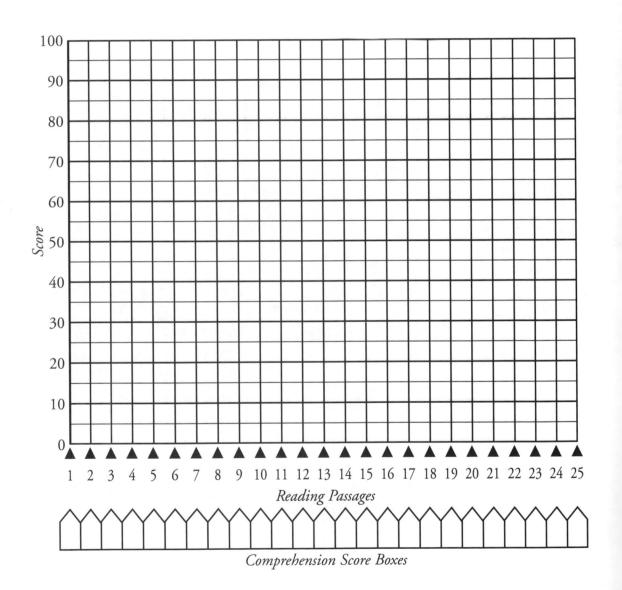

Progress Graph: Passages 26–50

Directions: Write your Total Score for each passage in the comprehension score box under the number of the passage. Then plot your score on the graph itself by putting a small *x* on the line directly above the number of the passage, across from the score you got for that passage. As you mark your score for each passage, graph your progress by drawing a line to connect the *x*'s.

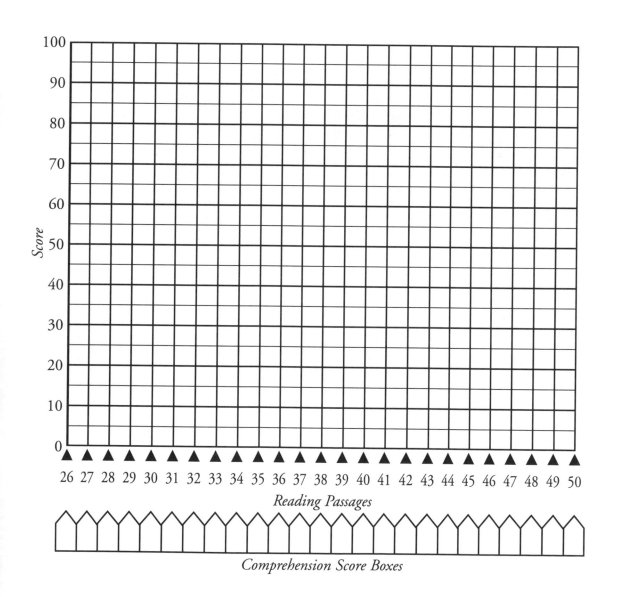

Reading Passages

Comprehension Score Boxes

Progress Graph: Passages 51–75

Directions: Write your Total Score for each passage in the comprehension score box under the number of the passage. Then plot your score on the graph itself by putting a small *x* on the line directly above the number of the passage, across from the score you got for that passage. As you mark your score for each passage, graph your progress by drawing a line to connect the *x*'s.

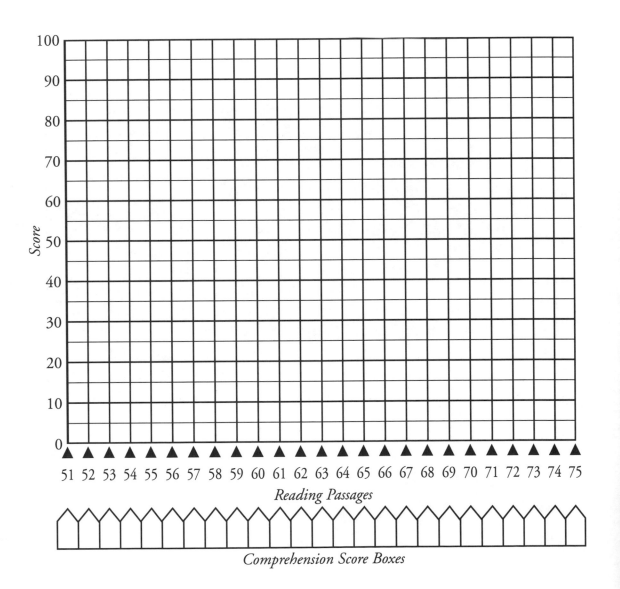

Reading Passages

Comprehension Score Boxes

Progress Graph: Passages 76–100

Directions: Write your Total Score for each passage in the comprehension score box under the number of the passage. Then plot your score on the graph itself by putting a small *x* on the line directly above the number of the passage, across from the score you got for that passage. As you mark your score for each passage, graph your progress by drawing a line to connect the *x*'s.

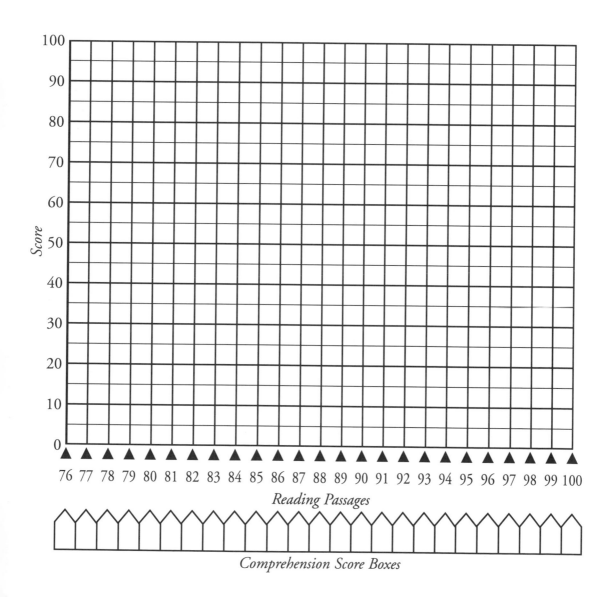

Reading Passages

Comprehension Score Boxes